Governing Solidarity in European Labour Markets

Across Western Europe, the rise of atypical employment has deepened insider–outsider divides. This book asks why two structurally similar countries – Portugal and Spain – pursued different routes to reduce labour market segmentation following the conclusion of the sovereign debt crisis. It argues that the composition of the governing social bloc drives the orientation of reform, while the choice of decision-making arena (parliamentary law-making versus tripartite social concertation) and the EU's evolving social governance shape the breadth and depth of reform.

Building on the distinction between competitive and inclusive solidarity, the book compares four domains: employment protection and collective bargaining; statutory minimum wages; regulation of ride-hailing platforms in passenger transport; and the regularisation of precarious public sector work. The analysis covers Portugal's progressive cycle (2015–2021) and Spain's coalition years (2019–2025), drawing on elite interviews, content analysis of parliamentary debates and media coverage, and official documents. The findings reveal a targeted, outsider-focussed strategy in Portugal and a more universal re-regulation in Spain.

Governing Solidarity offers a fresh framework and rich evidence for scholars of political economy and industrial relations, as well as advanced students and policymakers confronting labour market segmentation.

Paulo Marques is Associate Professor in the Department of Political Economy at ISCTE – University Institute of Lisbon, Portugal.

Rui Branco is Associate Professor in the Department of Political Studies at NOVA University of Lisbon, Portugal.

Óscar Molina is Associate Professor in the Department of Sociology at Autonomous University of Barcelona (UAB), Spain.

Renato Miguel Carmo is Associate Professor in the Department of Sociology at ISCTE – University Institute of Lisbon, Portugal.

Routledge Studies in Labour Economics

Trade Union Finance
How Labor Organizations Raise and Spend Money
Marick F. Masters and Raymond Gibney

India's Informal Economy
Contractual Labour in the Formal Manufacturing Sector
Bir Singh

The Political Economy of Immigration in The Netherlands
Population, Land and Welfare
Joop Hartog

Social Transformation and the Global Economy
Labour, Latin America and the Lefts
Ronaldo Munck

War Refugees and the Labour Market
Crisis-Driven Mobility in the Polish-Ukrainian Borderland
Ewa Łaźniewska, Joanna Kurowska-Pysz, Tomasz Górecki, Khrystyna Prytula, and Klaudia Plac

Technological Change and Labor Markets
Productivity, Job Polarization, and Inequality
Reyna Elizabeth Rodríguez Pérez and Liliana Meza González

Governing Solidarity in European Labour Markets
Atypical Employment and Minimum Wage Reform in Spain and Portugal
Edited by Paulo Marques, Rui Branco, Óscar Molina and Renato Miguel Carmo

For a full list of titles in this series, please visit: www.routledge.com/Routledge-Studies-in-Labour-Economics/book-series/RSLE

Governing Solidarity in European Labour Markets

Atypical Employment and Minimum Wage Reform in Spain and Portugal

Edited by Paulo Marques, Rui Branco, Óscar Molina and Renato Miguel Carmo

Routledge
Taylor & Francis Group
LONDON AND NEW YORK

First published 2026
by Routledge
4 Park Square, Milton Park, Abingdon, Oxon OX14 4RN

and by Routledge
605 Third Avenue, New York, NY 10158

Routledge is an imprint of the Taylor & Francis Group, an informa business

This work was funded by Portuguese public funds through FCT – Foundation for Science and Technology, under the project SOLID-JOB – Rebuilding Solidarity in an Age of Job Dualisation (project no. 06230; Reference: PTDC/CPO-CPO/6230/2020). DOI: https://doi.org/10.54499/PTDC/CPO-CPO/6230/2020.

For Product Safety Concerns and Information please contact our EU representative GPSR@taylorandfrancis.com. Taylor & Francis Verlag GmbH, Kaufingerstraße 24, 80331 München, Germany.

British Library Cataloguing-in-Publication Data
A catalogue record for this book is available from the British Library

ISBN: 978-1-032-85795-4 (hbk)
ISBN: 978-1-032-85801-2 (pbk)
ISBN: 978-1-003-51987-4 (ebk)

DOI: 10.4324/9781003519874

Typeset in Sabon
by Newgen Publishing UK

Contents

Figures

Tables

Preface and Acknowledgements

This book was conceived in the aftermath of two political turning points on the Iberian Peninsula. In Portugal, the parliamentary agreement between the Socialist Party (PS), the Portuguese Communist Party (PCP), the Left Bloc (BE), and "The Greens" (PEV) – known as the *Geringonça* (2015–2021) – committed a minority Socialist government to reversing crisis-era liberalisation and tackling precarious work. In Spain, successive Socialist Party governments culminating in the PSOE–*Unidas Podemos* coalition opened space for a negotiated re-regulation of core labour market institutions (2019–2025). The period that followed was one of rapid and measurable change in labour market segmentation, above all in the incidence of temporary contracts. Spain experienced a dramatic fall in temporary employment: among 15–64-year-olds, the share on temporary contracts declined from about 25% in 2021 to 16% by 2024; among 15–24-year-olds, it fell from 69.1% in 2021 to 44.3% in 2024. Portugal's reduction was more gradual but still notable: in the 15–64 cohort, the share moved from 22% in 2015 to 17% in 2021, while the youth rate fell from 68% in 2015 to 58% in 2021. Furthermore, between 2016 and 2022, the national minimum wage in Portugal experienced a cumulative nominal increase of approximately 40%, while in Spain, during the period from 2019 to 2025, it rose by about 61%, reflecting impressive strides in advancing inclusive wage policies in both countries. These trajectories underscore the empirical significance of the years covered here and motivate the comparative investigation that follows.

The reforms enacted by these two governments challenge the notion that dualisation can only be reduced by deregulating the labour market and exposing all workers to greater market risk. The Iberian experience documented here points instead to a second pathway: targeted re-regulation of atypical forms of employment (complemented by wage-floor policies) that curbs the use of temporary contracts and compresses the insider–outsider divide, while preserving, and in some cases reinforcing, the institutional bases of collective bargaining and other labour market institutions.

Notwithstanding episodic tensions, the new political arrangements proved durable for a considerable time. In Portugal, disagreement among the left partners crystallised on 27 October 2021, when the BE, PCP, and PEV sided with the centre-right opposition to defeat the State Budget Law, precipitating the dissolution of Parliament and a snap election on 30 January 2022. The PS secured an absolute majority (120 of 230 seats) – its first since 2005 – while the BE fell from 19 to 5 Members of Parliament and the PCP from 12 to 6. The rupture reflected the PS's refusal to accept the BE and PCP demands for increased investment in the National Health Service and for pending labour market reforms, notably the reintroduction of ultra-activity in collective bargaining and the reintroduction of the principle of the most favourable treatment. The subsequent PS government resigned in late 2023. By contrast, in Spain the left-of-centre coalition remains in office at the time of writing.

Beyond its scholarly contribution, this book also serves as a compact synthesis of the Iberian experience in these years. Unexpected developments – most notably agreements between the centre-left and the radical left – enabled substantial labour market reforms designed to stem liberalisation. At the same time, the period delivered encouraging outcomes in employment and economic growth. For example, between 2015 and 2021, the unemployment rate among individuals aged 15–64 in Portugal decreased significantly from 12.9% to 6.9%, while in Spain, it declined from 14.2% in 2019 to 11.4% in 2025. Our aim, therefore, is also to inform reflection within the left and the trade union movement on the strategies available to foster greater solidarity in the labour market – an endeavour that is especially pertinent amid the marked ebb of the left and organised labour in several European countries.

This edited volume was produced as part of the project *Rebuilding Solidarity in an Age of Job Dualisation* (SOLID-JOB), funded by the Fundação para a Ciência e a Tecnologia (FCT) under grant reference PTDC/CPO-CPO/6230/2020. The project was hosted by DINÂMIA'CET-ISCTE, with Paulo Marques as the Principal Investigator. We also gratefully acknowledge additional financial support from the Youth Employment Observatory (funding reference: UID/3127/2025, DINÂMIA'CET).

Although this is an edited collection, the chapters are tightly integrated by design. A collaborative process, anchored in a shared framework and a common empirical strategy, was essential to that coherence. We organised two internal workshops in Lisbon (January 2022 and February 2023) to refine the theoretical architecture and harmonise data collection; all empirical chapters were workshopped collectively. A concluding conference in Lisbon (January 2025), at which we presented the main findings, helped us to finalise the book and strengthen its comparative claims.

We are grateful to many colleagues for comments and encouragement at different stages. Chiara Benassi, who served as a project consultant, offered incisive feedback on early versions of Chapter 1 (ideal types of solidarity), namely during the first Lisbon workshop. Lisa Dorigatti commented on preliminary versions of Chapter 3, notably at the Council for European Studies conference in Iceland (2023). We also thank Arianna Tassinari for her remarks at the same CES conference, and Virginia Doellgast, who read the book proposal and encouraged us to pursue this project. Insights from seminar audiences across Portugal, and from reviewers of related journal articles, improved both our arguments and our evidence base. Any remaining errors are ours alone.

ISCTE – Instituto Universitário de Lisboa provided an excellent research environment. We are especially indebted to DINÂMIA'CET-ISCTE, which hosted the project and the workshops that underpinned the book's internal coherence. We are grateful, too, to students and research assistants who contributed to interviews, content analysis and data visualisation.

Finally, Paulo Marques dedicates his contribution to his father, António Marques, who passed away during the writing of this book. António Marques, a textile worker, was for nearly three decades a union leader in the southern textiles union within the CGTP and negotiated dozens of collective agreements. May the research assembled here contribute, in some measure, to the cause to which he devoted his life: building a more just and solidaristic world of work.

Lisbon

Contributors

Maria Asensio is Visiting Associate Professor in the Department of Political Science and Public Policy at ISCTE – University Institute of Lisbon, a Research Fellow at the Centre for Research and Studies in Sociology (CIES), and a Lead Researcher at the National Institute of Administration (INA). Her research focusses on comparative politics and public policy. She currently serves as a member of the board of the Institute for Public Policy (IPPS). She has published in leading international journals in political science, including *Social Policy & Administration* and the *Journal of Social Policy*.

Rui Branco is Associate Professor in the Department of Political Studies at NOVA University Lisbon and a Senior Researcher at IPRI/NOVA. His research examines comparative social and labour market regimes and policies. He has edited special issues and published in journals including the *Journal of Comparative Politics*, *Journal of Social Policy*, *New Political Economy*, *Social Policy & Administration*, *South European Society and Politics*, and *European Journal of Social Security*.

Renato Miguel Carmo is Associate Professor in the Department of Sociology at ISCTE – University Institute of Lisbon and a Research Fellow at the Centre for Research and Studies in Sociology (CIES), Portugal. He also serves as the Director of the Inequality Observatory. His research focusses on social and spatial inequalities, the welfare state, public policy, employment, labour markets, mobilities, and social capital. His recent work has been published in journals such as *Current Sociology*, *European Societies*, *Journal of Civil Society*, *Sociologia Ruralis*, *Time & Society*, *Geoforum*, *Community Development*, and *European Planning Studies*, among others.

Ana Costa is Associate Professor in the Department of Political Economy at ISCTE – University Institute of Lisbon, and a researcher at DINÂMIA'CET. She co-coordinates the PhD in Political Economy, an inter-institutional programme involving ISCTE – University Institute of Lisbon, the University of Coimbra, and the University of Lisbon. Her research focusses on issues such as the political economy of austerity, the theoretical and epistemological foundations of crises and the political responses to address them, the political economy of international economic organisations, and values and valuation. She has published in international journals including the *Cambridge Journal of Economics*, *Journal of Economic Issues*, *Ecological Economics*, *Environmental Values*, and *Transfer*.

Madalena Ferreira holds a degree in Political Science from ISCTE – University Institute of Lisbon and a master's degree in Development Studies from the same institution. She is currently a PhD candidate in Political Economy with an FCT research grant. She is also a researcher at the Centre for Research and Studies in Sociology (CIES). Previously, she worked as a research assistant on the project "Reconstructing Solidarity in an Era of Dualisation of Employment" (SOLID-JOB) at DINÂMIA'CET – ISCTE.

Luís Guerreiro is a PhD student in Public Policy at ISCTE – University Institute of Lisbon. His research focusses on political economy and the impacts of technology on the labour market. His PhD thesis compares the regulation of platform-mediated private transportation in Portugal and Spain. He has published in journals such as the *Revista Crítica de Ciências Sociais*.

Paulo Marques is Associate Professor in the Department of Political Economy at ISCTE – University Institute of Lisbon and a researcher at DINÂMIA'CET. His research focusses on comparative political economy, particularly labour market segmentation and labour market policies. He currently serves as the Director of the master's programme in Political Economy and also coordinates the Youth Employment Observatory. He has edited special journal issues and published in leading political economy journals, including the *Socio-Economic Review*, *British Journal of Industrial Relations*, *European Journal of Industrial Relations*, and *Comparative European Politics*.

Óscar Molina is Associate Professor in the Department of Sociology at the Autonomous University of Barcelona (UAB), and a researcher at the *Centre d'Estudis Sociològics sobre la Vida Quotidiana i el Treball* (QUIT) and the Institute for Labour Studies (IET). His main research interests include the study of industrial relations and collective bargaining from a comparative perspective; trade unions and neo-corporatism; social pacts and concertation; the political economy of southern Europe; and regional employment policies. He has edited special issues and contributed to several journals, including the *European Journal of Industrial Relations*, *Economic and Industrial Democracy*, *Annual Review of Political Science*, *Employee Relations*, *Industrial Relations Journal*, *Transfer*, *West European Politics*, and *South European Society and Politics*, among others.

Víctor Riesgo Gómez holds a PhD in Education, awarded by the National Distance Education University (UNED). His primary research focusses on transformations in the spheres of work, consumption, and sociability within the contemporary context of platform capitalism. He has published articles in both Spanish and international peer-reviewed journals, addressing topics such as the growth of the 'sharing economy' and the working conditions of platform drivers, including those employed by Uber and similar services, in Spain.

Nuno Rodrigues is a researcher at DINÂMIA'CET – ISCTE and an Associate Lecturer at IGOT – University of Lisbon. He holds a PhD in Human Geography from IGOT-UL (2024), where his thesis examined the digital transformation of urban space. He is currently the Principal Investigator of UrbanFrictions (2025–2026), a research project funded by FCT. His work focusses on digital geographies, exploring the intersections of digital and algorithmic mediations with urban and economic dynamics, while critically addressing the power relations embedded in these processes. His research has been published in international journals, including *Territory, Politics, Governance* and *Work Organisation, Labour & Globalisation*.

Introduction

Paulo Marques

Over the past three decades, the rapid spread of atypical employment has sharpened labour market dualisation in Western Europe, splitting workers into protected insiders – holding permanent contracts and covered by collective agreements and robust welfare entitlements – and a growing army of outsiders facing precarious contracts and patchy social protection (Rueda, 2007; Emmenegger et al., 2012; Emmenegger, 2014; Palier and Thelen, 2010). This divide is most acute in Southern Europe, where young people are disproportionately concentrated in the peripheral segment (Marques and Salavisa, 2017).

The European Union (EU) sovereign-debt crisis turned precariousness from a long-smouldering problem into an urgent political issue and triggered a wave of 'de-segmentation' reforms across the continent (Eichhorst and Marx, 2021; Emmenegger and Marx, 2021: 618; Marques et al., 2025). Portugal and Spain stand out in this process: between 2015 and 2025, progressive coalitions enacted an unusually dense package of measures, including major increases in the statutory minimum wage, programmes converting atypical public-sector contracts into permanent posts, labour-law reforms, and pioneering rules for digital-platform work.[1] Four factors help explain why both countries advanced this ambitious agenda. First, precarious workers were severely affected by the 2008–2010 and 2011–2014 economic crises: unemployment rose rapidly, and large waves of emigration particularly affected young labour market entrants (Marques and Hörisch, 2020; Marques and Videira, 2021). Second, social movements and trade unions placed the issue centre stage, with mass demonstrations in which precarious workers played a leading role (Carvalho, 2022; Fernandes, 2017). Third, elections in both countries saw radical-left parties – namely *Unidas Podemos* in Spain and the Left Bloc (BE) in Portugal – achieve significant results. In Portugal, the Portuguese Communist Party (PCP) also secured a substantial share of the vote (Marques and Fonseca, 2022). Indeed, after the sovereign-debt crisis, the radical left accounted for around 20% of the electorate in both countries. Finally, centre-left and radical-left parties agreed to support governments seeking to reverse policies implemented during austerity

DOI: 10.4324/9781003519874-1

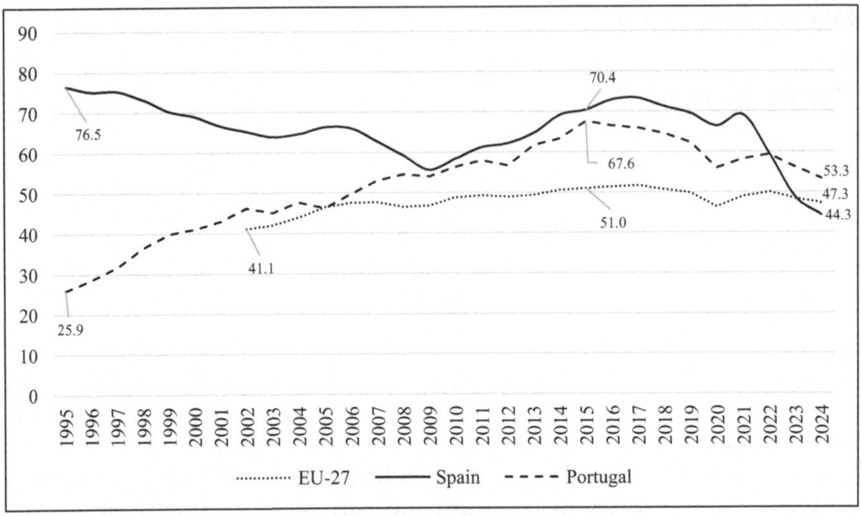

Figure I.1 Share of young employees on temporary contracts (15–24), Portugal, Spain and EU-27, 1995–2024.

Notes: EU-27 series available from 2002 onwards. Indicator covers employees only (excludes the self-employed). Age group 15–24.

Source: Eurostat, Labour Force Survey. See Eurostat (2025).

(2015–2021 in Portugal; 2019–2025 in Spain). Figure I.1 underscores the salience of these policies, showing a substantial decline in the proportion of workers in atypical employment over the period.

Despite these parallels, the two countries pursued different strategies. Portugal adopted a surgical focus on outsiders, whereas Spain embarked on a comprehensive re-regulation aimed at upgrading standards for all workers. This book explains this contrast in two steps. First, we distinguish between *competitive solidarity* – which reins in the most precarious contracts while leaving broader liberalisation largely intact and even expanding markets in certain domains – and *inclusive solidarity*, which seeks to re-embed labour market regulation on a universal basis. Second, we argue that reform trajectories are rooted principally in the composition of the governing social bloc, with decision-making arenas (whether the national parliament or social concertation), and the EU's evolving social governance operating as enabling (or constraining) conditions.

The Argument in Brief

Three decades of deregulation and crisis have contributed to spreading inequalities in Europe's labour markets, as shown in seminal studies of dualisation and insider–outsider politics (Rueda, 2007; Palier and Thelen, 2010). This book conceptualises two rival forms of solidarity capable of addressing that divide. *Competitive solidarity* reins in the most extreme forms of precarity – tightening rules on the most fragile contracts and expanding activation – while tolerating continued flexibility for insiders or other market-making policies. *Inclusive solidarity* rejects this trade-off and seeks a universal re-regulation of employment protection, collective bargaining, and welfare. The latter vision echoes Polanyi's (1944) claim that efforts to construct a 'self-regulating' market tear at the social fabric, particularly in the realm of labour, and that rebuilding solidarity therefore requires re-embedding and constraining markets rather than extending them into new domains.

This book analyses governing social blocs through an explicitly actor-centred lens, focussing on constellations of collective organisations – including political parties, governments, peak trade-union confederations, and employers' associations. These entities control access to decision-making arenas and mobilise institutionally defined resources, thereby directing reform strategies. Within each decision-making arena, the subset of authorised and capable actors forms the actor constellation. In Iberia, two distinct governing social blocs implemented labour market reforms during the two progressive coalitions, specifically what we refer to as the Centrist–Employer and the Left–Union governing social blocs. Centrist–Employer alignments (centrist parties, moderate unions, and employer associations) tend to favour competitive compromises. In contrast, Left–Union blocs – linking centre-left parties, radical left factions, and class-oriented unions – are more inclined to pursue inclusive re-regulation.

We argue that bloc composition fundamentally drives a reform's orientation (inclusive versus competitive), while the decision arena and the EU's stance act as sufficient conditions that can reinforce, mitigate, or obstruct the trajectory shaped by the bloc. Decision-making arenas exhibit asymmetries. Tripartite social concertation embeds a consent constraint, where employer assent functions as a de facto veto. Consequently, proposals that increase labour costs or restrict managerial discretion are often curtailed. Conversely, parliamentary law-making lacks an institutional employer veto, enabling cohesive left majorities to legislate closer to their policy preferences, albeit with employers retaining lobbying influence. The EU's role is conceptualised as a conditional external selector. In its 'liberal EU' configuration – grounded in fiscal surveillance and competitiveness-oriented coordination – European influence supports competitive policy outcomes and raises barriers to revisiting deregulatory measures (e.g., dismissal rules for open-ended contracts, decentralised wage setting). Alternatively, the 'social EU' configuration – embodied by the European Pillar of Social Rights, the Adequate Minimum Wages Directive, SURE, and the Recovery and Resilience Facility – creates legal and fiscal space for inclusive reforms, though it generally reinforces baseline protections without dismantling core crisis-era frameworks.

Taken together, the book demonstrates that labour market dualisation is not inevitable. The composition of the governing social bloc is the indispensable driver of change, yet its impact is conditioned by the institutional arena in which bargaining occurs and by the shifting currents of EU governance. By embedding the idea of solidarity within a political economy framework of coalitions and institutions, we explain why structurally similar economies embark on divergent trajectories of labour market reform to rebuild social solidarity.

Contextualisation of the Case Studies

This section situates the Portuguese and Spanish cases by outlining their shared historical and institutional legacies while specifying the key divergences rooted in distinct democratic transitions and subsequent trajectories of party politics, union organisation, employer representation, and labour market regulation. It sets the stage for the comparative analysis that follows by showing how these similarities and differences condition dualisation dynamics and inform the four policy arenas examined in the book.

The Portuguese political system and industrial relations were profoundly shaped by the revolutionary transition following the Carnation Revolution of 1974, marked by extensive nationalisations, land collectivisation, and progressive labour legislation (Campos Lima and Naumann, 2011; Campos Lima, 2019). The 1976 Constitution entrenched strong worker protections, while the 1979 collective-bargaining regime institutionalised principles such as ultra-activity, the favourability rule, and administrative extensions (Decree-Law No. 519-C1/1979). Politically, Portugal's left had long been divided between the centre-left and the radical left and had never governed together. Yet in the 2015 legislative election, the first after the austerity cycle, the combined vote of the PCP and the BE reached 18.4%, signalling a surge of radical-left support that paved the way for the subsequent parliamentary pact – the *Geringonça* – linking the centre-left Socialist Party (PS) with the PCP, BE, and the Ecologist Party "The Greens" (Fernandes et al., 2018).[2] The trade-union landscape remains politically divided, dominated by the communist-aligned General Confederation of Portuguese Workers (CGTP) alongside the socialist-leaning General Union of Workers (UGT-P) (Campos Lima and Naumann, 2011). Because the gains secured by workers in the immediate post-Revolution period were so substantial, the CGTP thereafter adopted a predominantly defensive strategy, centred on preserving those achievements, both in collective bargaining and in labour legislation. This fragmentation has perpetuated weak coordination and declining union density, now about 19% (Campos Lima, 2019). Employers, represented chiefly by the Confederation of Portuguese Industry and the Confederation of Commerce and Services, have also experienced falling density – from roughly 60% in 2002 to around 40% in recent years (OECD, 2017). Consequently, the state has played a central role in sustaining collective bargaining through administrative extensions, compensating for the structural fragility of social-partner organisations (Bulfone and Afonso, 2020; Garcia Calavia and Rigby, 2020).

Spain's democratic transition after Franco's death in 1975 unfolded gradually through negotiated pacts, the Moncloa Agreements, rather than through revolution, yielding a stable democracy that left many pre-existing power structures largely intact (Marques and Fonseca, 2022). Political parties and unions were initially ideologically polarised, but the latter gradually gained autonomy from political parties, most notably the General Workers' Union (UGT-S) and Workers' Commissions (CCOO) (Hamann and Lucio, 2003: 65; Molina and Rhodes, 2011: 183). In the post-austerity period, the radical left achieved unprecedented electoral success: Podemos secured 24.5% of the vote in 2016, outpolling the centre-left Spanish Socialist Workers' Party (PSOE). After a succession of inconclusive elections and failed investiture attempts between 2016 and 2019, *Unidas Podemos* (a coalition of *Podemos* and the Spanish Communist Party) ultimately entered Spain's first coalition cabinet of the democratic era, formed in January 2020 with the PSOE. This stands in sharp contrast to Portugal, where the left converged only through a parliamentary support agreement rather than by sharing ministerial posts. Employer representation remains fragmented between the Spanish Confederation of Employer Organisations and the Confederation of Small and Medium-Sized Enterprises, although employer-association density remains comparatively high at about 75%. Union density, by contrast, currently stands at roughly 14% (Rodríguez et al., 2019).

During the austerity years, dualisation in Iberia was deepened by a three-pronged liberalisation of labour law, public employment, and the minimum wage. In Portugal, the Troika Memorandum of Understanding (2011–2014) triggered successive Labour Code revisions that cut severance pay, expanded working-time 'banks,' trimmed overtime premia, and crucially made collective agreement extensions conditional on 50% employer coverage while letting ultra-activity lapse more readily. Spain's 2012 reform went further in recentring employer discretion: firm-level pacts were granted primacy over sectoral agreements, ultra-activity was time-limited, economic grounds for collective dismissals were widened, and redundancy compensation was reduced. In both countries, these moves hastened the shift from coordinated to fragmented bargaining, eroded coverage and compressed insider protections, leaving outsiders largely unshielded (Campos Lima et al., 2021; Rodríguez et al., 2016; Molina, 2014). Public administration underwent parallel internal devaluation. Portugal imposed wage cuts and freezes, strict hiring caps, and mobility/redundancy mechanisms that swelled the ranks of fixed-term and outsourced staff. Spain combined wage cuts, tight replacement rates, and decentralised head-count targets, pushing ministries and autonomous communities towards heavy reliance on temporary contracts; by mid-decade, over 30% of public-sector posts were non-permanent. Social protection narrowed as eligibility tightened, and benefit generosity fell. Minimum-wage policy completed the internal devaluation strategy: Portugal froze the statutory minimum wage at €485 from 2011 to 2014 under conditionality, while Spain's minimum wage stagnated in real terms, reaching a historic low relative to the median wage. In short, austerity-era liberalisation tightened managerial prerogatives, hollowed out collective bargaining, and shifted adjustment costs onto workers, entrenching a two-track labour market that post-2015 progressive coalitions would later attempt to reverse.

Against this backdrop, the book zooms in on four arenas where the insider–outsider tension is most visible – employment-protection legislation, minimum-wage governance, platform-work regulation, and the regularisation of precarious public-sector employment – to show how those austerity-era legacies conditioned subsequent reform choices. Taken together, these domains cover the key mechanisms through which dualisation is produced (contract rules, wage floors, new forms of work, and state employment). Examining them side by side allows us to trace how the same coalitional and institutional logics play out across distinct regulatory fields, revealing both common Iberian constraints and country-specific strategies for rebuilding labour market solidarity.

Employment-protection legislation has long been the principal engine of dualisation. Since the mid-1980s, almost every major reform in Iberia eased recourse to fixed-term contracts (Marques and Fonseca, 2022; Silva et al., 2018). Spain set the template in 1984 when a PSOE majority backed by the UGT-S but opposed by the CCOO authorised low-cost temporary hiring without touching permanent contract regulation: the archetypal two-tier reform (Rueda, 2007). Temporary employment soon exceeded 30% of the dependent workforce, and later reforms (1994, 2001, 2012) never structurally reversed that pattern.[3] Portugal followed a similar yet more contested path: attempts to deregulate permanents were blocked by general strikes and, twice, by the Constitutional Court, prompting governments to embrace 'flexibility at the margin,' most starkly in 2003, when the Social Democratic Party (PSD) – Christian Democrats (CDS-PP) coalition extended fixed-term durations to six years and allowed three renewals. Austerity programmes intensified this bias: EU-backed reforms in Lisbon (2012) and Madrid (2010/12) demanded internal devaluation and further liberalised temporary work. Marques and Fonseca (2022) demonstrate that the wider gaps in temporary-employment levels between Portugal and Spain in the 1990s and 2000s stem from the comparatively stronger radical left in Portugal, which, by exerting sustained pressure on the PS, prevented the centre-left from adopting a pro-insider strategy. Three decades of 'flexibility at the margin' have thus entrenched dualism, leaving progressive governments with the formidable task of dismantling a two-track employment protection legislation (EPL) regime that earlier reforms consolidated.

Minimum-wage policy provides the second crucial lens. Procedurally, both systems are state-centred: the executive sets the floor, but Portugal's

Council of Ministers can legislate only after the issue is tabled in the tripartite Council for Social Concertation, whereas Spain's Cabinet issues a *Real Decreto* largely at its own discretion (with, at most, a consultative opinion). Without automatic indexation, upratings are discretionary and politically contested (Afonso, 2019; Molina, 2021). These procedural nuances position the cases differently within academic typologies. On Dingeldey et al.'s (2021) continuum (measuring how closely the statutory rate tracks sectoral minima), Spain sits in 'distant interaction,'[4] whereas Portugal has shifted towards 'close interaction' as successive hikes pulled the floor up to negotiated minima. From Picot's (2023) governance perspective, both are "state-plus-collective" regimes: a binding national floor co-exists with high bargaining coverage. Pre-2015 trajectories reinforced these contrasts. Through the mid-1990s to the crisis, both countries used nominal upratings, often within social-pact deals (e.g., Portugal 2006), to narrow gaps with EU peers while courting employer consent (Campos Lima and Naumann, 2011). Austerity reversed course: Portugal froze the floor; Spain's micro-increases cut its relative value. By 2015, Portugal's minimum hovered near 60% of the median wage, Spain's around 41%, leaving Madrid much more room for 'catch-up' hikes thereafter.

Platform work in passenger transport surfaced as a policy challenge precisely when austerity suppressed demand and the taxi sector stagnated. Uber and others entered in 2014, exploiting different regulatory voids. Portugal's 1990 taxi framework, devolving licensing and prices to municipalities, never anticipated digital intermediaries, enabling platforms' rapid, largely uncontested expansion. Spain already had a secondary private hire vehicle (VTC) category capped at 1:30 taxis; a 2009 reform briefly lifted the cap, a 2013 law reinstated it, but a loophole let investors hoard VTC licences, fuelling concentrated growth in Madrid and Barcelona. As tourism rebounded, digital ride-hailing became strategically salient – lubricating visitor economies yet threatening entrenched taxi interests. This asymmetry made platform regulation a litmus test of state capacity to balance innovation, workers' rights, and incumbents' claims in a sector critical to post-austerity growth (Baccaro, 2022).

Public-sector employment had been quietly dualising since the mid-1990s, as both countries imported new public-management doctrines that replaced career civil-service recruitment with temporary, project-based, and outsourced contracts (Madureira, 2015; Molina and Godino, 2018). This produced growing stratification within the public sector. Austerity amplified the drift: wages were frozen, promotions suspended, and stringent hiring caps imposed. By 2015, temporary staff accounted for over 30% of public-sector employment in Spain, whereas in Portugal, the share hovered around 11–12%. Portugal, however, had greater experience with extraordinary regularisation – for example, António Guterres's 1998 programme. Thus, on the eve of the progressive turn, both systems had been liberalised, but Spain's problem was quantitatively larger, while Portugal had already experimented with corrective schemes.

In sum, Iberia's shared structural legacies of state-centred bargaining institutions and profound insider–outsider cleavages were filtered through divergent political trajectories. Democratic Portugal's revolutionary origins endowed workers with strong formal rights but left a legacy of partisan and organisational fragmentation; Spain's negotiated transition produced more balanced peak organisations. Austerity exposed common vulnerabilities, yet the subsequent radical-left surge and distinct alliance forms – Portugal's parliamentary support pact *versus* Spain's formal coalition – set partially divergent post-crisis paths. By tracing these coalitional and institutional differences across employment protection, wage setting, platform work, and public-sector precariousness, Chapters 3–6 show how similar constraints can generate contrasting reform strategies, offering a roadmap to the political dynamics of labour market solidarity.

Methodology and Case Selection

This book adopts a most-similar systems design (Gerring, 2007) to compare Portugal and Spain, two cases that are similar on structural dimensions that typically co-determine labour market outcomes, in order to isolate the causal role of the variables we theorise as decisive: the composition of the governing social bloc, the decision-making arena (social concertation versus parliamentary law-making), and the evolving role of the EU.

The dependent variable is the orientation of labour market reform during the years of progressive coalitions, specifically whether it aligns with competitive solidarity or inclusive solidarity. We code reforms as inclusive where packages raise universal floors (e.g., robust EPL for all contract types, sector-wide bargaining coverage, generous passive benefits) and do not offset such moves with new flexibility elsewhere; and as competitive, where gains for outsiders are combined with preserved or expanded flexibility for insiders, and where labour market policies prioritise social investment over passive policies. Hybrid episodes are coded on the dominant thrust.

The two countries are most similar in that both are Southern European, state-centred bargaining regimes with dualised labour markets; both democratised in the 1970s and acceded to the European Economic Community in the 1980s; both were severely affected by the global financial (2008–2010) and sovereign-debt (2011–2014) crises; and both share comparable economic specialisation profiles in which tourism, construction, real estate, and domestic demand are prominent (Baccaro et al., 2022; Baccaro, 2022). They also exhibit divided union representation and falling density, fragmented employer representation, and a common experience of fiscal consolidation under EU surveillance. Finally, in the aftermath of austerity, they were both governed by first-ever 'progressive coalitions' that challenged the post-transition scenario of a 'divided left' (Watson, 2015). Against this background of similarities, however, their post-austerity reform trajectories diverged: Portugal largely pursued what we term competitive solidarity, whereas Spain moved further towards inclusive solidarity. The most-similar systems design therefore provides analytical leverage to attribute this divergence to the theorised causal mechanism(s).

The period of empirical scrutiny spans 2015–2025, albeit asynchronously: 2015–2021 for Portugal (the '*Geringonça*' parliamentary-support arrangement) and 2019–2025 for Spain (the PSOE–*Unidas Podemos* coalition). The overarching most-similar systems design is retained across the empirical chapters, which compare Portugal and Spain domain-by-domain: EPL and collective bargaining; minimum-wage setting; platform-work regulation in the passenger-transport sector; and the regularisation of precarious public-sector employment. These policy domains were selected because, together, they cover the principal levers through which dualisation is produced and potentially undone (contract rules, wage floors, emergent forms of work, and the state as employer). In two of these domains, outcomes clearly diverge, enabling tests under conditions of contrast; in the remaining domains, apparent convergence masks different degrees of inclusiveness, which we explain through our theoretical triad of governing social blocs, decision arenas, and EU leverage. Within each domain, we use paired comparison to trace the mechanisms linking these variables to observed outcomes.

In the concluding chapter, we employ John Stuart Mill's (1843) joint method of agreement and difference.[5] We first apply a difference test to domains with opposite outcomes (employment protection/collective bargaining; passenger-transport platforms). We then apply an agreement test to domains with inclusive outcomes in both countries (minimum-wage upratings; regularisation of precarious public-sector employment). As shown in the conclusion, this joint test supports our claim that bloc composition is a necessary condition for inclusive reform, and that, when combined with parliamentary routes and strong EU push, it becomes jointly sufficient to reach the upper bound of inclusiveness.

The evidentiary base combines four types of data, allowing for methodological triangulation and cross-validation. First, we conducted 37 semi-structured elite interviews (24 in Portugal and 13 in Spain) with members of parliament and government, as well as representatives of trade-union confederations and employer associations.[6] Sampling was purposive (targeting actors directly involved in the reforms) and iterative (snowballing from references detected in parliamentary debates and press coverage); interviews were transcribed and coded thematically. Second, we performed a content analysis of the entire corpus of parliamentary debates linked to the reforms: 144 in Portugal and 99 in Spain, coded in MaxQDA using a template that combined deductive categories derived from our theoretical framework (bloc composition, decision arena, EU leverage, solidarity orientation) with inductively generated subcodes that captured emergent mechanisms (e.g., how specific European Court of Justice rulings or Recovery and Resilience Facility conditionalities were operationalised in domestic bargaining). Third, we analysed media coverage in leading newspapers – *Público*, *Expresso*, and

Diário de Notícias (Portugal); *El País*, *El Mundo*, and *ABC* (Spain) – to trace public framing, agenda-setting dynamics, and the salience of competing coalitional narratives. Finally, we reviewed all relevant official documents, including statutes, decrees, social-pact texts, EU legislation and soft-law instruments, European Court of Justice rulings, and Recovery and Resilience Facility regulations, in order to anchor our assessment of how supranational pressures were concretely translated into domestic reform design.

Our inference strategy is mechanism-centred. We specify *ex ante* the theoretical expectations linking governing-bloc composition to decision arenas and the EU's role to distinct solidarity orientations, and then trace the sequence of events in each reform to test whether the empirical record exhibits the predicted fingerprints (e.g., employer vetoes binding in social concertation; cohesive left coalitions using parliamentary majorities to legislate inclusively). We corroborate these narratives with quantitative indicators (e.g., the magnitude of minimum-wage increases and the breadth of public-sector regularisation). Following Gerring (2007), we treat convergent evidence and mechanism plausibility, rather than statistical identification, as the standard for causal warrant in small-N comparative research.

Two scope conditions qualify our claims. First, with only two most-similar cases, we do not claim that the mechanisms identified in this book are universally portable. Rather, we contend that the mechanisms we highlight – particularly the interaction among governing blocs, arenas, and EU leverage – are most likely to travel to other European state-centred and dualised labour market regimes, even if empirical thresholds (e.g., the magnitude of minimum-wage increases or the breadth of regularisation) remain context-specific. Second, although a most-similar systems design holds many structural features, constant, longer-run national legacies (Portugal's revolutionary transition; Spain's negotiated transition) continue to shape coalition strategies and veto structures. Our conclusions are therefore framed as bounded generalisations.

Structure of the Book

This Introduction is followed by Chapter 1, which lays the conceptual groundwork. It formulates the insider–outsider divide as the core analytical puzzle and elaborates two ideal-typical responses to it: competitive solidarity, which reins in the worst forms of precarity while tolerating continued flexibility for insiders; and inclusive solidarity, which seeks a universal re-regulation of employment protection, collective bargaining, and welfare. The chapter situates these models within classic and contemporary political economy debates, specifies how each can either mitigate or reproduce dualisation, and derives observable implications that orient the empirical inquiry.

Chapter 2 shifts from ideas to actors and institutions. It argues that the composition of the governing social bloc is the necessary driver of reform orientation: centrist alignments working with moderate unions and employer associations tend to produce competitive settlements, whereas cohesive Left–Union blocs are uniquely positioned to enact inclusive ones. It then demonstrates how arena asymmetries – a consent constraint in concertation versus the absence of an institutional employer veto in parliament – and EU configurations ('liberal' versus 'social') scale the reach of bloc preferences. Table 2.2 arrays eight stylised bloc–arena–EU combinations and derives expectations about when settlements will gravitate towards competitive or inclusive solidarity; crucially, arena choice is treated as endogenous to bloc priorities.

Chapters 3–6 operationalise the framework in four policy arenas where the insider–outsider tension is most acute. Each chapter offers a paired Portugal–Spain comparison that preserves the book's overarching most-similar systems design: broad structural commonalities are held constant so that the analysis can trace how different bloc–arena–EU constellations generate divergent (or, where relevant, convergent but differently scaled) outcomes.

Chapter 3 shows that, following the crisis-era deregulation of EPL, both countries sought to rebuild protections but pursued distinct routes. In Portugal (2015–21), a minoritarian centre-left (Socialist) government dependent on social concertation and right-wing abstentions tightened rules for atypical contracts yet preserved key employer veto points over the regulation of open-ended contracts and over crucial aspects of collective bargaining, an outcome consistent with competitive solidarity. In Spain (2019–2025), a cohesive PSOE–*Unidas Podemos* bloc used tripartite bargaining and narrow parliamentary majorities to restore the ultra-activity of collective agreements, re-establish sectoral primacy in bargaining, and sharply curtail temporary hiring, an inclusive turn. Although some Troika-era changes to open-ended contracts were not reversed, no further liberalisation of permanent contracts was enacted. The chapter demonstrates how bloc composition, decision arenas, and EU cues interacted to produce these contrasting orientations.

Chapter 4 analyses minimum-wage policy as a visible instrument of solidarity. Both countries ultimately converge on inclusive outcomes, albeit via different pathways. Portugal's negotiated incrementalism (regular upratings often bundled with compensatory measures for employers) reflects internal bloc constraints and the disciplining logic of concertation. Spain's programmatic, executive-led approach shows how stronger left-bloc cohesion and a less veto-laden arena can deliver faster, broader gains, aided by a supportive normative turn at the EU level.

Chapter 5 examines regulation of platform work in passenger transport, an emergent, weakly institutionalised field that stress-tests our framework. Portugal adopted permissive legislation with minimal protections, an archetypal competitive-solidarity compromise shaped by a centrist coalition and limited corporatist leverage. Spain, by contrast, enacted a more inclusive settlement that tightly constrained VTC licences and brought platforms under taxi-sector rules, driven by a cohesive left bloc, intense mobilisation, and decisive parliamentary action. EU leverage was negligible in both cases, underscoring the primacy of governing social blocs.

Chapter 6 turns to the state as employer, comparing Portugal's Programme for the Extraordinary Regularisation of Precarious Contracts in the Public Administration (PREVPAP) and Spain's *Ley de Interinos* on public-sector regularisation. Here, both countries move towards inclusivity, but with different depths and logics. The Portuguese programme was conditional and procedural, requiring individual proof of 'permanent need' and reflecting both looser bloc cohesion and limited supranational pressure. Propelled by European Court of Justice rulings and Recovery Fund milestones, the Spanish programme adopted a quasi-automatic regularisation model backed by sanctions on non-compliant administrations. The contrast again demonstrates how EU leverage and bloc cohesion jointly condition the breadth of inclusive outcomes.

Chapter 7 synthesises the findings through a two-stage comparative strategy. First, it contrasts domains with divergent outcomes (employment protection and collective bargaining *versus* platform regulation) to show that differences map consistently onto the proposed bloc–arena–EU configuration. Second, it scrutinises domains with convergent, inclusive outcomes (minimum-wage and public-sector regularisation) to explain why Spain's reforms were deeper and broader: stronger left-bloc cohesion, fewer employer vetoes in the arena, and more forceful EU leverage. The chapter thus refines the theoretical framework, reaffirms the governing social bloc as the necessary driver of reform orientation, and clarifies how decision arenas and EU instruments act as sufficient conditions that scale inclusivity up or down. It closes by drawing strategic lessons for unions and left parties and by outlining a research agenda on the durability, implementation, and diffusion of inclusive reforms.

Overall, the book demonstrates that labour market solidarity in Iberia is neither accidental nor preordained. It arises from the patterned interaction of governing social blocs, policymaking arenas, and supranational pressures. In Spain, a cohesive left bloc, frequent reliance on parliamentary routes, and strong EU leverage produced a near-uniform inclusive turn; in Portugal, oscillating, often centrist, governing blocs, heavier reliance on tripartite social concertation, and weaker EU leverage yielded competitive outcomes or diluted forms of inclusivity.

Notes

1 The empirical analysis covers 2015–2025. In Portugal, the progressive alliance governed from 2015 to 2021; whereas in Spain, the PSOE–*Unidas Podemos* coalition remains in office at the time of writing, so the Spanish period runs from 2019 to 2025.

2 "*Geringonça*", literally "contraption" or "makeshift gadget," was an expression previously used by the historian and columnist Vasco Pulido Valente. It was

recycled on 10 November 2015 by Paulo Portas, then leader of the CDS-PP and outgoing deputy prime minister, in his final speech in parliament: "I will borrow Vasco Pulido Valente's definition of your manoeuvre. It is not quite a government, it is a contraption." The label quickly stuck as shorthand for the Socialist Party's parliamentary agreement with the radical left.

3 The 1994 reform yielded some effects, but it never succeeded in reducing temporary employment to a level approaching the EU average.

4 Up until recently, collective scales remained well above the legal floor, but recent evidence points to a shift towards much closer interaction (Eurofound, 2025).

5 Mill's joint method of agreement and difference combines two tests: (i) among instances where the phenomenon occurs, identify a single circumstance common to all; and (ii) among instances where it does not occur, ensure that nothing is common except the absence of that circumstance. If both hold, that circumstance is the effect, the cause, or an indispensable part of the cause of the phenomenon (Mill, 1843: 284).

6 At the end of each chapter, we provide a list of the interviews used.

References

Afonso A. (2019) State-led wage devaluation in Southern Europe in the wake of the Eurozone crisis. *European Journal of Political Research* 58(3): 938–959.

Amable B. (2017) *Structural Crisis and Institutional Change in Modern Capitalism: French Capitalism in Transition*. Oxford: Oxford University Press.

Amable B. (2021) In search of the bloc bourgeois. Revue de la régulation – Capitalisme, institutions, pouvoirs 31.

Amable B. and Palombarini S. (2023) Multidimensional social conflict and institutional change. *New Political Economy* 28(6): 942–957.

Baccaro L. (2022) Is there a "Mediterranean" growth model? In: Burroni L., Pavolini E. and Regini M. (eds) *Mediterranean Capitalism Revisited: One Model, Different Trajectories*. 19–41. Ithaca, NY/London: Cornell University Press.

Baccaro L., Blyth M. and Pontusson J. (eds) (2022) *Diminishing Returns: The New Politics of Growth and Stagnation*. Oxford: Oxford University Press.

Branco R., Miro M. and Natili M. (2024) Back from the cold? Progressive politics and social policy in Southern Europe. *Politics & Society* 52(4): 630–661.

Bulfone F. and Afonso A. (2020) Business against markets: Employer resistance to collective bargaining liberalization during the Eurozone crisis. *Comparative Political Studies* 53(5): 809–846.

Campos Lima M. da P. (2019) Portugal: Reforms and the turn to neoliberal austerity. In: Müller T., Vandaele K. and Waddington J. (eds) *Collective Bargaining in Europe: Towards an Endgame?* Vol. III, 483–504. Brussels: European Trade Union Institute.

Campos Lima M. da P., Martins D., Costa A. C. and Velez A. (2021) Internal devaluation and economic inequality in Portugal: Challenges to industrial relations in times of crisis and recovery. *Transfer* 27(1): 47–73.

Campos Lima M. P. and Naumann R. (2011) Portugal: From broad strategic pacts to policy-specific agreements. In: Avdagic S., Rhodes M. and Visser J. (eds) *Social Pacts in Europe: Emergence, Evolution, and Institutionalization*. 147–173. Oxford: Oxford University Press.

Carvalho T. (2022) *Contesting Austerity: Social Movements and the Left in Portugal and Spain (2008–2015)*. Amsterdam: Amsterdam University Press.

Decree-Law No. 519-C1/1979 of 29 December. Law on collective labour regulation instruments [Lei dos Instrumentos de Regulação Coletiva do Trabalho]. *Diário da República*, Series I, No. 301, 29 December. Available at: https://diariodarepublica.pt/dr/detalhe/decreto-lei/519-c1-1979-157052

Dingeldey I., Schulten T. and Grimshaw D. (2021) Introduction: Minimum wage regimes in Europe and selected developing countries. In: Dingeldey I., Grimshaw D. and Schulten T. (eds) *Minimum Wage Regimes: Statutory Regulation, Collective Bargaining and Adequate Levels*. 1–16. London/New York: Routledge.

Eichhorst W. and Marx P. (2021) How stable is labour market dualism? Reforms of employment protection in nine European countries. *European Journal of Industrial Relations* 27(1): 93–110.

Emmenegger P. (2014) *The Power to Dismiss: Trade Unions and the Regulation of Job Security in Western Europe*. Oxford: Oxford University Press.

Emmenegger P., Häusermann S., Palier B. and Seeleib-Kaiser M. (eds) (2012) *The Age of Dualisation: The Changing Face of Inequality in Deindustrializing Societies*. Oxford: Oxford University Press.

Emmenegger P. and Marx P. (2021) The regulation of employment. In: Béland D., Morgan K. J., Obinger H. and Pierson C. (eds) The Oxford Handbook of the Welfare State (2nd ed.). 606–623. Oxford: Oxford University Press.

Erne R., Stan S., Golden D., Szabó I. and Maccarrone V. (2024) *Politicising Commodification: European Governance and Labour Politics from the Financial Crisis to the Covid Emergency*. Cambridge: Cambridge University Press.

Eurofound (2025) *Impact of National Minimum Wages on Collective Bargaining and Wages for Low-Paid Workers*. Luxembourg: Publications Office of the European Union.

Eurostat (2025) Labour Force Survey. Available at: https://ec.europa.eu/eurostat/databrowser/view/lfsa_etpgan__custom_18044211/default/table

Fernandes J. M., Magalhães P. C. and Santana-Pereira J. (2018) Portugal's leftist government: From sick man to poster boy? *South European Society and Politics* 23(4): 503–524.

Fernandes T. (2017) Late neoliberalism and its discontents: The case of Portugal. In: Della Porta D., Andretta M., Fernandes T., O'Connor F., Romanos E. and Vogiatzoglou M. (eds) *Late Neoliberalism and Its Discontents in the Economic Crisis: Comparing Social Movements in the European* Periphery. 169–200. Cham: Palgrave Macmillan.

Garcia Calavia M. and Rigby M. (2020) The extension of collective agreements in France, Portugal and Spain. *Transfer* 26(4): 399–414.

Gerring J. (2007) *Case Study Research: Principles and Practices*. Cambridge: Cambridge University Press.

Hamann K. and Lucio M. (2003) Strategies of union revitalization in Spain: Negotiating change and fragmentation. *European Journal of Industrial Relations* 9(1): 61–78.

Howell C. (2021) Rethinking the role of the state in employment relations for a neoliberal era. *ILR Review* 74(3): 739–772.

Madureira C. (2015) A reforma da Administração Pública Central no Portugal democrático: Do período pós-revolucionário à intervenção da troika. *Revista de Administração Pública* 49: 547–562.

Marques P., Benassi C., Costa A. and Pinto A. (2025) Under which conditions do unions succeed in pushing back dualization? A configurational study of collective agreements in Portugal. *British Journal of Industrial Relations* 63(1): 133–155.
Marques P. and Fonseca D. (2022) Understanding the positions taken by moderate union confederations and centre-left parties during labour market reforms in Portugal and Spain: Why the configuration of left parties and trade union confederations matters. *European Journal of Industrial Relations* 28(1): 65–84.
Marques P. and Hörisch F. (2020) Understanding massive youth unemployment during the EU sovereign debt crisis: A configurational study. *Comparative European Politics* 18(2): 233–255.
Marques P. and Salavisa I. (2017) Young people and dualisation in Europe: A fuzzy-set analysis. *Socio-Economic Review* 15(1): 135–160.
Marques P. and Videira P. (2021) Labour market policies to fight youth unemployment in Portugal: Between statism and experimentalism. In: Jagannathan R. (ed) *The Growing Challenge of Youth Unemployment in Europe and America: A Cross-Cultural Perspective*. 127–163. Bristol: Bristol University Press.
Mill J. S. (1882 [1843]) *A System of Logic: Ratiocinative and Inductive*. New York: Harper & Brothers.
Molina Ó. (2014) Self-regulation and the state in industrial relations in Southern Europe: Back to the future? *European Journal of Industrial Relations* 20(1): 21–36.
Molina Ó. (2021) Minimum wages in Southern Europe: Regulation and reconfiguration under the shadow of hierarchy. In: Dingeldey I., Grimshaw D. and Schulten T. (eds) *Minimum Wage Regimes: Statutory Regulation, Collective Bargaining and Adequate Levels*. 64–85. London/New York: Routledge.
Molina Ó. and Godino A. (2018) *Bargaining for social rights in the public sector: Spain*. Amsterdam: University of Amsterdam.
Molina Ó. and Rhodes M. (2011) Spain: From tripartite to bipartite pacts. In: Avdagic S., Rhodes M. and Visser J. (eds) *Social Pacts in Europe: Emergence, Evolution, and Institutionalization*. 174–201. Oxford: Oxford University Press.
OECD (2017) *OECD Employment Outlook 2017*. Paris: OECD Publishing.
Palier B. and Thelen K. (2010) Institutionalizing dualism: Complementarities and change in France and Germany. *Politics & Society* 38(1): 119–148.
Picot G. (2023) Minimum wages: By collective bargaining and by law. In: Clegg D. and Durazzi N. (eds) *Handbook of Labour Market Policy in Advanced Democracies*. 234–248. Cheltenham, UK: Edward Elgar.
Polanyi K. (2001 [1944]) *The Great Transformation: The Political and Economic Origins of Our Time*. Boston: Beacon Press.
Rhodes M. (2001) The political economy of social pacts: 'Competitive corporatism' and European welfare reform. In: Pierson P. (ed.) *The New Politics of the Welfare State*. 165–194. Oxford: Oxford University Press.
Rodríguez C., Rojo R. and Lucio M. (2016) Austerity and collective bargaining in Spain: The political and dysfunctional nature of neoliberal deregulation. *European Journal of Industrial Relations* 22(3): 267–280.
Rodríguez C., Rojo R. and Lucio M. (2019) Spain: Challenges to legitimacy and representation in a context of fragmentation and neoliberal reform. In: Müller T., Vandaele K. and Waddington J. (eds) *Collective Bargaining in Europe: Towards an Endgame*. 563–582. Brussels: European Trade Union Institute.

Rueda D. (2007) *Social Democracy Inside Out: Government Partisanship, Insiders, and Outsiders in Industrialized Democracies*. Oxford: Oxford University Press.
Silva M., Martins L. F. and Lopes H. (2018) Asymmetric labor market reforms: Effects on wage growth and conversion probability of fixed-term contracts. *ILR Review* 71(3): 760–788.
Traxler F. (2004) The metamorphoses of corporatism: From classical to lean patterns. *European Journal of Political Research* 43(4): 571–598.
Watson S. E. (2015). *The Left Divided: The Development and Transformation of Advanced Welfare States*. New York: Oxford University Press.

1 Competitive and Inclusive Solidarity in Contemporary Labour Markets

Two Ideal Types

Paulo Marques, Rui Branco, Óscar Molina, and Renato Miguel Carmo

Introduction

Labour market inequalities have spread across the Western world in recent decades. Key indicators, such as the share of atypical employment, illustrate the magnitude of the transformations that have occurred. In the European Union (EU), the share of young people (aged 15–24) on fixed-term contracts rose from 41.1% in 2002 to 51.0% in 2024 (Eurostat, 2025). This rise is notable given that incentives to use temporary contracts were arguably weaker than in the early 2000s, owing to the deregulation of permanent contracts in many EU countries over this period. Alongside the spread of atypical employment, other interrelated problems emerged. Workers with atypical contracts have lower collective bargaining coverage because they are over-represented in small firms and in sectors where coverage is lower (Palier and Thelen, 2010). Furthermore, their access to social protection is more precarious because eligibility for social benefits in many EU countries depends on prior contributions to social security (Palier, 2010). This problem is felt more acutely in Continental and Southern European countries due to the *Bismarckian* nature of their welfare regimes (Esping-Andersen, 1990; Ferrera, 1996). Because atypical workers tend to contribute more irregularly, they are adversely affected. Finally, their wages are, on average, lower than those of workers with permanent contracts.

Unsurprisingly, the issue of precariousness gained momentum in public debate from the 2000s, especially in the countries hardest hit by this problem, and it received increased attention after the sovereign debt crisis. Consequently, de-segmentation policies were implemented in many countries (e.g., Carver and Doellgast, 2021; Eichhorst and Marx, 2021; Marques et al., 2025). However, this was not a smooth process. While some de-segmentation policies focussed exclusively on improving the situation of precarious workers, others sought to re-regulate the labour market for the workforce as a whole. This leads to an interesting puzzle: most of the literature on de-segmentation policies defines solidarity as a new agenda aimed at overcoming dualised labour markets by improving the position of precarious workers, yet recent

DOI: 10.4324/9781003519874-2

experiences suggest that the process is more complex because conceptions of solidarity vary.

The existing literature often conceptualises solidarity as policies that increase the protection of the most vulnerable workers (Doellgast et al., 2018; Carver and Doellgast, 2021). Examples include revisions to labour law that further regulate temporary employment (fixed-term contracts or temporary-work-agency employment); legislative changes that seek to regulate platform work; collective agreements that contain clauses providing greater protection for precarious workers; the creation of, or increases in, the national minimum wage; special programmes aimed at converting atypical contracts into permanent ones; and reforms to social protection providing more generous support for atypical workers (e.g., making self-employed workers eligible for unemployment benefits). These measures strengthen vulnerable workers' protection against labour market risks. It is therefore a notion of solidarity focussed on policies rather than interpersonal relations. This is the understanding adopted in this book.

Nevertheless, this literature typically does not distinguish between different conceptions of solidarity. Carver and Doellgast (2021: 371) provide a good illustration. When categorising union strategies regarding precarious workers, they treat 'solidarity' as situations in which

> the union was able to improve working conditions for the peripheral workforce. This includes cases in which the union simultaneously improved conditions for the core workforce, as well as those in which the conditions for the core workforce remain stable or even declined.

In other words, they do not differentiate between cases where the position of the core workforce remains stable and those where it is weakened.

We argue that the main distinction is between what we call *competitive* and *inclusive* solidarity. The latter assumes that greater solidarity entails implementing reforms that increase the regulation of atypical employment and, at a minimum, keep intact the labour market position of workers with permanent contracts. Accordingly, resisting liberalisation is a precondition for further labour market solidarity (Streeck, 2009; Polanyi, 1944). This perspective challenges the view that the key division in contemporary labour markets lies between insiders and outsiders; instead, it posits that the major conflict is between organised labour and market forces. Competitive solidarity, by contrast, combines tighter regulation of atypical employment with labour market liberalisation in other areas. It is rooted in the idea that expanding markets in some spheres may enhance precarious workers' chances of entering the labour market and accessing good jobs. It sees the insider–outsider divide as a crucial feature of contemporary labour markets. However, it differs from traditional neoliberal economics in that it regards tighter regulation of non-permanent contracts as part of a strategy to foster labour market solidarity. More regulation of non-permanent contracts aims to establish a floor for competition in the labour market (akin to the role played by minimum wages). In addition, within this conception, active labour market policies (ALMPs) play a salient role because they assist precarious workers in job transitions. Again, this is a regulatory approach compatible with market expansion.

The main objective of the present chapter is to define these two ideal types of solidarity. The chapter begins by presenting the main building blocks of what we call competitive solidarity. Given that this literature dates back to the early 2000s, we engage with several research agendas, notably dualisation and welfare state literatures on new social risks, social investment, and flexicurity. We then set out the main features of what we call inclusive solidarity. We start by reviewing empirical studies that emphasise interdependencies within the labour force, before moving on to discuss the relationship between interdependence and de-segmentation policies, drawing on a Durkheimian understanding of social solidarity. The final section concludes the chapter.

Competitive Solidarity: Assumptions and Policy Toolkit

This section reviews the dualisation literature and the welfare state scholarship on new social risks, social investment, and flexicurity. We argue that these strands share common features in how they define the key conflicts in contemporary capitalism and how they should be addressed.

Dualisation: Insider–Outsider Logics

The dualisation literature draws substantially on the economic insider–outsider tradition (Blanchard, 2006; Lindbeck and Snower, 1988; Lindbeck and Snower, 2001), and is therefore aligned with many elements of neoliberal conceptions of labour market functioning (Rubery et al., 2016).

Liberalisation involved the deregulation of employment-protection legislation, a reduction in the scope of collective bargaining, and the retrenchment of generous welfare benefits. Neoliberal economics deemed wage flexibility crucial to the proper functioning of the labour market. Neoliberal thinkers argued that these three institutions hindered labour market functioning by impeding wage flexibility (Hayek, 1960: chs 18–19; Howell, 2005: ch. 1). The economic insider–outsider literature further developed this argument in the 1980s and 1990s. In addition to emphasising the need for deregulation to ensure wage flexibility, it highlighted how regulations protect some workers (insiders) while neglecting others (outsiders), thereby increasing segmentation. At its core, this approach assumes that market mechanisms are efficient and that outsiders remain excluded from the labour market and/or trapped in precarious conditions only because institutions impede competition. Hence, the interests of insiders and outsiders are conceived as antagonistic. As Alesina and Giavazzi (2007) put it:

> In Italy, Spain and France, the labour market is split. The young are hired with temporary contracts that offer no social security and no prospects [...] Reforms that eliminate this duality by making the entire labour market flexible, with an appropriate scheme of unemployment compensation, would not only reduce unemployment but, most importantly, favour the really poor and young entry-level workers. This is an example of a pro-market policy that favours the poor.

Dualisation posits that contemporary labour markets are divided into insiders and outsiders. Insiders hold permanent contracts, have access to standard social protection, and are covered by collective agreements; they therefore face better prospects for career progression and working conditions. Outsiders, by contrast, hold atypical contracts, face higher risks of unemployment, have access to lower-quality social protection and are often not covered by collective agreements. Unsurprisingly, outsiders' labour market conditions are worse than those of insiders.

Two principal arguments have been advanced to explain the causes of dualisation (Marques and Salavisa, 2017: 137–39). The first, associated with Rueda (2005; 2007; 2014), holds that dualisation results from insiders colluding with unions and centre-left parties to safeguard their position: centre-left parties maintain regulation and welfare generosity for insiders (e.g., generous unemployment benefits for workers who contribute regularly to social security and strict employment protection legislation), while worsening the position of outsiders (through deregulation of fixed-term contracts and limited investment in ALMPs). Since the 1980s, pressure to deregulate labour market institutions has intensified. Confronted with this trend, Rueda argues, the centre-left and unions have preferred two-tier labour market reforms, i.e., reforms that disproportionately affect outsiders. Unions are said to adopt this strategy because most of their members are insiders; moreover, such reforms did not jeopardise their organisational interests, notably their role in administering dismissals, which is paramount for unions in some EU countries (Davidsson and Emmenegger, 2013). By conceding on some issues (such as deregulating fixed-term contracts), unions retained influence over the direction of reform. For the centre-left, these reforms were electorally feasible because insiders constitute a core constituency. By avoiding deregulation of insiders' position, the centre-left protected its base while addressing rising unemployment, ostensibly by fostering job creation through greater labour market flexibility. In short, Rueda's contribution is closely linked to the economic insider–outsider literature, even though his focus is on the politics of segmentation; indeed, the label 'insider–outsider politics' has been used to characterise his approach. The second argument, developed by Palier and Thelen (2010), contends that labour market divisions in coordinated market economies have widened because regulations have been retained only in sectors where labour market institutions are essential to sustain institutional complementarities. Drawing on the 'varieties of capitalism' approach (Estevez-Abe et al., 2001; Hall and Soskice, 2001), they argue that institutions such as employment protection legislation, collective bargaining, and generous unemployment benefits are crucial to protect investment in specific skills, skills central to what they term the 'core manufacturing economy.' In the expanding service sector, these institutions are less pivotal, and deregulation can therefore proceed, especially when unemployment is high and flexibilisation is viewed as necessary for job creation. This dynamic, they argue, has widened divides in countries such as Germany and France, where regulation was maintained in industry (where specific-skills investment is important) but not in services, where flexible work arrangements and low-paid jobs proliferated during the 2000s. Consequently, there were transformations in social protection, particularly in conservative welfare regimes in which access depends on past contributions (Esping-Andersen, 1990). Workers unable to contribute regularly (outsiders) were not entitled to standard benefits and had to rely on second-tier provision (e.g., minimum income schemes), leading to a dualisation of social protection (Palier, 2010). As for collective bargaining, its scope narrowed as reforms promoted decentralisation. Germany is a case in point: sectoral bargaining coverage has declined substantially in recent decades, leaving workers outside industry with much poorer coverage than in the past (Streeck, 2009: ch. 2).

Beyond their distinct explanations of dualisation, two further differences distinguish this perspective from Rueda's. First, Palier and Thelen (2010) maintain that the centre-left and unions are not necessarily pro-insider. Dualisation is less pronounced where the centre-left is stronger, such as in Scandinavian countries, because social-democratic welfare regimes protect those most in need (Esping-Andersen, 1990). Owing to their universal character, these regimes are better suited to protecting outsiders. Second, unions are not inherently pro-insider: they are more likely to champion outsiders when marginal workers form part of their constituencies, as in Scandinavia (Thelen, 2014). Despite these differences, both approaches concur that contemporary labour markets are increasingly divided and that insiders' and outsiders' interests are in tension. Both also argue that existing regulatory tools affect the two groups differently, and they agree that dualisation can constitute a stable equilibrium in the long run because a deterioration in outsiders' position does not necessarily impinge on insiders.

New Social Risks, Social Investment, and Flexicurity

As noted in the introduction, atypical employment and new social vulnerabilities have risen since the 1990s. Scholarship on 'old' and 'new' social policies, social investment, and flexicurity – rightly highlighting these developments – has offered analytical frameworks and advanced reform proposals. This section engages these perspectives critically, arguing that they tend to view insiders' and outsiders' interests as being in conflict and therefore advocate de-segmentation policies that focus on the most vulnerable while retaining some labour market flexibility to safeguard outsiders' interests and the needs of post-industrial economies.

Set against the neoliberal era of permanent austerity and retrenchment, attention to political dynamics has remained central in the welfare state literature (Pierson, 2001; 2011). At the same time, an increasingly salient strand has examined how the transition from industrial to post-industrial economies and societies spawned *new social risk* groups and how, alongside efforts to contain social expenditure, new policies catering to these strata emerged over recent decades (Armingeon and Bonoli, 2006; Bonoli and Natali, 2012; Emmenegger et al., 2012; Taylor-Gooby, 2004). Deindustrialisation, rising employment in the service and knowledge economy (Wren, 2013), and the feminisation of the labour force have unsettled family structures and destandardised employment relations, creating new protection needs. For example, work–family balance, single parenthood, care for relatives or people with disabilities, and the updating of obsolete skills. Moreover, these risks tend to accrue to the same groups: migrants, young people, families with children, working women, the atypically employed, and the long-term unemployed. The protection needs of these groups – notably low-skilled immigrant parents, low-income working mothers, and low-skilled young unemployed people – often overlap, resulting in social exclusion (Bonoli, 2006).

Measures addressing industrial-era risks – e.g., the loss of the male breadwinner's income due to old age, unemployment, sickness, or disability – are designated 'old social policies' and mostly involve income replacement via 'passive' transfers and job protection regulation. By contrast, 'new social policies' target post-industrial risks such as atypical employment, long-term unemployment, in-work poverty, family instability, and low labour market participation. These latter policies aim to foster employability and activation, with a view to returning recipients to gainful employment and/or covering new risk groups that lack protection through employment. Thus, 'old' instruments – such as passive income-replacement benefits and employment protection – contrast with 'new' measures such as: ALMPs, training and skills formation, and needs-based income support for the (long-term) unemployed (Bonoli, 2006).

Häusermann's work (2012: 117) presents a policy matrix where each policy type can undergo either expansive or restrictive reforms. This 2×2 matrix juxtaposes 'old' and 'new' social policies against 'expansion' and 'restriction.' As simultaneous expansion or retrenchment of both policy types is rarely feasible, most reform trade-offs occur in two quadrants: welfare protectionism and welfare retrenchment. Welfare protectionism expands 'old' policies while constraining 'new' ones, shielding insiders and leaving outsiders under-protected; welfare retrenchment does the reverse, extending 'new' policies and tightening 'old' ones, thereby reallocating resources towards outsiders while reducing insiders' income security (Häusermann, 2012: 117–118). Post-war expansion predominated until the 1980s, after which fiscal and political constraints – social-spending cuts, weakened labour power, and labour market deregulation – curbed it (Streeck, 2014: ch. 1). Yet comprehensive retrenchment has also been limited by electoral costs and institutional veto points (Pierson, 1994; 2001). Hence, reform has largely proceeded within the two feasible quadrants, where the insider–outsider conflict precludes a straightforward win–win settlement.

According to Bonoli,

> [t]he extreme generosity of the post-war welfare state, the rapid process of population ageing and the weak political influence of new social risk groups makes it extremely unlikely that available resources will be assigned to the development of new social policies rather than keeping the post-war welfare state.
>
> 2006: 26

Thus, these scholars tend to argue that welfare protectionism was the most common outcome of the conflict between insiders and outsiders; this aligns closely with Rueda's view that two-tier labour market reforms were the most frequent outcome. Again, on this account, no win–win solution seems feasible. Additional factors also reinforce the framing of policy development in terms of trade-offs. First, the tightening of social expenditure and the allure of social or tax dumping in the pursuit of 'competitiveness,' foreign investment, and credit – compounded by the strictures of European economic and monetary integration – permanently constrained fiscal space and generated pressure to deregulate the labour market. Second, Western European countries crossed the post-industrial threshold at different times: the Nordic and British cases in the 1970s, continental countries in the 1980s, and, finally, third-wave democracies on the Southern rim in the 1990s. Consequently, the latter faced a peculiar modernisation challenge: matching a comparatively late expansion of old social policies ('catch-up convergence') with the need to address emerging new social risks. Thus, the conflict between insiders and outsiders was particularly acute in Southern Europe because both groups were demanding expansion in the same historical period. It is also interesting to note that these scholars argue that some degree of liberalisation benefits outsiders. For instance, Bonoli (2006: 26) claims that 'employment protection legislation is not only of little use to new social risk groups, but seems actually to be detrimental to them,' on the grounds that only insiders benefit from high job security. What outsiders require, by contrast, is the opportunity to compete with insiders for jobs and access to new social policies.

Following the term *social investment* state, coined by Giddens in *The Third Way – The Renewal of Social Democracy* (1998), and Esping-Andersen et al.'s (2002) agenda-setting *Why We Need a New Welfare State*, the 'emerging paradigm' of social investment became influential in welfare state and labour market reform. It has been mainstream in European discourse since the Lisbon Agenda (2000) and the subsequent Europe 2020 strategy, and is widely used by international organisations such as the OECD, UNICEF, and the World Bank. From the social investment perspective, social policy ought to address radically changed economic and social conditions. Knowledge drives productivity and economic growth in the post-industrial era, and the labour force must therefore adapt to ever-changing needs (Morel et al., 2012: 8). In the 2013 Social Investment Package, the European Commission called on national governments to prepare

> individuals, families and societies to respond to the new risks of a competitive knowledge economy, by investing in human capital and capabilities from early childhood through old age, rather than in policies that simply "repair" damages after moments of economic or personal crisis.
>
> (Hemerijck, 2017: 4)

Social investment is a paradigmatic 'new social policy' in that it seeks to modernise the welfare state to better address new social risks while shifting the welfare balance from ex-post compensation to ex-ante risk prevention. It does so via distinct welfare functions: supporting the efficient use and allocation of labour resources over the life course ('flow'), enhancing and maintaining human capital ('stock'), and mitigating social inequity while providing automatic macroeconomic stabilisers ('buffer'). These functions are 'consistent with widely shared normative aspirations of work for everyone, gender equality, and capacitating service provision as the foundations of solidarity in the competitive knowledge economy' (Hemerijck, 2017: 19–25). Although the 'buffer' pillar is part of this approach, and thus passive policies are not ignored, there is a clear emphasis on the other two pillars ('flow' and 'stock'). As social policy shifts from smoothing consumption (income replacement) to enhancing families' productive capacity, the focus moves from 'passive' protection via cash benefits (decommodification) to facilitating labour market participation (Jenson and Saint-Martin, 2003). Long-term investment in human capital, beginning with childcare, is the preferred path to social inclusion through the labour market, ensuring future productivity gains and the skills to seize opportunities in a knowledge economy and to break the intergenerational chain of poverty (Esping-Andersen et al., 2002: ch. 2). Overall, social protection shifts from collective to individual responsibility: the emphasis on paid employment entails a commitment to job search and the responsibility to accept suitable employment. A new balance between social rights and duties is thus established (Cantillon and Van Lancker, 2012).

The much-needed attention to the plight of outsiders, working mothers, the working poor, atypical workers, youth, and the long-term unemployed is sometimes framed in ways that downplay the importance of traditional labour market institutions. This is clear in Hemerijck's (2017: 25) contribution: '[r]estrictive employment protection with classical job security for insiders constrains labour market "flow" and employment growth.' Understanding the predicament as zero-sum tends to downplay the position of insiders. There is, therefore, a clear link between this strand and the literatures reviewed above (dualisation and new social risks).

Nevertheless, it is important to bear in mind that social investment is not a fully-fledged, coherent paradigm. This case therefore contains more varied ideas and interpretations of basic principles than new social risks. This variation can be traced back to two seminal works underpinning the social investment framework. Giddens's view of social investment, set out in *The Third Way* and ultimately replacing traditional forms of social protection, was highly influential in Third Way/*Die Neue Mitte* politics (Lister, 2004). By contrast, Esping-Andersen et al.'s *Why We Need a New Welfare State* (2002) draws on the social-democratic ideas of Myrdal in the 1930s (Morel et al., 2012) to argue, against Giddens, that social investment and traditional social protection are both indispensable; they maintain that the 'minimisation of poverty and income insecurity is a precondition for an effective social investment strategy,' and that the idea that activation can substitute for conventional income-maintenance guarantees is at best naïve optimism and at worst counterproductive (Esping-Andersen et al., 2002: 5). This inherent ambiguity has structured a lively critical discussion (see Hemerijck, 2017). Some have warned that reallocating spending from income support to activation undermines the mitigation of poverty and inequality (Morel et al., 2012; Van Kersbergen and Hemerijck, 2012). Others have pointed out that the already better-off gain when social spending is rechannelled to new social policies ('Matthew effects'); for example, middle-class families benefit disproportionately from public investment in childcare (Cantillon and Van Lancker, 2013). There is also the issue of those unable to participate in the labour market or engage in paid employment, such as people with disabilities and, more broadly, unpaid care workers. In short, despite differences within the social-investment literature, an important branch views further labour market competition (namely, less job protection and welfare generosity for insiders) combined with pro-outsider policies (investment in new social policies) as the appropriate approach for post-industrial economies. There is, therefore, continuity between some branches of social investment and the literatures reviewed above (dualisation and new social risks).

Since the 1990s, ascendant neoliberal theory has prescribed flexibilisation and deregulation of labour markets as the answer to persistent, widespread unemployment, particularly under the guise of 'Eurosclerosis.' The more atypical employment spread, the more the 'standard employment contract' was questioned as a reference for European countries. The erosion of employment and income security for many was accompanied by the segmentation of labour markets, in which well-protected core sectors coexist with relatively unprotected strata 'at the margin.' Thus, greater flexibility ought to be matched by adequate levels of security, in turn a precondition for skills improvement leading to sustainable labour market participation (Viebrock and Clasen, 2009). Rather than policies promoting either flexibility for employers or security for workers, *flexicurity* aims to do both, treating flexibility and security as complementary rather than contradictory. For Viebrock and Clasen (2009: 307), it charts a 'third way' between the flexibility of 'Anglo-Saxon' labour markets and the strict job security of (Southern) European countries, or between the flexibility of liberal market economies and the social safety nets of the traditional Scandinavian welfare states. As in some branches of social investment, this literature assumes contradictions between the interests of insiders and outsiders. The idea of flexicurity goes back to labour market reforms in the Netherlands and Denmark (Wilthagen and Tros, 2004). In the mid-1990s, the Dutch sociologist Hans Adriaansens introduced the concept with reference to the Dutch Flexibility and Security Act and the Act concerning the Allocation of Workers via Intermediaries. Both sought to add 'flexibility into the labour market by relaxing dismissal laws and the rules to start a temporary work agency [...] while generating a higher level of security for employees in flexible jobs' (Keune and Jepsen, 2007: 5). Dutch flexicurity combines atypical, flexible work with social-security rights aligned with standard employment (Van Oorschot, 2004), and has been described as 'normalising non-standard work' (Viebrock and Clasen, 2009: 315). Largely unconcerned with atypical forms of employment, Danish flexicurity builds on (*i*) flexible standard employment (low employment protection); (*ii*) extensive unemployment benefits offering income security; and (*iii*) ALMPs for skills formation and activation of the unemployed (Keune and Jepsen, 2007: 6). This mix – high occupational and geographical mobility via low employment protection, compensated by generous unemployment benefits and ambitious ALMPs aimed at skills formation and activation – came to be known as the Danish 'golden triangle' of labour market policy (Madsen, 2004: 101). Job security is replaced by employment security (Viebrock and Clasen, 2009: 313).

The influential 2007 European Commission interpretation starts from the pressure to adapt to the ever-changing demands of the global economy and the need for competitive European national economies (Bekker, 2012). Transitions between jobs and labour market statutes (employed, unemployed, inactive) are becoming increasingly common, so labour markets should adapt. As workers manage frequent transitions by remaining employable, security must be provided as a bridge to render mobility acceptable. Moreover, it is argued, flexicurity addresses enduring issues of labour market segmentation and precarious employment. Specifically, the European Commission (2007) outlines five key elements: contractual arrangements offering adequate flexibility for workers and employers; ALMPs to support transitions between jobs and from unemployment and inactivity; lifelong learning to boost employability; social security ensuring that all workers are adequately supported during absences from the labour market, easing mobility and transitions; and the involvement of social partners to achieve efficacy and legitimacy through consensus.

As with the dualisation, new social risks and social investment literatures, the insider–outsider split is also central to the flexicurity debate. The seminal work of Wilthagen and Tros (2004: 170) makes this clear in defining flexicurity policies:

> an essential element of our definition pertains to weaker groups, either in or outside the labour market. This means that policies or measures that enhance labour market flexibility and exclusively increase (employment, income, or social) security of stronger/insider groups are not to be counted as flexicurity policies or measures.

Competitive Solidarity: Summary

There is a common thread across the strands of literature reviewed in this section: the labour market is increasingly divided, and this division generates growing conflicts within the labour force. Moreover, these literatures posit a tension between labour market regulatory tools. While employment protection legislation for permanent contracts and passive labour market policies (unemployment benefits and early retirement) matter to insiders, they are less salient for outsiders. Outsiders benefit more from new social policies (e.g., ALMPs, investment in education, lifelong learning) and from tighter regulation of temporary contracts. At a time when expanding both sets of policies appears difficult, these authors view a mix of flexibilisation policies (which mainly affect insiders) and pro-outsider policies as the most feasible strategy. Solidarity, in this framing, means protecting outsiders by lowering the level of regulation for insiders. We call this *competitive solidarity* because greater market competition in some spheres forms part of the agenda (Streeck, 2004: 25). There are four reasons typically advanced. First, deregulation in some areas permits re-regulation in others. For instance, reduced generosity in unemployment benefits may allow governments to invest more in ALMPs. Another example concerns employment protection legislation: if job security for permanent contracts decreases, there is greater scope to regulate atypical employment more strictly, because the risks of job destruction are less acute when permanent contracts are less rigid. Second, deregulation for insiders narrows the regulatory gap between the two groups, enabling them to compete for the same jobs. Third, 'productive' social policies assist outsiders in flexible labour markets, notably by speeding up transitions between jobs; the favoured policy mix is compatible with greater labour market flexibility. Finally, it is argued that knowledge-intensive economies require higher degrees of labour market competition; greater flexibility accelerates this transition and thus boosts job creation, helping outsiders to enter the labour market. Despite commonalities with a purely neoliberal economic approach, there are differences. Competitive solidarity regards tighter regulation of non-permanent contracts as part of a strategy to foster labour market solidarity. More regulation for non-permanent contracts aims to establish a floor for competition in the labour market (akin to the role of minimum wages). In addition, within this conception of solidarity, public spending – particularly on ALMPs, education, and lifelong learning – may play a meaningful role in job creation.

Inclusive Solidarity: Interdependence and Re-Regulation

Recent studies suggest that workers with standard and atypical contracts do not necessarily have contradictory interests. We review these contributions and show that the notion of interdependence is central to the debate. We then deepen the discussion by drawing on Durkheim's conception of social solidarity. If the interests of the two groups are not contradictory, implementing de-segmentation policies implies resisting liberalisation and re-regulating the labour market for all workers. We conclude the section by summarising the main features of inclusive solidarity.

Interdependence in Practice: Mechanisms and Actors

Several recent studies argue that contemporary labour markets are characterised less by conflict of interests than by convergence, because workers are interdependent. We begin by explaining how interdependence affects individual workers' behaviour before considering its implications for unions and political parties.

Allowing atypical employment to spread through two-tier labour market reforms triggers its further expansion, which in turn puts pressure on workers with standard contracts (Baccaro and Benassi, 2017; Dorigatti, 2017; Eichhorst and Marx, 2021). When atypical employment grows rapidly, it also affects those with stable arrangements, because their conditions worsen in the face of large numbers of jobseekers willing to accept low pay and poor conditions. A classic example concerns former public utilities – such as telecommunications or postal services (Marques, 2015: ch. 5; Holst, 2014; Kornelakis, 2016) – where the spread of atypical employment led to deteriorating conditions for standard workers and increased pressure for collective dismissals. Before privatisations, most workers in these companies were directly employed on good terms. Many firms operated internal labour markets in which progression was based on seniority and job stability was very high (Doeringer and Piore, 1971; Grimshaw et al., 2001). After privatisations, challenger firms adopted different workforce strategies; agency work became common as deregulation permitted new hiring forms, and internal labour market structures were no longer used to manage staff. Competitive pressure forced former public firms to restructure substantially: they turned to outsourcing, reduced direct employment, and revised collective agreements that had guaranteed seniority-based progression. Studies also report that the spread of atypical employment extended to industry and negatively affected permanent employees (Benassi, 2017; Holst, 2014). In short, the diffusion of atypical employment can harm workers with standard contracts, fostering greater solidarity across the two groups as both experience deteriorating conditions.

Interdependence can also operate through the weakening of standard workers' position, which in turn harms atypical workers. As Tsakalotos (2004) argues, reforms that undermine employees with permanent contracts shift power towards employers, prompting regulatory change that damages all workers over time as labour markets become more unequal. Rubery et al. (2016: 240–41) add that, although standard workers may face more competition from precarious workers in flexible labour markets, many atypical workers belong to groups vulnerable to discrimination (e.g., women, ethnic minorities, disabled, and older workers). Exposing them to more frequent hiring competition increases encounters with prejudice and stereotyping. Emmenegger (2009: 135–136) notes household level channels: outsiders are often women or young men who are economically dependent on male insiders. If insiders' position is weakened, outsiders' position may deteriorate too. He further argues that dualisation – as a two-segment, reductionist approach – rests on limited mobility between groups, whereas people's economic fortunes are far more volatile. Atypical workers may reasonably expect to access more stable jobs over time; deregulating permanent contracts therefore also harms them, especially where such access is a realistic prospect. Taken together, this evidence supports the argument that convergence of interests can emerge.

Interdependencies also shape unions' positions. First, the expansion of atypical employment tends to weaken unions because density falls: atypical workers are harder to unionise. Not surprisingly, even when unions initially accept two-tier reforms, they often shift position once the long-term effects become apparent. Marques and Fonseca (2022) show that one of Spain's most representative confederations (General Workers' Union) agreed with the socialist party to implement a two-tier labour market reform in 1984. It quickly recognised the negative consequences, including a sharp drop in unionisation and the erosion of unions' legitimacy as class actors. It subsequently opposed further deregulation of temporary contracts. Interdependencies are at work here: permanent workers cannot safeguard their position if their primary representative, unions, are weak and unable to resist liberalisation. Moreover, the decoupling of unions and the centre-left (Howell, 2001; Piazza, 2001) increased the need to address precarious workers' concerns. Faced with this, unions had to rebuild organisational power; the size of atypical employment made these workers a necessary organising target. If standard workers wish to defend their position, they must attract the support of the most vulnerable, again encouraging convergence of interests.

For political parties, interdependence is also relevant. The rise of atypical employment influences party positions, with implications for standard workers. As the number of atypical workers grows, their electoral weight increases (Schwander, 2018). This poses two challenges to centre-left parties. If they focus solely on insiders, as the dualisation literature suggests (Rueda, 2007), other parties may attract these voters. On the left, radical-left parties acted as spokespersons for these workers during the 2000s; their electoral rise in some countries understandably concerned both centre-left and centre-right parties (Hall, 2007: 82–83). This was evident during austerity in Southern Europe, with parties such as *Podemos* in Spain and the *Bloco de Esquerda* and *Syriza* in Portugal and Greece, respectively. Unsurprisingly, some centrist parties enacted reforms increasing regulation of temporary contracts, for example, Portugal's 2019 reform (Marques and Fonseca, 2022). Some populist parties also sought to attract these workers. When the *Movimento Cinque Stelle* in Italy formed a coalition with the *Lega Nord*, it passed a law that substantially tightened regulation of atypical contracts (Eichhorst and Marx, 2021). In some instances, tighter regulation of atypical employment coincided with looser regulation of permanent contracts (e.g., Spain in 2001 and 2006, under centre-right and centre-left governments, respectively). In others, reforms improved the position of both groups (e.g., Italy under the *Lega Nord – Movimento Cinque Stelle*). This illustrates interdependence: as the number of precarious workers rises, parties cannot ignore their demands, and the resulting reforms may improve or worsen conditions for those on permanent contracts.

To sum up, recent empirical studies show that the interests of the groups are not necessarily contradictory and that there are strong reasons for key actors – unions and political parties – to represent precarious workers, especially where atypical employment is extensive. We now link interdependence to de-segmentation policies.

From Interdependence to De-Segmentation: A Durkheimian Perspective

Émile Durkheim's understanding of social solidarity is useful here, because interdependence, which he sees as a crucial building block of solidarity in contemporary societies, helps define what we call inclusive solidarity. We argue that the literature reviewed in Section 2 typically treats labour markets as segmented into groups that do not interact. From that perspective, deregulation affecting atypical workers has no consequences for the core workforce; dualisation is viewed as a stable equilibrium, and solidarity is conceived as intra-group rather than transversal. Drawing on Durkheim, we distinguish between approaches that treat segments as non-interacting fragments, thereby rendering solidarity across segments unlikely, and those that recognise interdependencies between segments, where cross-segment solidarity is possible.

In *The Division of Labour in Society* (1893), Durkheim analyses how societies are created and maintained. Social solidarity is necessary to prevent societies from falling apart, and its nature evolves over time. He identifies two types of solidarity: mechanical and organic (1893: chs 2–3). Mechanical solidarity is solidarity by likeness: in ancient societies, individuals were similar in terms of work tasks, education, values or religion, and solidarity emerged from similarity. Durkheim treats this as an ideal type, contrasted with organic solidarity. When providing real examples of mechanical solidarity, he refers to 'segments': closely integrated, locally situated groups, relatively isolated from others, leading a life of their own and presupposing separation from the outside. Many ancient societies, he argues, were composed of such segments (e.g., clans). Organic solidarity is different. In contemporary societies, greater complexity arises because individuals differ more. The division of labour – driven by population growth and rising 'material and moral density' (more people within a given territory and more intense communications and exchanges) – produces social differentiation and a new basis of solidarity. Rather than elimination through competition (as in the animal kingdom), differentiation provides a peaceful solution to the struggle for life: more people survive because each performs a different function. Solidarity emerges because individuals are interdependent. The farmer needs the blacksmith's tools; the blacksmith needs the farmer's produce. Cooperation arises because people need one another, unlike in ancient societies, where solidarity rested on similarity.

Applied to de-segmentation, the Durkheimian notion of interdependence is helpful. Where interests converge because of interdependence, de-segmentation policies follow a different logic. Rather than focussing narrowly on outsiders and increasing labour market competition, they entail re-regulation for the entire workforce and do not heighten competition. In this understanding, the main divide in contemporary labour markets is not insiders versus outsiders but workers versus employers (Table 1.1), since employers are the principal actors pushing for deregulation (commodification of labour), which affects those on standard and atypical contracts alike. Workers resist this by demanding greater regulation (decommodification of labour) (Polanyi, 1944). Many scholars argue that, unlike in the post-war era, when employers consented to higher regulation (Korpi, 2006), employers altered their strategies from the 1980s as political, economic, and social

Table 1.1 Linking labour market divides to de-segmentation strategies: two ideal types

Ideal Types	*Key Divide*	*De-Segmentation Strategy*	*Primary Regulatory Instruments*
Competitive solidarity	Conflicting interests between insiders and outsiders	Pro-outsider policies; increased labour market competition	New social policies; further regulation of atypical employment
Inclusive solidarity	Conflicting interests between workers and employers	Re-regulation for the entire labour force; reduced labour market competition	Traditional labour market institutions (employment protection legislation, passive labour market policies, and collective bargaining)

Source: Authors' elaboration.

conditions changed (Glyn, 2006; Streeck, 2009; Baccaro and Howell, 2017). This understanding of solidarity rests on three pillars: interdependence among workers; intensifying conflict between workers and employers in contemporary capitalism; and de-segmentation as re-regulating the entire labour market (strengthening traditional institutions such as employment protection legislation, passive labour market policies, and collective bargaining).

It follows that the greater the interdependence, the more likely solidarity across segments becomes. Interdependence is greater where atypical employment is more prevalent. It is also reinforced where the professional activities of precarious and permanent workers are closely connected – as can occur in public administration or industry when precarious and permanent workers operate side by side – thereby fostering interdependence between the two segments.

Inclusive Solidarity: Summary

The starting point for this conception of solidarity is that, although labour markets are segmented, this does not necessarily imply that workers' interests are contradictory. Indeed, owing to their interdependence, deregulatory policies affecting workers with atypical contracts inevitably also affect the conditions of those with permanent contracts (and *vice versa*). Labour market segmentation is not a stable equilibrium but a phase within a broader process of labour market flexibilisation. Furthermore, this ideal type rejects the notion of a conflict among labour market regulatory tools. What is needed is the strengthening of traditional institutions – such as employment protection legislation (for both permanent and temporary contracts), passive labour market policies, and collective bargaining – which benefits both precarious and standard workers. From this perspective, the key conflict in contemporary capitalism is between workers and employers: employers push for market expansion (deregulation), whereas workers demand stronger regulation. We call this *inclusive solidarity* because market expansion is ruled out (in contrast to competitive solidarity). Less labour market liberalisation is the best strategy for addressing growing labour market inequalities (Glyn, 2006; Streeck, 2009). It involves implementing de-segmentation policies that entail re-regulating the labour market for all workers, including those on standard contracts. A complete rejection of neoliberal economics lies at the core of this perspective.

Concluding Remarks

This chapter has developed a theoretical framework for studying labour market reforms implemented in Portugal and Spain during periods of progressive coalitions, but the framework can also be applied to labour market policies in other geographical and historical contexts. As ideal types are abstract categories, we should not expect to identify policies that fit perfectly into either of the two broad analytical categories (Hay, 2020). The empirical chapters of this book seek to locate policies along the continuum between the two extremes (competitive solidarity versus inclusive solidarity). The case studies therefore relate the content of each reform or policy to the two ideal types defined in this chapter.

Chapter 2 operationalises the framework in three steps. First, it specifies two governing social blocs (Centrist–Employer and Left–Union) and treats bloc composition as a necessary (though not sufficient) determinant of whether reform trajectories gravitate towards competitive or inclusive solidarity. Secondly, it contrasts the veto structures of the two principal decision arenas, arguing that tripartite social concertation embeds a consent constraint whereas parliamentary law-making contains no institutional employer veto. Thirdly, it conceptualises the EU as a conditional external selector whose liberal or social tilt modulates the feasible scope of change. Bringing these together, Chapter 2 arrays eight stylised combinations of bloc, arena, and EU stance, and derives expectations about when settlements will tend towards competitive or inclusive solidarity.

References

Alesina A. and Giavazzi F. (2007) Why the left should learn to love liberalism? *VoxEU*. Available at: https://voxeu.org/article/why-left-should-learn-love-liberalism.

Armingeon K. and Bonoli G. (eds) (2006) *Adapting Post-war Social Policies to New Social Risks*. London: Routledge.

Baccaro L. and Benassi C. (2017) Throwing out the ballast: Growth models and the liberalisation of German industrial relations. *Socio-Economic Review* 15: 85–115.

Baccaro L. and Howell C. (2017) *Trajectories of Neoliberal Transformation: European Industrial Relations After the 1970s*. Cambridge: Cambridge University Press.

Bekker S. (2012) *Flexicurity: The Emergence of a European Concept*. Antwerp: Intersentia.

Benassi C. (2017) Varieties of workplace dualisation: A study of agency work in the German automotive industry. *Industrial Relations Journal* 48(5–6): 424–441.

Blanchard O. (2006) European unemployment: The evolution of facts and ideas. *Economic Policy* 21(45): 5–59.

Bonoli G. (2006) New social risks and the politics of post-industrial welfare states. In: Armingeon K. and Bonoli G. (eds) *Adapting Post-war Social Policies to New Social Risks*. 3–26. London: Routledge.

Bonoli G. and Natali D. (eds) (2012) *The Politics of the New Welfare State*. Oxford: Oxford University Press.

Cantillon B. and Van Lancker W. (2012) Solidarity and reciprocity in the social investment state: What can be learned from the case of Flemish school allowances and truancy? *Journal of Social Policy* 41(4): 657–675.

Cantillon B. and Van Lancker W. (2013) Three shortcomings of the social investment perspective. *Social Policy and Society* 12(4): 553–564.

Carver L. and Doellgast V. (2021) Dualism or solidarity? Conditions for union success in regulating precarious work. *European Journal of Industrial Relations* 27(4): 367–385 (advance online publication).

Davidsson J. and Emmenegger P. (2013) Defending the organisation, not the members: Unions and the reform of job security legislation in Western Europe. *European Journal of Political Research* 52: 339–363.

Doellgast V., Lillie N. and Pulignano V. (2018) *Reconstructing Solidarity: Labour Unions, Precarious Work, and the Politics of Institutional Change in Europe*. Oxford: Oxford University Press.

Doeringer P. and Piore M. (1971) *Internal Labour Markets and Manpower Analysis*. Lexington, MA: Heath Lexington Books.

Dorigatti L. (2017) Trade unions in segmented labor markets: Evidence from the German metal and chemical sectors. *ILR Review* 70: 919–941.

Durkheim E. ([1893] 1933) *The Division of Labour in Society*. New York: Macmillan.

Eichhorst W. and Marx P. (2021) How stable is labour market dualism? Reforms of employment protection in nine European countries. *European Journal of Industrial Relations* 27(1): 93–110.

Emmenegger P. (2009) Barriers to entry: Insider/outsider politics and the political determinants of job security regulations. *Journal of European Social Policy* 19(2): 131–146.

Emmenegger P., Häusermann S., Palier B. and Seeleib-Kaiser M. (eds) (2012) *The Age of Dualisation: The Changing Face of Inequality in Deindustrializing Societies*. Oxford: Oxford University Press.

Esping-Andersen G. (1990) *The Three Worlds of Welfare Capitalism*. Cambridge: Polity Press.

Esping-Andersen G., Gallie D., Hemerijck A. and Myles J. (2002) *Why We Need a New Welfare State*. Oxford: Oxford University Press.

Estevez-Abe M., Iversen T. and Soskice D. (2001) Social protection and the formation of skills: A reinterpretation of the welfare state. In: Hall P. and Soskice D. (eds) Varieties of Capitalism: The Institutional Foundations of Comparative Advantage. 145–183. Oxford: Oxford University Press.

European Commission (2007) *Towards Common Principles of Flexicurity: More and Better Jobs through Flexibility and Security*. Brussels: European Commission.

Eurostat (2025) *Labour Force Survey*. Available at: https://ec.europa.eu/eurostat/databrowser/view/lfsa_etpgan__custom_18044211/default/table

Ferrera M. (1996) The southern model of welfare in Europe. *Journal of European Social Policy* 6(1): 17–37.

Giddens A. (1998) *The Third Way: The Renewal of Social Democracy*. Cambridge: Cambridge University Press.

Glyn A. (2006) *Capitalism Unleashed: Finance, Globalisation, and Welfare*. Oxford: Oxford University Press.

Grimshaw D., Ward K., Rubery J. and Beynon H. (2001) Organisations and the transformation of the internal labour market. *Work, Employment and Society* 15(1): 25–54.

Hall P. (2007) The evolution of varieties of capitalism in Europe. In: Hancké B., Rhodes M. and Thatcher M. (eds) *Beyond Varieties of Capitalism: Conflict, Contradictions and Complementarities in the European Economy*. 39–85. Oxford: Oxford University Press.

Hall P. and Soskice D. (2001) An introduction to varieties of capitalism. In: Hall P. and Soskice D. (eds) *Varieties of Capitalism: The Institutional Foundations of Comparative Advantage*. 1–68. Oxford: Oxford University Press.

Häusermann S. (2012) The politics of old and new social policies. In: Bonoli G. and Natali D. (eds) *The Politics of the New Welfare State*. 111–132. Oxford: Oxford University Press.

Häusermann S., Kurer T. and Traber D. (2019) The politics of trade-offs: Studying the dynamics of welfare state reform with conjoint experiments. *Comparative Political Studies* 52(7): 1059–1095.

Hay C. (2020) Does capitalism (still) come in varieties? *Review of International Political Economy* 27(2): 302–319.

Hayek F. (1960) *The Constitution of Liberty*. London: Routledge.

Hemerijck A. (ed) (2017) *The Uses of Social Investment*. Oxford: Oxford University Press.

Holst H. (2014) 'Commodifying institutions': Vertical disintegration and institutional change in German labour relations. *Work, Employment and Society* 28(1): 3–20.

Howell C. (2001) The end of the relationship between social democratic parties and trade unions? *Studies in Political Economy* 65: 7–37.

Howell D. (ed) (2005) *Fighting Unemployment: The Limits of Free Market Orthodoxy*. Oxford: Oxford University Press.

Jenson J. and Saint-Martin D. (2003) New routes to social cohesion? Citizenship and the social investment state. *Canadian Journal of Sociology* 28(1): 77–99.

Keune M. and Jepsen M. (2007) *Not Balanced and Hardly New: The European Commission's Quest for Flexicurity*. Brussels: ETUI-REHS.

Kornelakis A. (2016) Inclusion or dualisation? The political economy of employment relations in Italian and Greek telecommunications. *British Journal of Industrial Relations* 54(2): 385–408.

Korpi W. (2006) Power resources theory and employer-centred approaches in explanations of welfare states and varieties of capitalism: Protagonists, consenters, and antagonists. *World Politics* 58(2): 167–206.

Lindbeck A. and Snower D. (1988) *The Insider-Outsider Theory of Employment and Unemployment*. Cambridge, MA: MIT Press.

Lindbeck A. and Snower D. (2001) Insiders versus outsiders. *Journal of Economic Perspectives* 15(1): 165–188.

Lister R. (2004) The third way's social investment state. In: Lewis J. and Surender R. (eds) *Welfare State Change: Towards a Third Way?* 157–181. Oxford: Oxford University Press.

Madsen P. K. (2004) The Danish model of 'flexicurity': Experiences and lessons. *Transfer* 10: 187–207.

Marques P. (2015) *Young People and Labour Market Segmentation in Europe: An Institutionalist Perspective*. Doctoral thesis (PhD), ISCTE.

Marques P., Branco, R. and Guimarães, R. (2025) The politics of pro-outsider labour market reforms: A configurational study. *Comparative European Politics* 23(2): 159–184.

Marques P. and Fonseca D. (2022) Understanding the positions taken by moderate union confederations and centre-left parties during labour market reforms in Portugal and Spain: Why the configuration of left parties and trade union confederations matters. *European Journal of Industrial Relations* 28(1): 65–84.

Marques P. and Salavisa I. (2017) Young people and dualisation in Europe: A fuzzy set analysis. *Socio-Economic Review* 15(1): 135–160.

Morel N., Palier B. and Palme J. (eds) (2012) *Towards a Social Investment Welfare State? Ideas, Policies and Challenges*. Bristol: Policy Press.

Palier B. (ed) (2010) *A Long Goodbye to Bismarck? The Politics of Welfare Reform in Continental Europe*. Amsterdam: Amsterdam University Press.

Palier B. and Thelen K. (2010) Institutionalizing dualism: Complementarities and change in France and Germany. *Politics & Society* 38: 119–148.

Piazza J. (2001) De-linking labour: Labour unions and social democratic parties under globalisation. *Party Politics* 7: 413–435.

Pierson P. (1994) *Dismantling the Welfare State? Reagan, Thatcher and the Politics of Retrenchment*. Cambridge: Cambridge University Press.

Pierson P. (ed) (2001) *The New Politics of the Welfare State*. Oxford: Oxford University Press.

Pierson P. (2011) *The Welfare State Over the Very Long Run*. ZeS-Arbeitspapier No. 02/2011, Bremen: Universität Bremen, Zentrum für Sozialpolitik (ZeS).

Polanyi K. ([1944] 2001) *The Great Transformation: The Political and Economic Origins of Our Time*. Boston, MA: Beacon Press.

Rubery J., Keizer A. and Grimshaw D. (2016) Flexibility bites back: The multiple and hidden costs of flexible employment policies. *Human Resource Management Journal* 26(3): 235–251.

Rueda D. (2005) Insider-outsider politics in industrialised democracies: The challenge to social democratic parties. *American Political Science Review* 99(1): 61–74.

Rueda D. (2007) *Social Democracy Inside Out: Government Partisanship, Insiders, and Outsiders in Industrialised Democracies*. Oxford: Oxford University Press.

Rueda D. (2014) Dualisation, crisis and the welfare state. *Socio-Economic Review* 12(2): 381–407.

Schwander H. (2018) Are social democratic parties insider parties? Electoral strategies of social democratic parties in Western Europe in the age of dualisation. *Comparative European Politics* 17: 714–737.

Streeck W. (2004) International competition, supranational integration, national solidarity: The emerging constitution of 'Social Europe'. In: Kohli M. and Novak M. (eds) *Will Europe Work? Integration, Employment and the Social Order*. 21–34. London: Routledge.

Streeck W. (2009) *Re-forming Capitalism: Institutional Change in the German Political Economy*. Oxford: Oxford University Press.

Streeck W. (2014) *Buying Time: The Delayed Crisis of Democratic Capitalism*. London/New York: Verso.

Taylor-Gooby P. (2004) *New Risks, New Welfare: The Transformation of the European Welfare State*. Oxford: Oxford University Press.

Thelen K. (2014) *Varieties of Liberalisation and the New Politics of Social Solidarity*. Cambridge: Cambridge University Press.

Tsakalotos E. (2004) Market constraints, economic performance and political power: Modernizers versus leftists. *Socio-Economic Review* 2(3): 415–424.

Van Kersbergen K. and Hemerijck A. (2012) Two decades of change in Europe: The emergence of the social investment state. *Journal of Social Policy* 41(3): 475–492.

Van Oorschot W. (2004) Flexible work and flexicurity policies in the Netherlands: Trends and experiences. *Transfer* 10: 208–225.

Viebrock E. and Clasen J. (2009) Flexicurity and welfare reform: A review. *Socio-Economic Review* 7(2): 305–331.
Wilthagen T. and Tros F. (2004) The concept of 'flexicurity': A new approach to regulating employment and labour markets. *Transfer* 10(2): 166–186.
Wren A. (ed) (2013) *The Political Economy of the Service Transition*. Oxford: Oxford University Press.

2 Blocs, Arenas, and European Leverage in Iberian Labour Market Solidarity

Paulo Marques and Ana Costa

Introduction

This chapter serves as a hinge between the conceptual architecture set out in Chapter 1 and the country studies in Chapters 3–6. Chapter 1 developed the ideal-typical logics of competitive and inclusive solidarity at a deliberately high level of abstraction; the empirical chapters examine how Portuguese and Spanish governments have navigated those logics in practice. Situated between them, Chapter 2 both narrows and operationalises the argument. It identifies the causal mechanisms that account for the contrasting reform trajectories of the two Iberian cases while retaining sufficient generality to travel beyond them.

The first section connects the ideal types to distinct governing social blocs. The second section shifts focus from blocs to arenas, contrasting tripartite social concertation with parliamentary law-making. The third section introduces the supranational dimension, conceptualising the European Union (EU) as a conditional external selector. Finally, the concluding section synthesises these elements and advances the central claim that bloc composition is a necessary, albeit insufficient, determinant of reform orientation (inclusive versus competitive). Arena choice, viewed as endogenous to bloc priorities, and the direction of EU influence operate as conditional amplifiers or brakes, shaping the scope of change.

Governing Social Blocs

This section clarifies how we define the notion of governing social blocs and why it matters for the book's argument. By governing social blocs, we refer to constellations of collective organisations – parties, governments, as well as peak trade-union confederations and employers' associations – that, by controlling access to policy arenas and mobilising institutionally defined resources, steer the strategic direction of labour market reform. The section proceeds in three steps. First, it revisits Amable and Palombarini's understanding of social blocs and their crisis dynamics. Second, it explains why we adopt an explicitly actor-centred variant that foregrounds collective

DOI: 10.4324/9781003519874-3

organisations as the proximate makers of labour market reform. Third, it sets up the link from governing blocs to decision arenas and their modes of interaction, anticipating the comparative analysis of parliamentary law-making, tripartite social concertation, and the European level that follows.

According to Amable and Palombarini (2023: 945), a social bloc is a politically assembled alliance of social groups whose interests are neither pre-given nor immutable; they are perceived and articulated through ideology. Once organised, these groups advance policy demands that may diverge or even conflict. Bloc leaders decide which demands to accommodate, subject to economic feasibility and internal consistency, by weighing each group's capacity to supply decisive political support. The ensuing policy mix both binds the alliance and proclaims its claim to national relevance. This calculus generates an internal hierarchy: an indispensable core constituency and a more dispensable periphery whose allegiance can be withdrawn, or exchanged for alternative supporters, when shifting circumstances alter the coalition's electoral or programmatic needs (Amable, 2021: 6). Collective social actors – parties, trade unions, employer associations, professional bodies, think tanks – mediate these preferences, which endure only so long as members perceive a net benefit from the prevailing institutional order (Amable, 2017). A bloc becomes dominant when its programme secures both an organised social-producer alliance and an electoral majority, enabling it to steer institutional change and define the 'general interest' (Amable and Palombarini, 2023). Contrary to the original Gramscian conception, however, dominance does not require full hegemony: a bloc can govern effectively while leaving certain marginal interests unrepresented (Amable, 2021). Consequently, several social blocs may coexist and compete for political supremacy.

Amable and Palombarini (2023) add a dynamic twist by treating crises as moments when the dominant bloc fractures, forfeiting its ability to arbitrate conflicts and legitimise the institutional status quo. Political stability can be restored only if a new bloc succeeds in re-aggregating heterogeneous groups around a fresh policy compromise. Rupture alone does not guarantee recomposition: the rival alliances that surface in a crisis must devise a political strategy capable of reconciling the incompatible expectations that toppled the previous bloc, a task made easier when one coalition can present its project as both electorally majoritarian and materially compatible with the interests of pivotal producer groups. Where no such coalition emerges, the result is a systemic crisis, a prolonged period in which competing programmes, neither of which hegemonic, block one another, institutional drift accelerates, and policy oscillates or stalls (Amable, 2017). In short, crises mark the boundary between dominance and contestation: they either clear the way for a successor dominant bloc or reveal the absence of any bloc capable of imposing a new, coherent social compromise.

Amable (2017) illustrates the framework with four French blocs – bourgeois, traditional-left, social-right, and a latent anti-bourgeois configuration – each defined by distinctive party linkages, organisational backbones, and policy profiles. The example shows how a dominant bloc welds together a viable producer alliance with electoral backing, while crises fracture that dominance, opening space for recomposition. We draw on this logic, rather than on the French specifics, to structure our Iberian analysis.[1]

Beyond its analytical elegance, this framework is well suited to examining the Iberian Peninsula within the time frame analysed in the empirical chapters. Although initially developed to interpret French developments, it travels readily because Portugal and Spain share institutional traits that similarly structure the field of possible blocs. Both countries have historically fragmented systems of industrial relations in which reformist and class-struggle union confederations coexist, echoing the cleavage between moderate and militant unionism in France (Campos Lima and Naumann, 2011; Rodríguez et al., 2019; Afonso et al., 2022). Although Spain is less ideologically fragmented than Portugal, distinct historical affiliations persist. Second, in both party systems, centre-left parties can oscillate between coalitions with liberal centrists and alliances with the radical left (Marques and Fonseca, 2022). From 2015 onwards, in the aftermath of the sovereign-debt crisis, radical-left parties gained significant momentum, securing roughly 20% of the vote in national legislative elections. Socialist parties also garnered substantial support but fell short of outright majorities. Centre-right parties, responsible for implementing austerity (PSD–CDS-PP in Portugal; PP in Spain), subsequently lost their parliamentary majorities, yielding a landscape in which no clear dominant bloc emerged. Centre-left parties thus faced a strategic choice: ally with centre-right or radical-left forces to assemble a new dominant bloc. These parallels make the bloc perspective a particularly effective lens for analysing Lisbon and Madrid's divergent post-austerity trajectories: Portugal's 2015–2021 cycle of labour market re-regulation vs. Spain's 2019–2025 reform programme explicitly aimed at reversing labour market segmentation and austerity.

Given that our substantive interest lies in what governments did rather than in fluctuating electoral coalitions, we adopt an explicitly actor-centred variant: collective organisations – parties, governments, trade-union confederations, and employers' associations – are treated as the primary carriers of policy change. Following Scharpf's (1997) actor-centred institutionalism, purposive collective actors pursue their goals within arenas structured by distinct modes of interaction. In negotiated agreement, outcomes are produced through bargaining among interdependent actors who can move forward only by assent; the binding force and problem-solving capacity of such settlements depend on the institutional setting, ranging from minimal contracting environments to ongoing networks and joint-decision systems, and negotiations often unfold 'in the shadow' of a superior rule (a majority vote or hierarchical fiat) that can be triggered if talks fail.[2] In majority voting, choices are determined by decision rules that allow a winning coalition, typically in representative assemblies, to adopt policy without universal consent;

this mode presupposes more demanding institutional arrangements (associations/assemblies) and yields outcomes reflecting the preferences of decisive majorities rather than consensual bargains. In hierarchical direction, finally, a superior actor can unilaterally set binding strategies for subordinates, as in organisational or state settings; hierarchical structures can also cast a 'shadow of hierarchy' over negotiations and votes, shaping their terms even when authority is not directly exercised.

In our analysis, these generic modes map onto tripartite social concertation as a consensus-oriented joint-decision setting (negotiated agreement), ordinary parliamentary law-making as a majoritarian arena (majority voting), and the EU–national nexus as an arena with hierarchical features. This mapping underpins our actor-centred approach: collective organisations are the proximate carriers of labour market reform, but what they can achieve is mediated by the arena's interaction mode.[3]

In referring to *governing social blocs*, we denote an analytical construct: the prevailing constellations of collective organisations that, through controlling access to decision-making arenas and mobilising institutionally defined action resources, determine the strategic direction of labour market reforms. Unlike Amable and Palombarini's conceptualisation of social blocs, which associates organised actors with their underlying electoral bases, our definition is explicitly actor-centred and policy-focussed; hence, we prefer the term *governing* social blocs. While governing blocs may coincide with electoral majorities, this is not a requisite. In adopting this terminology, we draw upon Scharpf's (1997) actor-centred institutionalism, which emphasises purposive collective actors and the arena-specific rules that both enable and constrain them. We employ the term actor constellation to refer to the subset of collective organisations that are both institutionally authorised and practically capable of making decisions within a specific arena. These constellations are context-specific and arena-dependent; for instance, the actors pivotal in tripartite concertation may only partially overlap with those influential in parliamentary law-making.

In the subsequent discussion, we explicitly pair these actor constellations with the interaction modes structuring relevant arenas: negotiated agreement in tripartite concertation, majority voting in parliament, and hierarchical direction within the EU/national nexus. Before proceeding, we clarify the connections between governing social blocs and the ideal types presented in Chapter 1.

The Alignment of Governing Social Blocs with Competing Solidarities

This section makes the bloc–solidarity linkage explicit by pairing our two governing blocs with the two ideal-typical strategies of labour market solidarity introduced in Chapter 1. As detailed in Chapter 1, competitive solidarity conceives social protection as a trade-off: the state clamps down on the most precarious contractual forms, raises statutory floors, and invests in active labour market programmes, while simultaneously easing dismissal protection for open-ended contracts, tempering universal cash benefits or introducing other market-making policies. By contrast, inclusive solidarity proceeds from the premise that risks in precarious segments inevitably spill back onto standard employment. Enduring solidarity therefore requires comprehensive re-regulation: robust employment protection legislation for all types of contracts, encompassing collective bargaining, generous passive transfers, and universal public services.

Each strategy typically relies on a distinct constellation of actors, with centre-left parties functioning as a pivotal hinge between them. Competitive solidarity is usually championed by centrist parties, moderate trade union confederations, and employer associations. In contrast, inclusive solidarity is supported by coalitions linking the centre-left with radical-left parties and class-oriented unions. Using Amable and Palombarini's terminology, these alignments correspond respectively to the *bourgeois* and *traditional-left blocs*. However, in post-austerity Iberia, the salient cleavage no longer opposes liberalisers to anti-liberalisers in the abstract; it differentiates coalitions that selectively roll back the most precarious features of austerity while maintaining flexibility elsewhere from coalitions that seek a comprehensive re-regulation of employment relations. We therefore designate these two governing social blocs as the Centrist–Employer bloc and the Left–Union bloc, respectively, to reflect clearly each coalition's pivotal social actors.[4]

Competitive solidarity appeals to the Centrist–Employer bloc not only because its pivotal actors value competitiveness, but also because the bloc's internal hierarchy is best served by the pattern of risks and rewards the strategy entails. Centrist parties – the bloc's strategic core – can support such flexibilisation provided that a robust floor for temporary work, well-funded activation policies, and enforceable minimum standards protect precarious workers from a race to the bottom. Employer associations enjoy a dual advantage: lower separation costs for permanent staff and public co-financing of up-skilling (Martin, 2004; Cronert, 2018). Because the package channels resources into 'productive' programmes while curbing universal transfers, it remains fiscally lean, electorally palatable to middle-class voters, and discursively consonant with the EU's social-investment narrative (Morel et al., 2012; Hemerijck, 2018). Moderate unions may support this approach so long as reforms do not excessively undermine insiders and the gains for outsiders enhance unions' capacity to fight back against the expansion of precarity, recruit new members, and reinforce their role in social concertation (Marques and Fonseca, 2022: 76). In short, competitive solidarity sustains governing-bloc cohesion by maximising core benefits, compensating the pivotal ring (employers and centrist parties), and limiting concessions to the peripheral moderate unions.

Conversely, inclusive solidarity underpins the Left–Union bloc, whose internal cohesion relies on universal guarantees that counter labour market segmentation. Class-oriented unions and radical left parties provide the organisational strength needed to sustain these arrangements. Achieving electoral hegemony, however, usually requires participation by the centre-left, highlighting the crucial role played by its more progressive factions in preserving bloc unity. Inclusive solidarity, therefore, raises regulatory standards across all employment contracts, couples higher minimum wages with non-wage labour-cost increases that are not offset elsewhere, and treats generous passive benefits as indispensable complements to active labour market measures. These policies simultaneously redistribute income and standardise bargaining conditions across the workforce. Because such policies impose tangible costs on employers and higher-income groups, assembling a broader electoral coalition that spans the full left-wing spectrum becomes essential. Occasionally, the coalition may incorporate peripheral actors – such as domestic-market-oriented employers or those fearing even more radical left-wing reforms – who participate as a second-best strategy, typically as consenters. Although such alliances tend to be temporary, they nonetheless serve to legitimise the coalition, enhancing its broader appeal and political viability. By delivering comprehensive economic security and maintaining inclusive bargaining frameworks, inclusive solidarity unifies the bloc's diverse constituents: insiders safeguard existing standards, outsiders acquire enforceable rights, and political leaders can credibly present policy outcomes as collective goods rather than zero-sum concessions.

Throughout, we treat these mappings as ideal types; concrete reform episodes often display hybrid features as leaders balance partially conflicting demands within each bloc. This caveat matters because the empirical chapters examine specific reforms supported in parliament by varying majorities and backed (or opposed) by social partners. Consequently, policy packages often display hybrid characteristics – for instance, competitive measures introduced to placate employer constituencies within predominantly inclusive coalitions, or vice versa – and may evolve as the internal balance of power shifts. Recognising this intrinsic heterogeneity leaves analytical space for the hybrid or nuanced outcomes documented in the empirical chapters, ensuring that ideal types serve as flexible guides rather than rigid templates (Hay, 2020).

In sum, this section has shown how each bloc's material interests and normative outlook align with one of the two solidarity logics outlined in Chapter 1: competitive solidarity coheres the Centrist–Employer bloc, whereas inclusive solidarity underpins the Left–Union bloc. Yet this pairing is only a point of departure. Whether a given governing social bloc can translate its preferred solidaristic orientation into binding rules depends on the locus of policy decision, whether at the bargaining table of social concertation or on the floor of parliament, arenas that differ in their majoritarian requirements and veto structures. The institutional channel through which these bloc preferences are translated into binding rules is therefore pivotal. We now turn to the contrasting veto structures of tripartite social concertation and parliamentary law-making, which condition both the feasible scope and the durability of solidaristic change.

Table 2.1 Ideal types of solidarity and their governing social-bloc foundations

Ideal type of solidarity	*Core policy mix*	*Governing social bloc most likely to back it*	*Key social actors*
Competitive solidarity	Stricter regulation of extreme precarity Expanded active labour market policies and portable training rights Lighter employment protection legislation for open-ended contracts Lean, 'productive' social spending	**Centrist-Employer bloc**	*Key social actors (core):* centrist parties and employers' organisations *Key social actors (periphery)*: moderate unions willing to trade some limited insider safeguards for relevant outsider gains
Inclusive solidarity	Universal employment protection legislation and extension to new contract types Sector-wide/national bargaining coverage Generous passive benefits and public services Upward adjustment of statutory minimum wage	**Left-Union bloc**	*Key social actors (core):* centre-left parties (progressive factions), class-oriented unions, and radical-left parties *Key social actors (periphery)*: domestic-market-oriented small and medium enterprises that benefit from stable demand; employers fearing even more radical left-wing reforms (support is episodic and legitimising)

Source: Authors' elaboration.

Decision Arenas: Social Concertation Versus the National Parliament

Two institutional arenas structure labour market policymaking in Iberia: tripartite social concertation and ordinary parliamentary legislation. Either can, in principle, widen or narrow solidarity, but they diverge sharply in terms of veto structures, bargaining logics, and modes of legitimation. These contrasts condition the room for manoeuvre of the governing social bloc, shaping both the feasible policy mix and the durability of change. We argue that whereas parliamentary majorities can legislate at or near their partisan ideal points, tripartite concertation embeds a consent constraint. Because employer approval is priced into the decision rule, measures that raise labour costs or curtail managerial discretion face a de facto veto threshold; inclusive packages, therefore, require either unusually favourable bargaining conditions or credible non-concertation fallbacks.

Concertation brings governments, peak-level unions, and employer confederations to a single negotiating table. In our terms, these actors are the primary collective decision-makers in the concertation arena, those whose consent is institutionally required for a binding agreement. By contrast, in parliamentary law-making, the relevant collective decision-maker is the governing-bloc majority in the legislature. While the concertation arena can broaden the social legitimacy of reforms, the institutional requirement of employer assent confers an effective veto over measures that threaten profits or managerial autonomy.

Scharpf's (1988) 'joint-decision trap' captures decision settings that approximate unanimity: when each organised participant holds a veto, negotiations gravitate towards least-common-denominator outcomes or stalemate. In such arenas, side-payments and agenda-narrowing become routine, and unilateral adjustment is pre-empted. Tripartite concertation exhibits these features whenever employer assent is indispensable (Scharpf, 1988: 273). The result is a systematic dilution of measures that would materially redistribute power or income towards labour.[5]

Comparative research shows that executives, especially those heading fragile or divided coalitions, have repeatedly used tripartite pacts to secure the participation of producer groups and to legitimise restructuring while sidestepping open parliamentary confrontation (Rhodes, 2001; Traxler, 2004; Branco and Cardoso, 2022). Howell (2021: 760) terms this pattern 'neoliberal concertation': state-directed bargaining designed to legitimise and enable austerity and deregulation by offering unions symbolic or compensatory side-payments while embedding a deregulatory core. This shift exemplifies a broader transformation of Europe's collective-bargaining regimes: institutions have been re-engineered in ways that favour employers' interests and weaken labour's capacity to forge solidaristic, redistributive compromises (Baccaro and Benassi, 2017; Baccaro and Howell, 2011; Lethbridge et al., 2014; Umney et al., 2018). The state has been central to this reconfiguration, steering employment relations towards liberalisation under conditions of financialisation and a push towards export-oriented growth models (Crouch, 2009; Baccaro and Howell, 2017; Howell, 2021).

Portugal and Spain exemplify this process. Over time, the state's role shifted from empowering collective regulation – including the extension of sectoral agreements in contexts of union fragmentation, weak employer organisation, and the prevalence of small firms – to dismantling collective-bargaining institutions and eroding union power, thereby facilitating labour market liberalisation and austerity while prioritising minimal individual rights (Campos Lima, 2019). This aligns with Howell's characterisation of a "resurgence in state intervention in the regulation of class relations" alongside "a collapse in collective self-regulation" (Howell, 2021: 740). In Iberia, this transformation acquired an exceptional edge during the Troika's adjustment programmes: austerity and internal devaluation accelerated liberalisation via decentralisation of collective bargaining to the firm level, abolition of the favourability principle, unilateral expiry (caducity) of collective agreements, and restrictions on extension mechanisms (Molina and Miguelez, 2013; Campos Lima et al., 2021; Branco and Cardoso, 2022). Because Iberian bargaining had long relied on state enforcement, these measures severely hindered collective-bargaining dynamics.

These developments matter for the present argument because the state-led reconfiguration of collective bargaining in the austerity decade lowered unions' organisational capacity and strike leverage while preserving, and in some respects strengthening, employers' outside options. In contemporary Iberian concertation rounds, this asymmetry sharpens the consent constraint: employers can credibly threaten non-agreement knowing that the liberalised baseline endures, whereas unions face weaker threat points. Under these conditions, the unanimity-like logic that defines tripartite pacts translates into a structurally tighter veto against far-reaching re-regulation, unless governments wield a credible legislative fallback.

In practice, the breadth of advances is further conditioned by EU-level fiscal and legal constraints. The next section shows how shifts in European governance alternately tighten and relax these constraints, thereby modulating how far governing blocs can travel along the inclusive–competitive axis. Before delving into the European dimension, the following section will analyse the interplay between concertation, parliamentary dynamics, and the two ideal types of solidarity.

Concertation, Parliament, and the Two Ideal Types of Solidarity

These institutional characteristics map asymmetrically onto the ideal-typical solidarities set out in Chapter 1. Competitive solidarity, combining limited new protections for outsiders with continued flexibility for insiders, fits neatly with tripartite concertation and aligns with the preferences of Centrist–Employer blocs, because it is compatible with the liberalisation of employment relations. Its policy mix offers unions incremental gains while delivering to employers lighter employment protection rules and flatter wage structures, thereby providing the material for a classic 'political exchange' (Pizzorno, 1978; Avdagic et al., 2011). Since these bargains hinge on employer consent, they typically preserve the core of crisis-era liberalisation and confine redistributive effort to what Bulfone and Tassinari (2021: 510, 513–515) term the corollary sphere, that is, measures such as active labour market policies, transitional subsidies, or training credits that do not revisit the deregulatory core. Inclusive solidarity, by contrast, seeks comprehensive re-regulation policies (stricter dismissal constraints, stronger sectoral bargaining, higher minimum wages, and more generous passive benefits) that raise labour costs, increase the reservation wage, and curb employers' discretionary power. In the neo-corporatist channel where employer approval is indispensable, business has little incentive to endorse such packages, making tripartite concertation an inhospitable route for fully inclusive reform. In the electoral channel, parliamentary arenas can deliver inclusive outcomes when a cohesive Left–Union governing bloc commands sufficient votes to overcome business political resistance, particularly if EU fiscal or legal instruments reduce the budgetary cost.

The relationship is not mechanical. Tripartite bargains can move closer to inclusive outcomes when the employer side is internally fragmented, when transfers soften the fiscal burden of new protections or European hierarchical policy orientations apply, and when employers adopt a defensive strategy. Fragmentation often reflects a cleavage between firms dependent on domestic demand – such as typically small and medium-sized enterprises in sheltered, lower-productivity sectors – and export-oriented or multinational producers competing primarily on international markets. The former gain when higher household purchasing power fuels domestic demand and from curbing low-wage competition; they may therefore endorse increases in the statutory minimum wage, tighter limits on temporary contracts, or stronger sectoral bargaining, whereas the latter tend to view such measures as a cost burden jeopardising external competitiveness, and thus lobby against them. Governments can leverage these divergent preferences by offering selective tax credits or EU-financed up-skilling funds to outward-oriented firms, thereby peeling away opposition among exporters and easing the passage of inclusive provisions. A third pathway to greater inclusivity lies in employers' defensive participation. When a cohesive left-of-centre majority signals that it can legislate unilaterally, business organisations may join concertation to temper reforms rather than block them outright – mirroring the role played by moderate unions during the austerity period, whose participation was justified as a means of containing the scope of liberalisation (Branco and Cardoso, 2022). By entering negotiations, employer confederations seek to shift the agenda towards productivity-oriented activation or transitional subsidies and away from sweeping re-regulation of dismissal rules or collective-bargaining structures. Their very presence, however, allows governments to claim cross-class endorsement for reforms that still expand the protective floor. Under these conditions, the resulting pact edges towards inclusive solidarity, albeit usually at the price of postponing the costlier redistributive steps and preserving elements from the earlier liberal policy regime.

In short, under current conditions of eroded union bargaining power, social concertation is structurally predisposed to generate competitive solidarity because employer consent is priced into the decision rule. By contrast, parliamentary legislation offers the institutional channel through which inclusive solidarity can be realised – provided that supportive coalitions command the requisite votes and are willing to deploy them effectively.

European Union Leverage

The EU functions as an external selector whose stance can both constrain and facilitate solidaristic reform. For the purposes of this chapter, we distinguish analytically between a 'liberal EU' configuration – dominated by hard conditionality under the Excessive Deficit Procedure and competitiveness-oriented Country-Specific Recommendations – and a 'social EU' configuration, where the European Pillar of Social Rights, recent labour directives (adequate minimum wages, predictable working conditions, pay transparency), and crisis instruments such as SURE and the Recovery and Resilience Facility play a crucial role. Elements of both may coexist, which prevails hinges on macro-fiscal conditions and the partisan balance at EU level. In what follows, we outline why the EU should be viewed as simultaneously enabling and limiting reforms aimed at enhancing labour market solidarity.

The EU has constrained the scope for more solidaristic compromises through four main channels. First, during the sovereign-debt crisis, the Union sought to overhaul Southern European labour market institutions – seen as overly rigid and detrimental to external competitiveness (Perez and Matsaganis, 2019). Within the euro area, bailout strategies hinged on internal devaluation, i.e., restoring competitiveness through lower nominal wages and reductions in the price of non-tradables relative to tradables. In an influential paper published before the onset of the crisis, Blanchard (2007: 14) described the "Portuguese labour market" as "dysfunctional," with a "high degree of employment protection" identified as the central problem. The Troika's conditionality combined extensive labour market reforms to enhance flexibility and restrain wages with fiscal consolidation: reductions in the generosity of unemployment benefits; revisions to fair-dismissal clauses in the labour law and lower severance payments; promotion of flexible working-time arrangements; and wage restraint via minimum-wage freezes, decentralisation of collective bargaining, and cuts to nominal public-sector wages with career-progression freezes (Armingeon and Baccaro, 2012; Moreira, et al., 2015; Cardoso and Branco, 2018; Campos Lima et al., 2021; Tassinari et al., 2023: 469–72). According to Bulfone and Tassinari (2021), the common core of these reforms lay in weakening employment protection rules for open-ended contracts and decentralising collective bargaining. Around this core, countries adopted different compensatory measures (adjustments to unemployment benefits and assistance, revised rules for temporary contracts, and new active labour market policies). Consequently, post-austerity attempts to re-regulate these core areas were likely to encounter stronger opposition from EU institutions. Second, EU leverage did not disappear once Portugal and Spain returned to international financial markets. Through the European Semester, the Commission continued to scrutinise labour market policy closely, linking its recommendations to fiscal surveillance under the Excessive Deficit Procedure, with particular attention to the domains reformed during 2010–2014. It is worth recalling that Spain's Excessive Deficit Procedure, triggered in 2009, was only closed in 2019, while the Portuguese case, also initiated in 2009, was concluded in 2017. Thus, even after bailout conditionality formally ceased, the Commission retained powerful instruments to influence national reforms. Third, especially since Maastricht and the European Monetary Union in the 1990s, the trajectory of European integration has privileged liberalisation in employment relations (Howell, 2021). In a monetary union such as the euro area, adjustment to external imbalances relies primarily on relative price changes, notably by holding down wage growth in deficit countries; the result is a deflationary bias that weighs more heavily on debtor states (Mundell, 1961; De Grauwe, 2016). Howell (2021: 757) argues that European integration adds another layer to the political dynamics driving liberalisation. Likewise, Johnston and Matthijs (2022: 119) contend that the European Economic and Monetary Union "explicitly prioritised export-led growth and effectively cut off growth strategies that revolved around buoyant domestic consumption." Fourth, prior to the Portuguese and Spanish cases, Greece attempted to reverse austerity-era labour market measures under the *Syriza* government. Although a new dominant coalition gained office, its programme was effectively blocked by the Troika of lenders. This episode signalled to subsequent Portuguese and Spanish left-of-centre governments that any radical departure from the liberalising trajectory would face intense opposition from EU institutions.

With the 'social turn' in European governance, the EU's role has appeared to shift towards the active facilitation of greater labour market solidarity. First, in Member States with large shares of temporary employment and weak protection for non-standard contracts, Brussels has promoted what it calls 'de-dualisation,' that is, the tightening of rules for atypical work and expanding active labour market policies (Marques et al., 2025). Second, as unemployment fell after 2014, resistance to more ambitious re-regulation eased, making it easier for national governments to strengthen labour protections. Third, the Union's social turn has supplied fresh normative and legal resources. The 2017 European Pillar of Social Rights and, above all, the 2022 Directive on Adequate Minimum Wages require Member States with statutory minimum wages to promote adequacy – using reference values (60% of the median and 50% of the average wage) as guidance – and to produce action plans where collective-bargaining coverage falls below 80% (Erne et al., 2024). Together with newer directives on predictable working conditions and pay transparency, this marks a shift away from the wage-restraint prescriptions of the post-2008 era. Fourth, the EU's pandemic response reinforced this trajectory. The SURE facility underwrote short-time-work schemes across the Union, enabling firms to retain workers and signalling a preference for job retention over further liberalisation (Erne et al., 2024). National recovery plans then channelled sizeable EU funds into more inclusive reforms. Notwithstanding this turn, most enabling instruments widen statutory and institutional floors rather than directly reversing the crisis-era core of liberalisation – namely, lighter dismissal protection for standard contracts and decentralised wage-setting. Their structural effects depend on national transposition choices and enforcement capacity; where governments use EU templates to recalibrate extension rules or to raise collective-bargaining coverage, the resulting changes may nevertheless be far-reaching.

These mechanisms do not bear uniformly on domestic arenas. Under tripartite concertation, conditionality and competitiveness-centred Semester recommendations raise employers' reservation point and thus tighten the consent constraint identified in the previous section; by contrast, directives and EU-financed programmes expand governments' legislative fall-back and allow executives to bound the bargaining space ex ante. In parliamentary arenas, the same instruments lower the political cost of unilateral re-regulation by supplying legal mandates and fiscal cover. In short, EU leverage tends to amplify the asymmetries between the two arenas described above.

In sum, the Union acts as a conditional external selector. In its liberal configuration, the dominance of fiscal surveillance and competitiveness-oriented coordination raises the political price of revisiting the deregulatory core (dismissal rules for open-ended contracts; decentralised wage-setting) while leaving room for targeted upgrades at the margins. In its social configuration, legal templates and fiscal instruments expand the feasible set for inclusive change – most visibly in statutory wage floors, the extension of collective-bargaining coverage, and investment in activation – without, by themselves, overturning the crisis-era core. Because these levers interact differently with domestic arenas, they strengthen competitive settlements negotiated via concertation and, when a cohesive left bloc commands parliament, provide cover and resources for more inclusive legislation.

The EU and the Two Ideal Types of Solidarity

In the recent past, the EU has neither imposed a uniform liberal blueprint nor rubber-stamped domestic agendas; instead, its actions have involved filtering national reform projects through a shifting set of fiscal rules, legal templates, and discursive frames that map unevenly onto the two ideal types of solidarity set out in Chapter 1.

During the sovereign-debt crisis, the Union's economic governance toolkit – memoranda of understanding, Country-Specific Recommendations, and surveillance under the Excessive Deficit Procedure – rewarded strategies combining tighter fiscal control with greater labour market flexibility. That configuration dovetailed with competitive solidarity: it aligned with the Centrist–Employer bloc's priorities (lighter employment protection legislation for insiders, lean 'productive' spending, activation) and granted national reformers external leverage to overcome organised resistance. The political salience of competitiveness and the Commission's emphasis on de-dualisation through targeted active labour market policies provided both the narrative and the procedural channels through which centrist governments could pursue selective re-regulation of precarious work. However, during the austerity years, deep cuts to public expenditure made this strategy difficult to implement, as active labour market policies are costly (Marques and Hörisch, 2020). Moreover, with unemployment around 20% in many Southern European countries, tighter regulation of temporary employment was widely viewed as detrimental to job creation. In the immediate post-crisis years, therefore, competitive solidarity retained momentum and remained the approach most readily backed by the EU.

Yet EU influence appears to be contingent, not deterministic. As macro-fiscal conditions eased, unemployment dropped, and the Union embarked on its social turn, the same governance architecture began to supply resources more compatible with inclusive solidarity. The European Pillar of Social Rights, the 2022 Directive on Adequate Minimum Wages and initiatives to strengthen collective bargaining, together with the COVID-era SURE facility, endowed domestic coalitions with fresh legal mandates, funding streams and legitimacy to raise statutory wage floors, and extend collective bargaining coverage. Crucially, however, these instruments operate primarily within what Bulfone and Tassinari (2021) call the corollary/compensatory spheres. The core elements of the austerity-era settlement, lighter employment protection rules for open-ended contracts, and decentralised wage-setting, remain structurally embedded and far harder to reverse. Because the new EU tools still require fiscal plausibility and compatibility with the single market and monetary union, they leave the foundational liberalising reforms largely intact while widening the scope for incremental improvements at the margins. In short, Brussels now broadens the policy space in which Left–Union coalitions can pursue additional protections; yet the heart of the crisis-period liberalisation endures as a constraint.

The Union therefore operates as a conditional selector between the two solidarities. Where national actors frame reforms as instruments of competitiveness, fiscal sustainability, and activation, EU surveillance and funding tend to reinforce competitive solidarity. Conversely, when governments present broader re-regulation as advancing the Pillar's principles, meeting wage-adequacy benchmarks or delivering 'resilient' growth, Brussels can become an ally – or at least a tacit supporter – of inclusive solidarity. Ultimately, whether the EU acts as brake or driver hinges on the alignment of three moving parts: (*i*) the prevailing macro-fiscal regime; (*ii*) the strategic orientation of the domestic governing bloc; and (*iii*) the capacity of reformers to frame their agenda as contributing to the Union's evolving social-convergence narrative. When these elements combine in a mutually supportive way – such as the post-pandemic suspension of the Stability and Growth Pact's fiscal clauses, the activation of short-time work schemes, and the implementation of the Minimum Wage Directive – the EU can operate as a catalyst for inclusive change. Where they diverge, it retains considerable capacity to constrain.

Governing Social Blocs as the Pivotal Determinant of Solidaristic Outcomes

The preceding sections have shown that three proximate factors – (*i*) the governing social bloc, (*ii*) the decision-making arena, and (*iii*) the orientation of EU leverage – shape the trajectory of labour market reform. We now draw these factors together. Our core claim is that the composition of the governing bloc is the necessary condition for steering reforms towards either competitive or inclusive solidarity; the decision-making arena and the supranational context are important, yet merely sufficient conditions, serving to magnify, attenuate, or block the direction already established by the bloc. At the same time, the governing bloc's discretionary actions are not exempt from the influence of the EU's economic surveillance. For the avoidance of ambiguity in causal language, by 'necessary' we mean that, absent a Left–Union or a Centrist–Employer governing bloc, national policy orientation will not systematically gravitate towards inclusive or competitive solidarity, respectively. The governing bloc, however, is not sufficient on its own for the full realisation of either orientation. Arena-specific veto structures and the evolving EU macro-fiscal and legal stance operate as conditional moderators that shape the scope of change.

First, a bloc anchored in the Left–Union alliance is the only configuration capable of sustaining an inclusive-solidarity agenda. Radical-left parties, class-oriented unions, and progressive centre-left factions share a distributive preference for raising universal floors and re-embedding markets. Where they constitute the dominant coalition, inclusive proposals enter the policy agenda; where they do not, such proposals rarely move beyond rhetoric. By contrast, a Centrist–Employer bloc systematically privileges competitive solidarity: it can live with selective upgrades for outsiders, but only so long as insider flexibility remains intact. Second, the decision-making arena conditions how far either logic can be pushed. Parliamentary arenas, which rest on partisan majorities, allow an inclusive bloc to legislate without granting employers a structural veto; in parliamentary arenas there is no institutional employer veto – although employer organisations retain significant lobbying capacity – which enables left governing majorities to legislate closer to their ideal points; parliamentary arenas likewise permit a centrist coalition to move decisively towards competition when the electoral calculus points that way. Tripartite concertation, by contrast, embeds employer consent within the decision rule. It therefore acts as a brake on ambitious inclusive projects – though not an insurmountable one when employers are divided, when transfers soften the fiscal burden of new protections or when employers fear more far-reaching unilateral legislation – and as an accelerator for competitive solutions that already align with business interests (Traxler, 2004; Howell, 2021). Third, the EU exerts a variable external constraint. During periods of hard conditionality, or when European Semester recommendations stress cost competitiveness, EU pressure buttresses competitive projects and raises the political price of inclusive reforms that touch the core of crisis-era liberalisation (Bulfone and Tassinari, 2021). In those contexts, it becomes very difficult to pass inclusive reforms, as the Greek example has shown. In more permissive phases – exemplified by the 'social turn' inaugurated with the European Pillar of Social Rights, the Adequate Minimum Wages Directive, and the SURE facility – EU instruments provide legal templates, funding streams, and discursive resources that an inclusive bloc can appropriate, while a centrist bloc may still instrumentalise them for selective outsider protection (Erne et al., 2024). Because governments can choose between concertation and parliamentary channels, arena selection is itself endogenous to bloc priorities and anticipated vetoes. We therefore treat arena choice as a strategic variable and derive typological expectations that are explicitly conditional on the chosen arena. Putting the pieces together, eight stylised combinations emerge (Table 2.2).

These combinations demonstrate that the governing bloc establishes the polarity (inclusive or competitive) while the decision-making arena and the EU stance determine the degree of movement along that polarity and the conditions under which it can be maintained. Shifts in either of the latter factors can alter the intensity and sequencing of reform, but are unlikely to reverse the fundamental direction of travel established by bloc composition. Inclusive reforms adopted through concertation in a liberal-leaning EU phase will be incremental and less ambitious; competitive reforms passed in parliament during a social-turn moment may incorporate more generous side-payments, yet the deregulatory core remains intact. Conversely, without a Left–Union majority, even the most favourable combination of arenas and European incentives will struggle to break decisively with the competitive template.

Concluding Remarks

The chapter has argued that the orientation of labour market reforms – whether they reinforce competitive or inclusive forms of solidarity – hinges, first and foremost, on which governing social bloc is dominant. Only a dominant Left–Union governing bloc places comprehensive re-regulation on the agenda; by contrast, a Centrist–Employer constellation is prepared to trade limited outsider protections for enhanced flexibility. Yet bloc dominance alone does not dictate the depth of reform or guarantee its sustainability. Outcomes are sharpened, or blunted, by the institutional arena in which decisions are made and by the direction of EU leverage.

Parliamentary arenas, free of an employer veto, allow dominant governing social blocs to legislate closer to their ideal points and thus avoid the 'joint-decision trap,' whereas concertation channels policy towards compromise. This is because, in a context of the state-led reconfiguration of collective-bargaining institutions and the erosion of union power, the capacity to reinforce inclusive forms of solidarity through concertation is further

Table 2.2 Combinations of social bloc, decision arena, and EU stance, and their expected solidarity outcomes

	Governing constellation	*Expected solidarity outcome*	*Intensity/typical scope*
1	**Left–Union bloc + Parliament + Social EU**	Inclusive	*Maximal*. Able to revisit the deregulatory core; employer veto absent; EU resources and legal frames expand fiscal and political room for manoeuvre
2	**Left–Union bloc + Parliament + Liberal EU**	Inclusive	*High but bounded*. Inclusive reforms advance, yet fiscal and competitiveness warnings curb reach; priority on upgrading 'corollary' elements
3	**Left–Union bloc + Concertation + Social EU**	Inclusive	*Medium*. EU funding/legal hooks help unions push beyond cosmetic gains, but employer presence trims redistributive ambition; core deregulation only partially revisited
4	**Left–Union bloc + Concertation + Liberal EU**	Inclusive	*Low-to-medium*. Tripartite bargaining plus liberal EU tilt limit changes to wage-floor hikes or tighter rules on the most precarious contracts; core remains largely intact
5	**Centrist–Employer bloc + Parliament + Liberal EU**	Competitive	*Maximal*. Fast-track deregulatory packages; few compensations; EU fiscal surveillance reinforces downward pressure on labour costs
6	**Centrist–Employer bloc + Parliament + Social EU**	Competitive	*High but moderated*. Parliament can legislate flexibly, yet EU social directives compel some protective add-ons (e.g., minimum-wage thresholds, coverage-action plans)
7	**Centrist–Employer bloc + Concertation + Liberal EU**	Competitive	*Strong*. Classic 'neoliberal concertation': pacts entrench lighter employment protection legislation and decentralised bargaining, with token activation or training credits
8	**Centrist–Employer bloc + Concertation + Social EU**	Competitive	*Medium*. Social-turn EU injects modest inclusive elements (e.g., active labour market policies funding), but employer veto in the pact arena keeps reforms within a competitive template

Source: Authors' elaboration.

constrained. Nonetheless, tripartite bargains can move beyond minimalism when employer interests are internally fragmented, governments compensate employers, and employers adopt a defensive strategy. Likewise, the EU, in a 'social turn' phase, supplies funding, legal templates, and discursive cover that widen the scope for inclusion, while a liberal-leaning EU raises the cost of diverging from competitiveness imperatives. Yet these instruments typically widen statutory floors and procedural requirements rather than overturn the crisis-era liberalising core. Furthermore, at the EU level, tensions between the consolidation and expansion of the European Social Agenda and the fiscal governance of the euro area remain unresolved. Therefore, although inclusive reforms are possible in certain historical contexts, such advances are reversible in a different EU context, given the path the EU has followed since the Maastricht Treaty.

The empirical chapters that follow investigate how these theoretical expectations play out across employment protection, minimum-wage setting, platform work regulation, and public employment in Portugal and Spain, while Chapter 7 revisits the framework in light of the comparative evidence.

Notes

1 This differs little from the typology subsequently proposed by Bulfone and Tassinari (2021: 514), who distinguish four models of labour market reform pursued by Southern European governments: (i) the preservation of the social-democratic coalition, (ii) the creation of a centrist, pro-EU coalition, (iii) a neoliberal rupture, and (iv) the coalescence of a challengers' coalition.

2 See Scharpf's Table 2.1 on page 47.

3 We employ Scharpf's conceptual vocabulary – actors, constellations, arenas and modes of interaction – without adopting the game-theoretic reconstruction associated with some applications; the empirical analysis proceeds in a historically institutionalist vein.

4 We restrict the discussion to these two governing social blocs. Our objective is to compare the strategies of the progressive coalitions that entered office after the austerity years, rather than to catalogue all potential political configurations. In this spirit, we focus on coalitions committed to promoting the two solidarities theorised in Chapter 1.

5 The same applies when right-wing governments seek the support of trade unions within the framework of social dialogue. In such cases, liberalising reforms may encounter significant obstacles, as the balance between governmental interests and trade union demands necessitates concessions that can constrain both the scope and the pace of these reforms.

References

Afonso A., Dorigatti L., Molina O. and Tassinari A. (2022) Labor market (de)regulation and wage-setting institutions. In: L. Burroni L., Pavolini E. and Regini M. (eds), *Mediterranean Capitalism Revisited: One Model, Different Trajectories*. 115–148. Ithaca and London: Cornell University Press.

Amable B. (2017) *Structural Crisis and Institutional Change in Modern Capitalism: French Capitalism in Transition*. Oxford: Oxford University Press.

Amable B. (2021) In search of the bloc bourgeois. *Revue de la régulation – Capitalisme, institutions, pouvoirs* 31: 1–24.

Amable B. and Palombarini S. (2023) Multidimensional social conflict and institutional change. *New Political Economy* 28(6): 942–957.

Armingeon K. and Baccaro L. (2012) Political economy of the sovereign debt crisis: The limits of internal devaluation. *Industrial Law Journal* 41(3): 254–275.

Avdagic S., Rhodes M. and Visser J. (eds) (2011) *Social Pacts in Europe: Emergence, Evolution and Institutionalisation*. Oxford: Oxford University Press.

Baccaro L. and Benassi C. (2017) Throwing out the ballast: Growth models and the liberalization of German industrial relations. *Socio-Economic Review* 15(1): 85–115.

Baccaro L. and Howell C. (2011) A common neoliberal trajectory: The transformation of industrial relations in advanced capitalism. *Politics & Society* 39(4): 521–563.

Baccaro L. and Howell C. (2017) *Trajectories of Neoliberal Transformation: European Industrial Relations After the 1970s*. Cambridge: Cambridge University Press.

Blanchard O. (2007) Adjustment within the Euro: The difficult case of Portugal. *Portuguese Economic Journal* 6(1): 1–21.

Branco R., and Cardoso, D. (2022) The politics of change: Coalitional politics and labour market reforms during the sovereign debt crisis in Portugal. *Journal of Social Policy* 51(1): 39–57.

Bulfone F. and Tassinari A. (2021) Under pressure: Economic constraints, electoral politics and labour market reforms in Southern Europe in the decade of the Great Recession. *European Journal of Political Research* 60(3): 509–538.

Campos Lima M. da P. (2019) Portugal: Reforms and the turn to neoliberal austerity. In: Müller T., Vandaele K. and Waddington J. (eds) *Collective Bargaining in Europe: Towards an Endgame?* Vol. III, 483–504. Brussels: European Trade Union Institute.

Campos Lima M. da P., Martins D., Costa A. and Velez A. (2021) Internal devaluation and economic inequality in Portugal: Challenges to industrial relations in times of crisis and recovery. *Transfer* 27(1): 47–73.

Campos Lima M. da P. and Naumann R. (2011) Portugal: From broad strategic pacts to policy-specific agreements. In: Avdagic S., Rhodes M. and Visser J. (eds) *Social Pacts in Europe: Emergence, Evolution and Institutionalisation*. 147–173. Oxford: Oxford University Press.

Cardoso D. and Branco R. (2018) Liberalised dualisation: Labour market reforms and the crisis in Portugal: A new departure. *European Journal of Social Security* 20(1): 31–48.

Cronert A. (2018) Accommodation or extraction? Employers, the state, and the joint production of active labor market policy. *Politics & Society* 46(4): 539–569.

Crouch C. (2009) Privatised Keynesianism: An unacknowledged policy regime. *The British Journal of Politics and International Relations* 11: 382–399.

De Grauwe P. (2016) The legacy of the Eurozone crisis and how to overcome it. *Journal of Empirical Finance* 39: 147–155.

Erne R., Stan S., Golden D., Szabó I. and Maccarrone V. (2024) *Politicising Commodification: European Governance and Labour Politics from the Financial Crisis to the COVID Emergency*. Cambridge: Cambridge University Press.

Hay C. (2020) Does capitalism (still) come in varieties? *Review of International Political Economy* 27(2): 302–319.

Hemerijck A. (2018) Social investment as a policy paradigm. *Journal of European Public Policy* 25(6): 810–827.

Howell C. (2021) Rethinking the role of the state in employment relations for a neoliberal era. *ILR Review* 74(3): 739–772.

Johnston A. and Matthijs M. (2022) The political economy of the Eurozone's postcrisis growth model. In: Baccaro L., Blyth M. and Pontusson J. (eds) *Diminishing Returns: The New Politics of Growth and Stagnation*. 117–142. Oxford: Oxford University Press.

Lethbridge J., Greer I., Kretsos L., Umney C. and White G. (2014) *Industrial Relations in Central Public Administration: Recent Trends and Features*. Dublin: Eurofound.

Marques P., Branco R. and Guimarães R. (2025) The politics of pro-outsider labour-market reforms: A configurational study. *Comparative European Politics* 23(2): 159–184.

Marques P. and Fonseca D. (2022) Understanding the positions taken by moderate union confederations and centre-left parties during labour market reforms in Portugal and Spain: Why the configuration of left parties and trade union confederations matters. *European Journal of Industrial Relations* 28(1): 65–84.

Marques P. and Hörisch F. (2020) Understanding massive youth unemployment during the EU sovereign-debt crisis: A configurational study. *Comparative European Politics* 18(2): 233–255.

Martin C. J. (2004) Reinventing welfare regimes: Employers and the implementation of active social policy. *World Politics* 57(1): 39–69.

Molina O. and Miguélez F. (2013) From negotiation to imposition: Social dialogue in austerity times in Spain. DIALOGUE Working Paper, No. 51. Geneva: International Labour Office (ILO), Governance and Tripartism Department.

Moreira A., Alonso Dominguez A., Antunes C., Karamessini M., Raitano M. and Glatzer, M. (2015) Austerity-Driven labour market reforms in Southern Europe: Eroding the security of labour market insiders. *European Journal of Social Security* 17(2): 202–225.

Morel N., Palier B. and Palme J. (eds) (2012) *Towards a Social Investment Welfare State? Ideas, Policies and Challenges*. Bristol: Policy Press.

Mundell R. A. (1961) A theory of optimum currency areas. *The American Economic Review* 51(4): 657–665.

Perez S. A. and Matsaganis M. (2019) Export or perish: Can internal devaluation create enough good jobs in Southern Europe? *South European Society and Politics* 24(2), 259–285.

Pizzorno A. (1978) Political exchange and collective identity in industrial conflict. In: Crouch C. and Pizzorno A. (eds) *The Resurgence of Class Conflict in Western Europe since 1968: Volume 2: Comparative Analyses*. 277–298. London and Basingstoke: Palgrave Macmillan.

Rhodes M. (2001) The political economy of social pacts: 'Competitive corporatism' and European welfare reform. In: Pierson P. (ed) *The New Politics of the Welfare State*. 165–194. New York: Oxford University Press.

Rodríguez C., Rojo R. and Lucio M. (2019) Spain: Challenges to legitimacy and representation in a context of fragmentation and neoliberal reform. In: Müller T., Vandaele K. and Waddington J. (eds) Collective Bargaining in Europe: Towards an Endgame? 563–582. Brussels: European Trade Union Institute.

Scharpf F. W. (1988) The joint decision trap: Lessons from German federalism and European integration. *Public Administration* 66(3), 239–278.

Scharpf F. W. (1997) *Games Real Actors Play: Actor-Centered Institutionalism in Policy Research*. Boulder, CO: Westview Press.

Tassinari A., Bulfone F. and Gago A. (2023) Labour market policy reforms in Southern Europe: Too much of the wrong medicine? In: Clegg D. and Durazzi N. (eds) Handbook of Labour Market Policy in Advanced Democracies. 463–477. Cheltenham: Edward Elgar.

Traxler F. (2004) The metamorphoses of corporatism: From classical to lean patterns. *European Journal of Political Research* 43(4): 571–598.

Umney C., Greer I., Onaran Ö. and Symon G. (2018) The state and class discipline: European labour market policy after the financial crisis. *Capital & Class* 42(2): 333–351.

3 Employment Protection and Collective Bargaining Reforms after Austerity

Divergent Paths in Portugal and Spain

Rui Branco, Paulo Marques, Óscar Molina, and Madalena Ferreira

Introduction

Policies implemented during the Great Recession overhauled the institutional architecture governing labour markets and systems of industrial relations in Iberia. Although earlier reforms had already paved the way for labour-market flexibilisation and the erosion of employment protection through two-tier changes, the measures adopted under the conditionality attached to the Memorandum of Understanding in Portugal and under austerity politics in Spain not only accelerated these trajectories but also recast core pillars of the employment-relations edifice, thereby weakening the capacity of social partners to regulate working conditions.

Iberian crisis-era reforms depleted the regulatory and protective force of employment legislation and collective bargaining. Deregulation of employment protection, together with expanded employer discretion over working conditions, served the strategic objective of internal devaluation in pursuit of cost-competitiveness. The Iberian model of sectoral bargaining was profoundly reshaped; the *favor laboratoris* principle was derogated; the administrative extension of agreements was curtailed; and expiry regimes for collective agreements were established (introduced in Spain in 2012 and already in place in Portugal since 2003).

These reforms acquired strong symbolic significance for trade unions and left-wing parties, over and above their measurable effects on inequality and working conditions. In the post-crisis period, left parties and trade unions placed the reversal of labour-market reforms at the centre of their programmes and used it as a key device to mobilise voters. The limited capacity of austerity-era measures to address soaring unemployment and inequality, together with declining productivity and stagnant economic growth thereafter, created a favourable environment for electoral upheaval in the Iberian countries and the formation of left-leaning coalitions. The objective was to reduce dualisation by promoting inclusive solidarity that would enhance the rights and protection of outsiders while maintaining, or increasing, those of insiders.

DOI: 10.4324/9781003519874-4

Following the accession of progressive left coalitions to office in Portugal (2015) and Spain (2019), Iberian governments embarked upon labour-market reforms designed to reverse key elements of the austerity settlement. Coalition governments in both countries relied on social dialogue to bolster the legitimacy of the reforms, whilst also undertaking inter-party negotiations to secure parliamentary approval. Despite broadly similar trajectories and political contexts, notable differences emerged in both the process and the substance of the reforms enacted.

The chapter is organised as follows: the first section sets out the institutional and policy trajectories of Iberian labour markets; the second section analyses the 2019 Portuguese reform, first through social concertation and then through the parliamentary legislative process; the third section examines Spain's 2021 reform, likewise via social dialogue and its passage through the *Cortes*; the fourth section undertakes a systematic Portugal–Spain comparison; and the final one presents the discussion and conclusions.

Throughout, we align concepts with Chapter 2 in three respects. First, arena choice is treated as endogenous to bloc priorities. Secondly, concertation is analysed as a joint-decision setting that embeds a consent constraint on measures raising labour costs or curbing managerial discretion. Thirdly, we characterise the EU as a conditional external selector that oscillates between 'liberal' and 'social' configurations.

Iberian Labour Market Institutions and Policy Trajectories

Iberian labour markets show the typical features of the Mediterranean model of industrial relations (Afonso et al., 2022: 117–120). State intervention is extensive, via strong statutory legislation; legal support for, and procedural regulation of, multi-employer collective bargaining (e.g., state-backed sectoral extensions of collective agreements). Highly fragmented and competitive unions and employers' organisations generate a weak capacity for autonomous coordination and cooperation (Crouch, 1993; Molina and Rhodes, 2007: 225–227), a deficiency that has been offset by state intervention.

The industrial relations system is broadly adversarial. Unions and employers' organisations struggle to aggregate internal interests and to reach autonomous compromises. Historically, weak national-level corporatist structures mean that the political relations of unions and employers with the state combine confrontation with occasional accommodation through incorporation. Neither producer group played a role in the development and management of welfare-state institutions (Andreotti et al., 2001: 49), nor have they been routinely incorporated into policymaking through institutionalised corporatist concertation, unlike in Northern Europe. Even so, they have at times acted as veto players through union mobilisation and disruption during industrial conflict.

The state has engaged in tripartite political exchange with social partners to secure their acquiescence and collaboration in policy reforms and in the coordination of industrial relations, to overcome veto powers, and to resolve distributive conflicts (Molina, 2006). Tripartite social concertation has often been used to facilitate wage moderation or labour-market flexibilisation (Ebbinghaus and Hassel, 2000; Hancké and Rhodes, 2005; Molina and Rhodes, 2007).

Portugal's social-revolutionary transition to democracy divided trade unions along ideological and partisan lines and, despite a few, but important, unitary actions such as general strikes, this produced endemic organisational weakness in the labour movement. The early hegemony of the General Confederation of Portuguese Workers (CGTP) was challenged in 1978 by the creation of the General Union of Workers (UGT-P). The former represents 62% of unionised workers and maintains strong links with the Portuguese Communist Party (PCP), while the latter has close relations with the centre-left Socialist Party (PS) and the centre-right Social Democratic Party (PSD), the main governing parties (Campos Lima and Naumann, 2011). CGTP has retained an adversarial, class-struggle approach, whereas UGT-P adopts a social-partnership, reform-oriented stance. CGTP has greater mobilisation capacity; UGT-P prioritises social concertation. Combined membership fell from about 1.5 million in 1980 to 0.5 million in 2015, and union density declined from a peak of 60% in the 1970s to 19% in 2016 (Campos Lima, 2019).

Employers are likewise fragmented across several organisations. At the macro level they split along sectoral lines: the Confederation of Portuguese Industry (CIP) for manufacturing industries, the Portuguese Confederation of Farmers for agriculture, the Confederation of Commerce and Services of Portugal, and the Confederation of Portuguese Tourism. Attempts to create a single peak organisation have failed. While the larger CIP has pressed for a united institutional front, the others have resisted in order to preserve organisational autonomy. Membership rates fell from nearly 60% in 2002 to under 40% in 2011 (Lisi and Loureiro, 2022).

In Spain, the weakness of civil society and social partners is a critical legacy of the 40-year dictatorship. The trade-union movement that emerged during the transition to democracy is an attenuated duopoly of two large national confederations – the General Workers' Union (UGT-S) and the Trade Union Confederation of Workers' Committees (CCOO) – alongside a number of small professional and/or regional confederations. The different ideological and associational traditions of the two main confederations, the CCOO and the UGT-S, produced divergent strategies: bottom-up and top-down, respectively. The CCOO arose from clandestine worker mobilisation in the industrial belt of Barcelona and enjoyed stronger roots at company level, a more decentralised organisation, and a relatively robust capacity for mobilisation. By contrast, the UGT-S returned to Spain immediately after democratisation and looked to the state to build organisational strength, making it more supportive of pacting than its rival, at least until the late 1980s. Its close links with the Spanish Socialist Workers' Party (PSOE) also made it more inclined to cooperate via pacts, whereas the most powerful influence within the CCOO, albeit declining from the late 1980s, was the Spanish Communist Party. Inter-union competition for members and votes in workplace elections prevented strong labour-movement unity until the mid-1990s.

Organisational weakness was even more pronounced among employers. The Spanish Confederation of Employers' Organisations (CEOE), created in 1977, had a highly fragmented membership and lacked disciplinary control over its constituency. Its organisational structure has always been highly complex: in 1985 there were 114 sectoral associations and 50 territorial associations (firms are usually affiliated to these organisations rather than to the peak CEOE), with both numbers increasing in subsequent years (Eurofound, 1999). As a result, the CEOE has had an ambivalent view of concertation. While organisational weakness has obliged it to take a critical position towards pacts, from which employers expect to obtain less than unions, participation has also provided it with influence.

The most enduring feature of Iberian labour markets has been acute dualism, generating a large share of temporary employment, compounded by occupational and fragmented social insurance, thereby reinforcing insider–outsider divides. Since the mid-1980s, two-tier reforms have emerged as a politically viable way to circumvent the 'Maginot line' of stricter employment protection for standard workers. Shortly thereafter, labour markets developed intense dual segmentation (in terms of employment protection and dismissal costs), producing the largest share of atypical employment in Europe. A pattern took root: low annual transition rates to open-ended employment created a growing periphery of insecure workers trapped between recurring spells of temporary work and unprotected unemployment.

Consider the paradigmatic Spanish two-tier reform of 1984. The 1980 Workers' Statute restricted the use of temporary contracts to less than 10% of all contracts. Facing an economic downturn in the wake of the second oil-price shock, mass unemployment, and social unrest, the PSOE cabinet pursued labour-market liberalisation as the route out of 'Eurosclerosis' towards job creation. Given trade-union opposition to deregulating permanent contracts, relaxing the regulation of fixed-term contracts presented the path of least political resistance. Henceforth, temporary workers could be hired to perform permanent activities and dismissed at much lower cost. The 'employment-promotion contract' carried severance of 12 days' wages per year of service (maximum duration three years), while other forms of fixed-term contracts carried none. Severance for permanent contracts in cases of fair and unfair dismissal remained at 20 and 45 days' wages per year of service (capped at 12 or 42 months' wages, respectively). The differential in termination costs, combined with a pre-determined expiry date, incentivised employers to deploy fixed-term work not only to meet seasonal needs but also to adjust to the economic cycle, or even as a cheaper, more pliable substitute for permanent, structural labour needs. By the early 1990s, the share of temporary contracts was approaching 35%, and it never fell below 30% until the Great Recession (Marques and Fonseca, 2022). High turnover, eased by access to unemployment benefits, translated into low annual conversion rates into permanent contracts.

In both countries, segmentation by contract type (compounded by age and gender) separates a core of standard workers from a growing periphery of insecure workers who bear the brunt of adjustment. Stable employment trajectories for the former contrast with the latter's entrapment between recurrent bouts of unemployment and short-term work. Distinctively, Spain has the largest share of temporary employment and the lowest transition rate to permanent employment in Europe, together with persistently high unemployment. Portugal, by contrast, faces particularly acute age-based labour-market inequalities: young people are disproportionately represented in the sizeable temporary segment and among the unemployed, while enjoying far less protection from unemployment insurance and social security more generally (Marques and Salavisa, 2017; Branco, 2022).

Portugal's 2019 Labour Market Reform (Law 93/2019)

This section examines the Portuguese reform's policymaking process in two stages: social dialogue culminating in the 2018 tripartite agreement and the subsequent parliamentary debate. To appreciate the scope of the 2019 reform, it is necessary to recall the main features of the austerity-era legislation it was meant to revise. During the Troika period (2011–2014) the labour code was liberalised in ways that simultaneously reduced employment protection legislation and weakened multi-employer bargaining. Severance pay for standard workers was cut from 30 to 20 days per year of tenure and then to 18 days, and compensation for new fixed-term workers was likewise lowered from 36 or 24 days to 20 days and then to 18 days. The definition of fair dismissal was broadened beyond 'just cause' to include unsuitability or redundancy, while the ranking criteria introduced in 2014 prioritised the dismissal of workers with low performance, few qualifications, or higher labour costs. The requirement to redeploy redundant workers to alternative posts was removed, making dismissals simpler and cheaper.

At the same time, the conservative government tried to decentralise collective bargaining and strengthened employer prerogatives. The threshold for works councils to negotiate firm-level agreements was reduced from 500 to 150 employees, allowing non-union bodies to conclude company agreements with union authorisation. Company agreements were given priority over sectoral agreements and employers were empowered to unilaterally change working conditions. Extensions of sectoral agreements were made conditional on the representativeness of the employer associations. The ultra-activity regime was weakened: collective agreements could be terminated unilaterally after three rather than five years, and expired agreements only remained valid for 12 rather than 18 months, after which firms could withdraw without providing reasons or submitting to arbitration. Companies in financial difficulty were authorised to suspend agreements temporarily.

The formation of the centre-left minority government in 2015 with parliamentary support from the PCP and the Left Bloc (BE) created a window of opportunity for reform. The government issued a Green Book on labour relations and, after negotiations with employers and the moderate trade union UGT-P, signed a tripartite agreement in June 2018 aimed at combating precariousness, revitalising collective bargaining, and strengthening public regulation. Unlike the radical left parties, the government did not seek to restore the pre-2003 collective bargaining regime or the full favourability principle, and it signalled that the end of the ultra-activity regime of collective agreements would remain part of Portugal's labour law tradition.

The 2019 reform reflected this compromise. On the one hand, it strengthened the regulation of non-standard employment (Table 3.1). With respect to fixed-term contracts, the law removed 'first-job seekers' as a lawful justification and confined their use to genuine temporary needs, long-term unemployed persons and new activities; the threshold for start-ups was lowered from firms with fewer than 750 workers to 250 workers, and contracts linked to the start-up of a new activity could only be concluded within the first two years of that activity. The maximum cumulative duration of successive fixed-term contracts was reduced from three years to two years, although the number of successive contracts remained four. The maximum duration of contracts of uncertain duration was reduced from six to four years. Compensation for temporary workers remained at 18 days of base salary per year of tenure and the trial period remained 30 days for contracts longer than six months and 15 days for shorter contracts. Regulation of

Table 3.1 Portugal – Employment protection legislation: Crisis-era changes (2012–2014) and the 2019 reform

Dimension	*Troika-era reforms (2012–2014)*	*2019 reform (Law 93/ 2019)*
Permanent contracts: severance pay	Severance compensation cut from 30 to 20 days per year of tenure and then to 18 days; capped at one year's wages	Unchanged: compensation remains at 18 days per year of tenure, with the same cap
Permanent contracts: fair dismissal criteria	Broadened definition of fair dismissal (unsuitability, redundancy); 2014 ranking rules prioritise dismissal of workers with lowest performance, qualifications, or higher labour costs	Unchanged: same broad definition and ranking criteria

Table 3.1 (Continued)

Dimension	*Troika-era reforms (2012–2014)*	*2019 reform (Law 93/ 2019)*
Permanent contracts: trial period	General probatory period: 90 days; 180 days for complex jobs; 240 days for managers	General probatory period unchanged; new 180-day trial period for first-time job-seekers and long-term unemployed
Fixed-term contracts: valid cases	Allowed for temporary needs, launching new activity, hiring first-job seekers and long-term unemployed, and start-ups (<750 employees)	Use limited to temporary needs, new activity and long-term unemployed; start-ups threshold lowered to <250 employees and only within 2 years of the start-up; first-job seekers removed
Fixed-term contracts: max successive contracts	4 contracts (plus transitional extensions)	4 contracts
Fixed-term contracts: max cumulative duration	Standard cap 3 years (with exceptions up to 4.5/ 5.5 years)	Cap reduced to 2 years
Fixed-term contracts: severance pay	Initially 20 days per year of tenure; cut to 18 days in 2013	18 days per year of tenure (unchanged)
Fixed-term contracts: trial period	30 days for contracts >6 months; 15 days otherwise	Unchanged
Uncertain-duration contracts: max duration	6 years	4 years
Temporary agency work: max duration and renewals	Assignments up to 2 years; renewals allowed if justification persists	Assignments up to 3 years; 6 renewals (unlimited for substituting absent workers)
Bogus self-employment	Presumption of employment triggered when a worker derives ≥80% of income from a single client	Threshold lowered to 50% of income from one client

Source: Authors' own elaboration.

temporary agency work was tightened by imposing a cap of six renewals and increasing the maximum duration of assignments from two to three years. A further novelty was a presumptive test against bogus self-employment: the threshold of income derived from a single client triggering a presumption of employment was lowered from 80% to 50%.

On the other hand, the reform barely altered job security for permanent contracts. Severance pay for standard workers remained at 18 days per year of service, and the broad definition of fair dismissal and ranking criteria adopted in 2014 were untouched. The general probation period remained 90 days, but a new six-month (180-day) trial period was introduced for first-time job-seekers and long-term unemployed workers, a measure justified by the government as a way of discouraging recourse to temporary contracts.

In collective bargaining, the law made only partial changes (Table 3.2). It retained the priority of firm-level agreements and left unaltered the shortened deadlines for unilateral termination (three years) and the 12-month validity of expired agreements. Employers in financial difficulty were, however, deprived of the unilateral right to suspend collective agreements. At the same

Table 3.2 Portugal – Collective bargaining and wage-setting: Crisis-era changes and the 2019 reform

Dimension	*Troika-era reforms (2012–2014)*	*2019 reform (Law 93/2019)*
Who can negotiate?	Company-level bargaining open to works councils with a union mandate (companies with ≥150 workers); union and employer federations can negotiate multi-employer agreements	Unchanged
Favourability principle	Collective agreements allowed to derogate from statutory minima in areas such as working time and severance pay	Areas in which agreements can derogate from statutory law curtailed; individual contracts can only override collective agreements when more favourable to workers
Priority of company agreements	Company agreements take precedence over sectoral agreements	Unchanged
Ultra-activity (expiry of agreements)	Unilateral termination allowed after 3 years (down from 5); expired agreements valid for 12 months (down from 18); firms in difficulty could opt out temporarily by agreement	Deadlines unchanged (3 years and 12 months); companies in difficulty can no longer unilaterally suspend agreements
Extension of agreements	State extensions conditional on employer-representativeness: unions must represent ≥50% of workers or ≥30% of small and medium-sized enterprises (SMEs)	No representativeness criteria: government may extend sectoral agreements administratively

Source: Authors' own elaboration.

time, the government resumed the use of the extension mechanism without the representativeness criteria introduced during the Troika period, once again allowing sectoral agreements to be extended by administrative decision. The ability of collective agreements to derogate from statutory minima was curtailed: areas in which agreements could set terms less favourable than the law were restricted and individual employment contracts could only override collective agreements when providing more favourable conditions to workers.

From the standpoint of the Socialist government, the reform represented a pragmatic compromise that responded to concerns about precariousness while preserving a degree of labour market flexibility. For the PCP, the BE, and the CGTP, it fell short of restoring pre-crisis standards because it did not reverse the reduction in severance pay, nor restore the ultra-activity of collective agreements. Conversely, employer organisations were reassured that the core liberalising features of the Troika reforms were left intact.

Social Concertation: The 2018 Tripartite Agreement

Given the political composition of the *Geringonça*,[1] a tripartite agreement offered the government a way to circumvent longstanding ideological disputes with its radical-left partners. In doing so, however, it also generated internal tensions, as we shall see. Crucially, the balance of political power in parliament differed from that within social concertation. Whereas social concertation inherently grants employers and the moderate trade union UGT-P a *de facto* veto, the parliamentary arena was more amenable to the left parties, whose potential withdrawal of support could bring down the minority PS government. In Chapter 2's terms, concertation embeds a consent constraint: because employer approval is priced into the decision rule, measures that raise labour costs face a *de facto* veto threshold. This pushes settlements towards least-common-denominator outcomes or to the corollary sphere, unless governments wield a credible legislative fall-back.

For the government, securing the social partners' buy-in was vital for reasons of legitimacy, policy coordination, and the mitigation of opposition. A negotiated solution was politically more robust. As one MP explained, social concertation 'insulates' political initiatives from present and future challenges arising from the electoral cycle on both the left and the right, as well as from 'external pressures' (Interview 11). As a PS MP stated in Parliament:

> The role of social concertation [...] is essential to protect the measures combating precariousness from future drifts from the right, as well as external pressures from international institutions that are only interested in flexibilization and cuts.
>
> (MP Tiago Ribeiro, 07/07/2018)

Conversely, an MP from the radical-left BE was dissatisfied with the limited capacity to effect changes to the content of legislation flowing from the tripartite social pact into parliament, viewing that process, steered by the incumbent centre-left PS, as an attempt to circumvent parliament's legislative role and as a debasement of 'our democratic decision-making system on labour laws [...] through a kind of neo-corporatist bias' (Interview 2).

In 2016, the government issued the *Green Book on Labour Relations* with the involvement of the social partners, whose key role was to delineate the perimeter of discussion by establishing which issues were 'on the bargaining table' and which were not. The Green Book prioritised 'combating precarious work and labour-market segmentation,' 'dignifying working conditions,' and 'revitalising collective bargaining' (Dray et al., 2016). Notably, it omitted both the restoration of the ultra-activity regime and the full reinstatement of the favourability principle.

Subsequently, in June 2018, the Socialist cabinet, UGT-P, and the employers' confederations signed a tripartite agreement that sought to: 'fight precariousness and reduce labour-market segmentation'; 'promote the dynamism of collective bargaining'; and 'reinforce the public means and instruments of labour regulation' (CPCS, 2018). In parliament, the Socialist Minister of Labour, Solidarity and Social Security explained that the executive did not favour restoring the ultra-activity of collective agreements, as the existing expiry regime was 'part of the history and tradition of the Socialist Party.'[2] The party had adopted this regime during a previous term in office when it passed the 2009 labour market reform, again on the basis of a tripartite social pact. A former cabinet member with direct responsibility in this area stated:

> For the PS, there was never a question of re-introducing the ultra-activity of collective agreements, nor was it admissible; not for ideological reasons, but because this was seen as returning to a past of stalled collective bargaining, which does not help collective bargaining to become more relevant.
>
> (Interview 4)

UGT-P explained that the 2018 tripartite agreement curtailed both the maximum duration and the lawful scope of fixed-term contracts and opened the possibility of "eliminating individual working-time banks." On the expiry regime, UGT-P "never advocated the reversal tout court," since its introduction back in 2003 had "brought about a renewal of collective agreements." Before then, some agreements had remained unchanged "for over thirty years," resulting in "disharmonised wage scales across sectors." Nonetheless, UGT-P lamented employers' abusive use of the expiry clause and called on future reforms to require a reasoned expiry claim or an arbitration procedure (Interview 8).

It is perhaps unsurprising that CGTP did not sign the social pact, arguing that the agreement did not address "structural issues" from a class-based perspective: it failed to resolve "the problems of the expiry regime of collective agreements and the full restoration of the *favor laboratoris*, combat the spread of precariousness, or respond to the problems that arise from a fairer distribution of wealth" (Interview 7).

The government's stance reflects endogenous arena selection by a Centrist–Employer bloc (see Chapter 2) seeking the legitimising benefits of pacting while maintaining control over the agenda perimeter.

Legislative Process in the Assembleia da República *(2018–2019)*

From the outset, the legislative process was shaped by divergent strategic orientations among the left parties, the right-wing parties, and the Socialist government.

On the left, BE and PCP argued that parliamentary discussion ought not to be constrained by the social pact, given parliament's exclusive legislative competence over matters related to social concertation. Between 2016 and 2018, both parties repeatedly introduced bills that embodied a clear reform agenda: regulation of atypical employment; derogation of the expiry regime; full reinstatement of the favourability principle; and the reversal of crisis-era liberalisation of dismissals for permanent contracts. These initiatives were repeatedly voted down by a majority composed of the PS and the right-wing PSD and CDS – People's Party (CDS-PP).[3]

For the right-wing parties, no labour-code reform was needed. Failing that, they sought to keep legislation strictly within the four corners of the 2018 social pact. As a rule, "whatever is decided in social concertation, we follow," stated a PSD MP (Interview 10). Social concertation "is where employers and workers are represented and where the Government, which is also an employer and exercises political power, arbitrates to find some consensus between these two sides" (CDS-PP MP, Interview 6). MPs from both parties advanced these positions in parliament from 2016 to 2018.[4]

For the minority Socialist government, within social concertation employers' associations were the crucial constituency to secure for the social pact (given UGT-P's alignment and CGTP's exit option), whereas in parliament the radical-left parties held the pivotal votes. If they withdrew support, the PS would have to rely on the right – exactly what happened. As a CDS-PP MP put it, the PS ended up 'relying on the right-wing votes [to pass the reform bill] so as to foil PCP's and BE's proposals. PCP and BE were left utterly dissatisfied' (Interview 6). In July 2018, the government submitted Law Proposal 136/XIII – *Altera o Código de Trabalho, e a respetiva regulamentação, e o Código dos Regimes Contributivos do Sistema Previdencial de Segurança Social* – thereby initiating a legislative process that concluded in July 2019. Following this proposal, the left parties (PCP, BE, and Ecologist Party "The

Greens" (PEV)) alongside People-Animals-Nature (PAN) presented several bills.[5]

To explore the dynamics between parties and the government during the legislative discussion, we analyse the parliamentary debates using the MAXMaps tool in MAXQDA (Figure 3.1). The map displays relationships between key themes in the legislative process and political actors, as well as the intensity of those connections. The circles represent both the categories of analysis and the political actors; the lines represent the connections (the thicker the line, the stronger the connection). As regards the government, while it is connected to themes such as precariousness, segmentation, and collective bargaining – similarly to the left parties – it takes a different view of these issues. One of the most prominent points of contention was the proposal to extend the trial period from 90 to 180 days, presented as a way to limit the use of fixed-term contracts, particularly for young workers.[6] The left parties are strongly connected to themes such as collective bargaining, the favourability principle, and precariousness, and are at odds with the government. They are also linked to the idea of trade-offs – measures compensating employers – as well as to the theme of parliament's legitimacy to reform labour law. These parties were highly critical of extending the trial period, which they argued increased job insecurity and offered employers

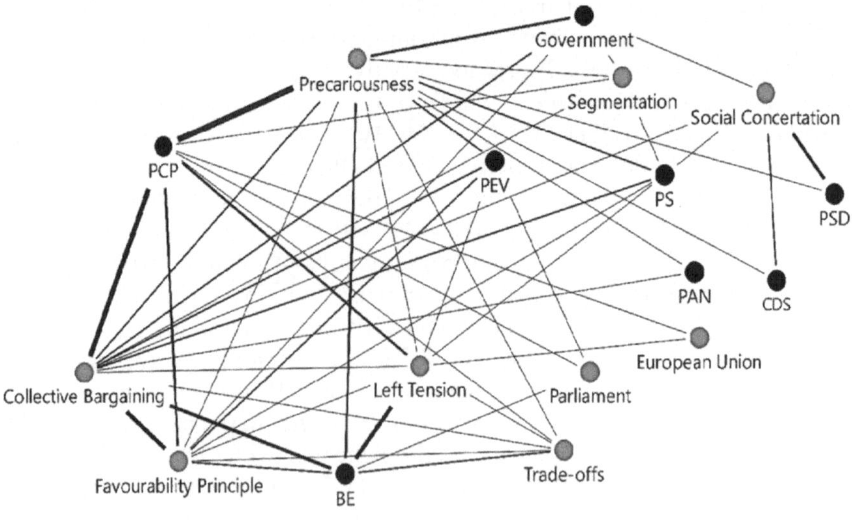

Figure 3.1 Portugal (2016–2019): Connections between key themes and political actors in legislative debates.

Source: Own elaboration using the MAXMaps tool from the MAXQDA programme.

Note: Key: black: political actors (parties and the government) | grey: dimensions of analysis.

unwarranted compensation for accepting pro-outsider regulation. Several parliamentary speeches illustrate their position:

> [the extension of the trial period] cannot be traded off against limiting fixed-term contracts to young people and long-term unemployed.
>
> (PCP MP Rita Rato)

> The Government sought precarity measures negotiated with employers and supported by the right: very short-duration oral contracts for all sectors of activity, new working time accounts outside collective bargaining and the doubling of the duration of the trial period for first-time job seekers and long-term unemployed.
>
> (BE MP José Soeiro)

> [O]ne cannot trade the trial period extension for limits on fixed-term contracts for young people and the long-term unemployed – which is, in fact, a measure we appreciate – because it would assume the Government's combat against precariousness is taking a step forward and another step back.
>
> (PEV MP José Luís Ferreira)[7]

By contrast, the right-wing parties exhibit stronger connections to social concertation, a theme also linked to the government and the PS:

> PSD respects and will always respect social concertation.
>
> (PSD MP Susana Lamas)

> [W]e are available to pass what was agreed [in social concertation]; anything that falls short or goes beyond the tripartite agreement will clearly meet our opposition.
>
> (CDS-PP MP António Carlos Monteiro)[8]

The lengthy parliamentary discussion reveals a clear pattern of alignment. The PS concurred with the radical left on tighter regulation of atypical employment and on restoring an unbridled sectoral extension of collective agreements, but not on the expiry regime and the favourability principle. Nor did they agree on job security for permanent contracts: the PS was unwilling to reverse the Troika-era reforms in that domain and was, indeed, prepared to extend the trial period. Reflecting these cleavages, the final version was approved in July 2019 with votes in favour from the minority PS, abstentions from PSD and CDS-PP, and votes against from PCP and BE.

The episode illustrates Chapter 2's expectation that parliamentary arenas lack an institutional employer veto, yet when a Centrist–Employer bloc chooses to root the package in concertation, inclusive amendments face a higher hurdle and are more easily diluted.

The radical left parties (PCP and BE) assessed that the gains made in the re-regulation of atypical employment were poisoned by concessions to employers (the extended trial period) and by the government's refusal to oppose policy orientations attributed to European institutions, notably regarding collective bargaining and the regulation of permanent contracts (Interviews 1 and 2). The right secured the best outcome available on the table: the final legislation remained within the four corners of the 2018 tripartite agreement. The CDS-PP "did not let the agreement be distorted, we were in the first line of defence of social concertation" (MP António Carlos Monteiro, 19/07/2019). The PSD claimed it had done "everything in its power to ensure the [tripartite agreement] was respected" (MP Susana Lamas, 19/07/2019). The government's strategic aim, a pro-outsider recalibration, was fully achieved, as a Socialist MP acknowledged: it addressed "the dualisation of the labour market [...] the problem of great precariousness of labour relations, visible above all, but not only, in the situation of younger workers [...] (not just) bogus independent work, but also fixed-term contracts" (Interview 11).

Spain's 2021 Labour Market Reform (Royal Decree-Law 32/2021)

This section analyses the Spanish labour market reform agreed at the end of 2021 and enacted as Royal Decree-Law 32/2021. The law, settled in tripartite concertation on 23 December 2021 and approved in parliament in March 2022 by a single vote, has been celebrated by the coalition government as a flagship achievement in reducing labour-market dualisation. As with the Portuguese case, its significance can only be appreciated in light of the crisis-era reforms it partially reverses.

The unilateral 2012 reform enacted by the conservative People's Party (PP) government liberalised both employment protection and collective bargaining (Malo, 2012). In the domain of employment protection, it broadened the grounds for fair dismissal to encompass economic, technical, organisational, or production causes and allowed firms to dismiss workers when turnover declined for three consecutive quarters. Compensation for unfair dismissal under open-ended contracts was shortened to 33 days' wages per year of service (with a cap of 24 months), and a new 'contract to support entrepreneurs' was set up, allowing for a 12-month probationary period. The requirement of administrative authorisation for collective dismissals was abolished, limiting reinstatement rights. On the collective bargaining front, the reform privileged company-level agreements over sectoral agreements in wage setting, job classification, working time, contract types, and other matters, eased employers opting out of collective agreements unilaterally and shortened the ultra-activity of agreements to one year after which the agreement would expire, accelerating decentralisation and eroding sectoral coordination (Molina, 2014).

The 2021 reform sought to generalise permanent employment, curb the abusive use of temporary contracts, and rebalance collective bargaining.

Severance pay for unfair dismissal remained unchanged at 33 days per year of service, but the 'entrepreneurial' contract and its year-long probation were abolished. Firms must now reinstate employees unfairly dismissed within five days. The law severely restricted fixed-term hiring: the long-standing contract for works and services was abolished and temporary contracts can only be concluded for 'production circumstances' – that is, temporary and unforeseen increases in activity – or to substitute an absent worker; production contracts may last six months (extendable to 12 by sectoral agreement), while contracts designed to cover predictable but short-lived peaks may not exceed 90 days in a calendar year. Workers engaged by the same employer for more than 18 months in a 24-month period acquire permanent status. A new indefinite *fijo-discontinuo* contract is to be used for seasonal or intermittent work. Apprenticeship and training contracts were rationalised but maximum trial periods remained six months for highly qualified workers and two months (one month for contracts shorter than six months) for other employees. The reform also introduced a presumption of employment for digital-platform workers, targeting bogus self-employment (Table 3.3). In collective bargaining, the 2021 law marked a partial return to pre-2012 rules. Company-level agreements continue to prevail over sectoral agreements only

Table 3.3 Spain – Employment protection legislation: The 2012 and 2021 reforms

Dimension	*2012 labour reform (Real Decreto-Ley 3/2012)*	*2021 labour reform (Real Decreto-Ley 32/2021)*
Permanent contracts: severance pay	Compensation for unfair dismissal shortened to 33 days per year of service (capped at maximum 24 months)	Unchanged at 33 days per year of service
Permanent contracts: fair dismissal grounds	Fair dismissal permitted for economic, technical, organisational, or production reasons; firms could dismiss after three consecutive quarters of declining revenue	Same causes; additional ground of maladaptation but greater emphasis on reinstatement for unfair dismissal
Permanent contracts: trial period	New 'contract to support entrepreneurs' with a 12-month probation; other contracts: 6 months (qualified), 2–3 months (others)	Entrepreneurial contract abolished; probation periods remain 6/2/1 month depending on qualification and contract length

(*Continued*)

Table 3.3 (Continued)

Dimension	*2012 labour reform (Real Decreto-Ley 3/2012)*	*2021 labour reform (Real Decreto-Ley 32/2021)*
Permanent contracts: reinstatement	Limited reinstatement following unfair dismissal	Employer must reinstate worker within 5 days when dismissal is declared unfair
Fixed-term contracts: valid cases	Multiple categories, including replacement, temporary market needs, training contracts, and the contract for work or services	Temporary hiring restricted to production circumstances (temporary and unforeseeable increases in activity) or substitution of a worker; contract for work or services eliminated
Fixed-term contracts: maximum duration	Specific tasks: 3 years + 12 months extension; temporary increase in workload: 6–12 months; conversion to permanent after 24 months in a 30-month period	Production contracts: 6 months (extendable to 12 by sectoral agreement); occasional predictable peaks: 90 days per year; conversion to permanent after 18 months in a 24-month period
Fixed-term contracts: severance pay	12 days per year of service (phased in from 8 days in 2011 to 12 days from 2015)	Same schedule (12 days per year)
Fixed-term contracts: trial period	6 months (qualified technicians), 2 months (others), 3 months in small firms	Unchanged; but 1-month probation for contracts shorter than 6 months
Successive contracts and conversion to permanent	Permanent status after 24 months of employment within a 30-month period	Permanent status after 18 months of employment within 24 months
Seasonal work	No specific contract; seasonal work often covered by fixed-term contracts	Introduction of the indefinite discontinuous (*fijo-discontinuo*) contract for seasonal or intermittent work

Table 3.3 (Continued)

Dimension	*2012 labour reform (Real Decreto-Ley 3/2012)*	*2021 labour reform (Real Decreto-Ley 32/2021)*
Temporary agency work	Allowed for temporary needs, replacement of absent workers and specific projects; no limit on renewals	Contract for works and services removed; general rules align with fixed-term contracts; conversion to permanent after 18 months in 24 months
Bogus self-employment	No presumption of employment	Presumption of employment introduced for sectors with high rates of digital-platform work

Source: Authors' own elaboration.

in certain domains (overtime pay, working schedules, job classification, contract types, and work–life balance), while others (basic wage scales and salary supplements) once again fall under sectoral agreements. The ultra-activity of collective agreements was restored: agreements remain in force until replaced rather than expiring after 12 months. Extension mechanisms were broadened so that any bargaining party may request the extension of a collective agreement, replacing the earlier restriction to the National Consultative Commission. The favourability principle remains limited by statutory exceptions, but overall the reform strengthens sectoral coordination while preserving some company-level flexibility (Table 3.4).

From a political economy perspective, the 2021 reform illustrates how European conditionality, social-partner consensus, and coalition politics moderated but did not fully overturn the 2012 liberalisation. Employers were able to retain many of the dismissal regulations, while unions achieved tighter regulation of temporary work and restoration of ultra-activity. The coalition government could therefore present the reform as progress towards reducing Spain's entrenched labour-market segmentation.

Social Concertation: Towards the 2021 Tripartite Agreement (2020–2021)

For years, trade unions and the main left-wing parties (PSOE and *Podemos*), as well as left-wing nationalist parties such as *Euskal Herria Bildu* (EH-Bildu)

Table 3.4 Spain – Collective bargaining and wage-setting: The 2012 versus the 2021 reform

Dimension	*2012 labour reform*	*2021 labour reform*
Who can negotiate?	Most representative unions and employer associations at national or regional level	Unchanged
Favourability principle	National agreements prevail over industry-level agreements and the latter over company agreements; derogations allowed for economic or organisational reasons	Unchanged
Priority of company agreements	Company agreements take precedence over sectoral agreements in basic pay, supplements, overtime pay, schedules, job classification, contract types, and work–life balance	Company agreements prevail only for overtime pay, schedules, classification, contract types, and work–life balance; basic salary and supplements revert to sectoral bargaining
Ultra-activity	Expired collective agreements remain in force for 12 months; 2-year limit to negotiate a new agreement	Restored: agreements remain effective until replaced by a new one (indefinite ultra-activity)
Extension mechanisms	Only the National Consultative Commission on Collective Agreements can extend agreements; rarely used	Any bargaining party can request extension of an agreement

Source: Authors' own elaboration.

in the Basque Country and *Esquerra Republicana de Catalunya* (ERC) in Catalonia placed the reversal of the 2012 labour-market reform at the forefront of their agendas. Party representatives repeatedly stated:

> We must derogate the PP's labour-market reform [...]
> (*Unidas Podemos* (UP) MP Echenique Robba)

> What matters to us is that the labour reform is derogated in order to restore all the aspects that have curtailed the rights of workers. [...] This is not simply tackling the temporary nature or the simplification of contracts — with which we very much agree, by the way – but also recovering the prevalence of sectoral agreements, ultra-activity, severance payments that were brutally cut with the labour reform of the PP, the processing of wages or the necessary administrative authorisation of the ERE.
> (MP Matute García de Jalón, EH-Bildu)[9]

In the November 2019 elections, the centre-left PSOE won a plurality of the vote and opened negotiations to form a new government. The following month, PSOE and *Unidas Podemos* signed an agreement to form the first left coalition government since the transition to democracy. Formally appointed on 7 January 2020, the government presented an ambitious programme to combat precariousness and promote job quality, pledging *inter alia* to derogate the 2012 labour-market reform and to work within social dialogue to deliver a new Labour Code for the 21st century combining workers' protection with social, technological, and environmental challenges.[10]

The government quickly signalled its commitment to social dialogue. The first meeting of the tripartite social dialogue table on employment and employment relations was held in January 2020 with the two most representative union confederations (CCOO and UGT-S) and the main employers' organisations (CEOE and Spanish Confederation of Small and Medium-Sized Enterprises (CEPYME)). One of the first laws enacted by the new executive was the 2020 minimum wage increase, previously agreed with the social partners (Molina, 2022). As the Prime Minister Sánchez underlined: the government "firmly believes in social dialogue, in reaching agreements, which is why we propose to rebuild broken consensus and repeal the labour market reform of 2012."[11]

The COVID-19 pandemic, erupting just two months after the government took office, compelled a shift in priorities and temporarily postponed several planned reforms, including the derogation of the 2012 reform. This generated tensions within the coalition, particularly regarding the social agenda and the appropriateness of delaying reforms in the prevailing context. Social dialogue played a more central role in many policy responses than during the Great Recession and helped mitigate labour-market impacts through innovative instruments for recovery, including the mechanism designed to alleviate the employment effects of the pandemic (renewed several times) and the agreement on telework (Molina, 2022).

Once the worst of the pandemic had passed, the government and social partners returned to labour-market reform. Negotiations began in March 2021, immediately after approval of the 'Rider Law' regulating platform work, itself negotiated with the social partners. Sensing a favourable political climate, CCOO and UGT-S pressed for dismantling the 2012 reform under the slogan 'Now it's time!' Employers' organisations CEOE and CEPYME were reluctant to amend a reform they regarded as effective and endorsed by international organisations. The president of CEOE even argued that this was the worst possible moment to consider derogating the reform (Europa Press, 2020).

The European dimension proved pivotal. Interviewees agreed that the EU played a key role in creating a favourable environment for agreement on reducing temporary employment, following repeated failed attempts to do so. First, curbing labour market dualisation by lowering Spain's high share of temporary employment had long featured in the Country-Specific

Recommendations. Secondly, European Court of Justice rulings in June 2021 cautioned against wrongful renewals and the fraudulent use of temporary contracts in the public sector, particularly in the healthcare system. Finally, within the Recovery and Resilience Plan, the government committed to negotiating a reform by 31 December 2021 and to penalising the excessive use of very short-term contracts and labour fraud. The stated aims were to universalise the permanent contract; restore causality to temporary contracts; simplify hiring by revising contractual modalities; and introduce a new, permanent model of temporary employment regulation files (ERTEs), which had functioned as an alternative flexibility instrument to external employment adjustment in the face of negative shocks.

What the social partners and coalition parties perceived as a supportive setting was, for the right-wing PP, the sole reason the government pursued agreement:

> [Y]ou have come to legislate dragged by the halter and you have done so by the European requirement both at the level of rulings of the European Court of Justice and the conditionality of the Transformation, Recovery and Resilience Plan to access funds.
>
> (MP Martín Martín)[12]

Despite the favourable context, negotiations were beset by obstacles and unfolded in two phases. The first addressed matters where consensus was easier, notably collective bargaining. Here, agreement coalesced around restoring ultra-activity and introducing adjustments to the 2012 reform to ensure the prevalence of sectoral collective bargaining in key domains. As several interviews indicated, unions and employers had already developed mechanisms that de facto prolonged the ultra-activity of collective agreements, while reaffirming the importance of sectoral agreements as coordination devices. As a CEOE representative put it:

> [The reform] consolidates what was already happening in the realm of collective bargaining, because what the 2012 reform had done was to make all non-renewed agreements expire within one year, unless otherwise agreed. In truth, the bargaining partners had either prolonged that year down the road or directly stated that the collective agreement would hold until jointly renewed.
>
> (Interview 15)

The second phase centred on the most contentious issues: reforming temporary employment; introducing new flexibility mechanisms for firms; the structure of collective bargaining; and the articulation between company- and sector-level agreements. Several hurdles emerged. Employers strongly opposed the proposal to cap the share of temporary employees within firms. Interviewees also noted tensions within government, notably between the

Labour Minister, closer to *Unidas Podemos*, and the finance minister from the PSOE with a more technocratic profile. The latter was critical of some of the Labour Ministry's more radical proposals, particularly those limiting temporary contracts. Despite progress, no agreement had been reached by early December 2021.

The government then held daily meetings with social partners to conclude a deal before the 31 December deadline. Three issues remained unresolved one week beforehand. First, the creation of a new, permanent mechanism of temporary employment regulation files to provide an internal-flexibility alternative to external adjustment during negative shocks, building upon the pandemic experience. Secondly, the application of sectoral collective agreements in outsourcing and subcontracting: the government proposed applying the client company's sectoral agreement to the outsourced firm, whereas employers wanted the latter to apply the agreement corresponding to its own activity. Thirdly, the manner of limiting temporary employment, with employers rejecting a maximum percentage cap. As the CEOE representative explained:

> [T]he key issues were those on the table and those outside the negotiation perimeter that had not been addressed [...] such as changes to the subcontracting regime, changes to the way working conditions are defined, the issue of subrogation. These were very important issues for the business community because they were key to internal flexibility.
>
> (Interview 15)

A tripartite agreement was signed on 27 December by both employers' associations and union confederations. CCOO characterised it as a highly positive compromise:

> [E]verything hinged upon a lot of political will, a lot of willingness by the unions and also commitment from the employers' organizations in reaching a compromise agreement [...] [we believe] the success of this reform was reached by seeking the necessary balance between government, unions and employers, each of which has very different preferences and looks out for different rights.
>
> (Interview 12)

Subsequently, several organisations within CEOE voiced dissatisfaction with the decision to sign, including the powerful Foment, CEOE's Catalan federation, which publicly criticised the reform as inimical to its interests. The right-wing PP also attacked CEOE, opening an unprecedented rift between the main employers' confederation and the party. Criticism arose on the trade-union side as well, notably from smaller confederations that viewed the outcome not as a reversal but as a marginal adjustment to the 2012 reform.

Some left-wing parties likewise faulted social dialogue for enabling employer vetoes and producing a toothless reform.

Employers' defensive participation in concertation, entering to temper a left-legislative threat rather than block it, matches a Chapter 2 pathway whereby pacting edges towards inclusivity while preserving aspects of the earlier core.

Legislative Process in the Cortes Generales *(2021–2022)*

Despite the agreement with social partners, the reform attracted criticism from both sides of the political spectrum. On the right, it precipitated an historic split between the PP and CEOE. Shortly after the tripartite deal, the PP initially dismissed the reform as effecting no derogation; it then distanced itself from CEOE, contending the reform lacked broad support within the confederation and insisting that parliamentary prerogatives should not be displaced by social dialogue. On the left, smaller unions and several parties, including ERC, previously supportive of the government on other bills, also criticised the reform.

In parliament, right-of-centre parties opposed reversing the 2012 reform. Framed against the post-pandemic recovery, they argued for more, not less, flexibility:

> [M]ore flexibility, more negotiation capacity, more capacity within the company to be able to adopt flexible mechanisms, more efficiency and a favourable environment for employment.
>
> (MP Gamarra Ruiz-Clavijo)[13]

Some regional right-wing parties adopted a more nuanced stance, accepting the revision of specific aspects while retaining others seen as beneficial:

> We do not want a complete repeal, but we do want a modification of the labour reform on the issue of the primacy of sectoral agreements, ultra-activity and many others.
>
> (MP Bel Accensi)

> We believe there are some aspects in need of reform: the ultra-activity of [collective] agreements, the fight against temporary employment, the issue related to relief contracts and how to promote them, or our proposal to the introduction of the so-called Austrian backpack in labour regulations.[14] We believe that measures and issues [...] can be used to create a new labour framework, which will surely also have to take into account the new economy and, therefore, the whole issue of teleworking that has appeared with the pandemic.
>
> (MP Boadella Esteve)[15]

The only centre-right parties voting in favour were *Ciudadanos* and the PDCAT. *Ciudadanos* offered a positive assessment of the tripartite agreement and underscored the value of a negotiated reform for access to European funds. In its view, the law delivered improvements:

> [Such as] narrow the menu of [temporary] contracts in favour of the indefinite contract and combat temporary employment. But this regulation will also give Spain credibility with a view to receiving European funds, which was one of the commitments that our country obtained from our partners. Why? Because it is endorsed by the social partners. This is the government's reform, but the reform of a country endorsed by the social partners, which is much better than what *Podemos* would like to have done and what Mr. Sánchez would like to have done.
>
> (MP Arrimadas Garcia)[16]

Although left parties broadly supported the initiative, not all voted in favour. Left nationalist parties in Galicia, the Basque Country, and Catalonia, including ERC, opposed the bill. They offered similar reasons: the reform lacked ambition, failed fully to derogate the 2012 changes, and retained problematic elements such as the liberalisation of employment protection for permanent contracts. Whether this opposition reflected substantive disagreement or an electoral strategy to distinguish themselves from the governing left coalition and reclaim votes on the left is difficult to determine.

The Cortes' majoritarian logic allowed the Left–Union bloc to pass the pact intact, underscoring the difference between negotiated agreement and majority voting that Chapter 2 highlights. The result is an inclusive-leaning settlement that remains bounded by what the employer consent constraint could accept at the bargaining table.

The analysis of the parliamentary debates using the MAXMaps tool helps to summarise differences in the discourse and policy priorities of the political actors involved in the legislative process (Figure 3.2). As with the Portuguese map, it represents the connections between key themes in the legislative discussion and the political actors, and the intensity of those connections. Regarding the different levels of decision-making, policy concertation and social dialogue appear to be of particular importance to the Government, while the EU and the parliamentary arena are salient for the PP and the regional left parties, respectively. Although regional right parties are also connected to the parliamentary arena, this concern was expressed more strongly by MPs from left parties, who favour Parliament over social concertation as the legitimate policymaking body. The stronger role played by the EU in the PP's discourse is likely linked to the reform's placement within a broader spectrum of measures under the Recovery and Resilience Plans, and to the fact that approval by the social partners was a necessary condition for access to European funds; this also led left parties to criticise some of the concessions made. Regarding party positions on the reform, the

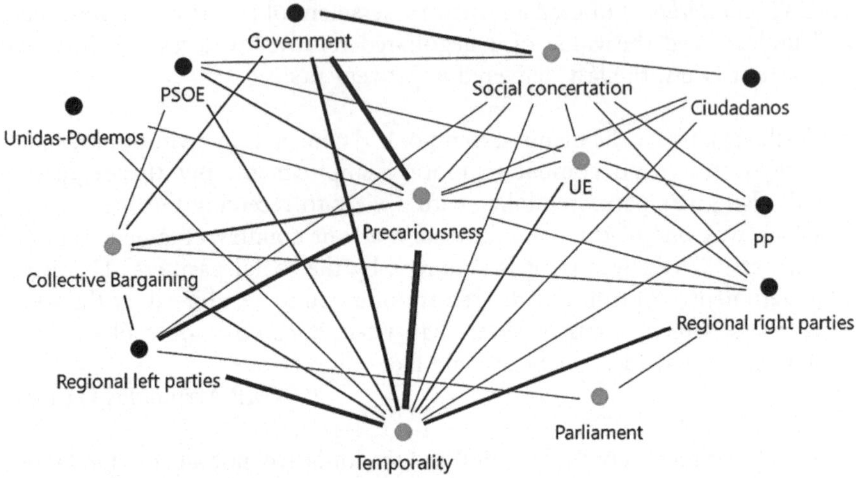

Figure 3.2 Spain (2020–2022): Connections between key themes and political actors in legislative debates.

Source: Own elaboration using the MAXMaps tool from the MAXQDA programme.

Note: Key: black: political actors (parties and the government) | grey: dimensions of analysis.

PP and regional parties (both right and left) opposed it, albeit for different reasons. The regional left parties considered that the tripartite agreement conceded too much to employers in key areas, most notably the limitation of temporary contracts and the precedence of regional collective agreements over national-sectoral ones. The latter issue was also raised by regional right parties. The themes such as precariousness, collective bargaining, and temporality emerged as highly important to the left parties (both regional and *Unidas Podemos*-PSOE) and to the Government (mainly precariousness and temporality).

Comparative Assessment: Portugal (2019) and Spain (2021)

The two reforms display distinct conceptions of how to rebuild labour-market solidarity after a period of liberalisation and dualisation. In Portugal, the 2019 reform constitutes a partial and asymmetrical reversal: it substantially re-regulates non-standard employment while preserving the core liberalising pillars introduced during the Troika period for standard workers and the structure of collective bargaining. In Spain, the 2021 reform is broader in scope: it tightens regulation across several dimensions, notably temporary hiring and collective bargaining, whilst leaving in place some elements of the 2012 settlement for permanent contracts.

In the Portuguese case, the thrust of policy reform is unambiguous on atypical work. Fixed-term contracts were confined to genuine temporary needs, the cumulative duration of successive contracts was reduced, and the presumptive test against bogus self-employment was strengthened. By contrast, the reform leaves the priority of company-level agreements over sectoral agreements unchanged and does not alter the shortened deadlines governing the expiry of collective agreements; the extension mechanism was, however, reinstated without representativeness thresholds. On permanent contracts, protection is broadly stable, albeit with a slight net commodification effect arising from the introduction of a six-month trial period for first-time job-seekers and the long-term unemployed. For temporary agency work, the net effect is best characterised as broadly neutral: the maximum assignment length was increased (from two to three years), but a cap on renewals was introduced, which offsets the deregulatory component. On balance, and as summarised in Table 3.5, the direction of change combines a strong positive change (++) for fixed-term contracts and bogus self-employment; no net change (=) for the articulation of bargaining levels and for ultra-activity; a strong positive change (++) for extensions; and a neutral to negative outcome (=/–) for permanent-contract regulation.

Spain's 2021 reform follows a different trajectory. The negotiated package severely curtails abusive temporary hiring and, in collective bargaining, both restores ultra-activity and rebalances the articulation between company and sectoral levels in key domains. Although it does not fully undo the 2012 changes to permanent-contract protection, it marginally increases the security of standard workers relative to the 2012 baseline. The overall configuration is therefore one of across-the-board re-regulation, captured in Table 3.5 as a strong positive change (++) for fixed-term contracts and

Table 3.5 Portugal (2019) and Spain (2021) compared: Qualitative direction of regulatory change by domain

Regulatory dimensions	*Portugal 2019*	*Spain 2021*
	Direction of change	
Job security for permanent contracts	=/–	=/+
Job security for fixed-term contracts	++	++
Job security for temporary agency work	=	=/+
Regulation of bogus self-employment	++	++
Articulation between company and sectoral level agreements	=	=/+
Ultra-activity of collective agreements	=	++
Extension regime of collective agreements	++	++

Source: Authors' own elaboration.

Notes: Key: direction of change in regulation: increasing/decreasing.
–: large decrease | =/–: slight decrease | =: no change | =/+: slight increase | ++: large increase.

ultra-activity; a neutral to positive outcome (=/+) for temporary agency work and for the company–sector articulation; a strong positive change (++) for extensions; and a neutral to positive outcome (=/+) for permanent-contract regulation.

Taken together, the Iberian comparison underscores how similar political economies, operating under a more socially balanced European governance framework, can deliver different solidaristic settlements. Portugal resolved distributional conflicts by relying on social concertation to re-regulate outsiders while maintaining the main competitive features of the post-crisis regime for insiders. Spain, benefiting from a broader coalition and a later, post-pandemic timing in the European 'social turn,' advanced a more encompassing recalibration that narrows the insider–outsider divide and strengthens the capacity of collective bargaining to coordinate wage-setting and working conditions. Table 3.5 sums up the differences that help explain why the reforms differ in their likely effects on dualisation: mitigation without full closure in Portugal versus substantial narrowing of segmentation in Spain.[17]

Discussion and Conclusions

The Iberian reforms pursued after the Great Recession regulated atypical employment more ambitiously than at any point in recent decades, yet they did so with divergent orientations and scopes. Portugal's 2019 reform amounted to a partial and asymmetrical reversal: it tightened rules on non-standard contracts while leaving core elements of the crisis-era settlement in place (including the expiry regime and a truncated favourability principle). Spain's 2021 reform, by contrast, combined a far-reaching re-anchoring of open-ended contracts with selective recentralisation of bargaining rules, thereby improving conditions for both outsiders and insiders, even if it stopped short of fully undoing the 2012 deregulation of unfair-dismissal remedies and the opting-out regime for employers. This divergence requires explanation.

The governing social bloc was decisive in shaping the direction of policy change. In Portugal, a PS-centred alliance with employer confederations and the moderate union (UGT-P) channelled reform through social concertation, where employer vetoes were structurally priced in. This produced a regulatory tightening of fixed-term contracts, whilst retaining the central pillars of the post-2003/2012 bargaining settlement and even expanding trial periods – precisely the kind of trade-off associated with competitive solidarity. In Spain, a PSOE–*Unidas Podemos* coalition with strong union participation negotiated a tripartite pact that subsequently passed intact in the *Cortes*, restoring ultra-activity and sectoral precedence in wage-setting while generalising indefinite employment. Employers consented, but the 2012 dismissal regime and opt-outs survived largely unscathed, delineating the boundary of the inclusive turn.

As predicted by Chapter 2, concertation, a joint-decision setting with a built-in consent constraint, compresses inclusive ambitions, whereas parliamentary arenas, lacking an institutional employer veto, permit legislation closer to bloc ideal points. The Portuguese centre-left executive's reliance on social concertation, leaving left parties in parliament with limited capacity to shape policy, insulated the reform politically but narrowed its breadth; by contrast, the Spanish coalition government's combination of social dialogue and parliamentary rule-making delivered a broader re-regulatory sweep, though keeping employers on board nonetheless reduced the scope of the reform.

The EU acted as a conditional selector and amplifier rather than a simple constraint. In the Eurozone crisis, EU leverage pushed liberalising internal-devaluation agendas (Scharpf, 2016; Perez and Matsaganis, 2018); thereafter, a 'social turn' rebalanced governance via the 2017 European Pillar of Social Rights (European Commission, 2017), implemented via the 2021 Action Plan (European Commission, 2021), the EU directives on transparent and predictable working conditions (Directive 2019/1152) and adequate minimum wages/collective bargaining coverage (Directive 2022/2041), and the Next Generation EU facility (Kyriazi and Miró, 2023; Petmesidou et al., 2023). Spain's reform was further enabled by European Court of Justice jurisprudence censuring abusive temporariness in the public sector (CJEU, 2016; CJEU, 2020), and by the Recovery and Resilience Plan milestones that favoured negotiated re-regulation; Portugal legislated earlier, with weaker EU social support and stronger domestic constraints tied to concertation. These supranational shifts help explain why regulation of temporariness became politically feasible – and why more was achieved in Spain.

Bringing these strands together, the contrast with Table 2.2 (Chapter 2) is instructive. Portugal exemplifies a configuration that combines a centrist government aligned with employer interests, social concertation as the main arena of decision-making, and an early and attenuated turn in EU social policy. Taken together, these features predict competitive solidarity of partial scope. Spain, by contrast, illustrates a configuration that combines a left government aligned with trade unions, social dialogue alongside Parliament as the arenas of decision-making, and strong EU social leverage. Taken together, these features predict a tendency towards inclusive solidarity of broader scope. Elements retained from the 2012 reform continue to delineate the negotiated frontier.

In sum, Iberia's post-crisis labour market reforms were not merely two national iterations of a single script. Each reform embodies a distinct political settlement: on the one hand, Portugal's competitive solidarity recalibration, insulated from partisan meddling through social concertation and bounded by pre-existing veto points; on the other hand, Spain's inclusive-leaning bargain, bolstered by a supportive EU conjuncture and consolidated in parliament. The comparative lesson is that, in post-austerity Europe, the restoration of solidarity to labour markets, whether of the inclusive or the competitive type, requires not only favourable supranational winds but also domestic coalitions to propel them and political venues capable of harnessing them.

Notes

1 "*Geringonça*," shorthand for the PS–left support pact in 2015–2021.
2 Parliamentary record, session 10/02/2017.
3 See interventions in the debates of 10 February 2017 and 9 June 2017 by MPs António Filipe and Rita Rato (PCP), José Luís Ferreira (PEV), and Isabel Pires and José Soeiro (BE).
4 See interventions in the debates of 10 February 2018 and 28 February 2018 by MPs António Carlos Monteiro (CDS-PP) and Maria das Mercês Soares (PSD).
5 In total, 18 bill proposals were discussed alongside the government's bill.
6 Statement by the Labour Minister, José Vieira da Silva, session of 31 May 2019.
7 *Diário da Assembleia da República* (parliamentary record), sessions of 19 July 2019, 10 June 2019, and 9 May 2019, respectively.
8 Both interventions are recorded in the *Diário da Assembleia da República* (parliamentary record), session of 2 July 2019.
9 *Diario del Congreso de los Diputados* (parliamentary record), sessions of 20 December 2020 and 19 May 2021, respectively.
10 Prime Minister Pedro Sánchez's investiture speech is available at: www.lamoncloa.gob.es/presidente/intervenciones/Paginas/2020/prsp04012020.aspx (accessed 10 September 2025).
11 *Diario del Congreso de los Diputados* (parliamentary record), session of 1 April 2020.
12 *Diario del Congreso de los Diputados* (parliamentary record), session of 21 December 2021.
13 *Diario del Congreso de los Diputados* (parliamentary record), session of 24 March 2021.
14 On this see: Sousa et al. (2022).
15 *Diario del Congreso de los Diputados* (parliamentary record), sessions of 7 March 2020 and 13 April 2021, respectively.
16 *Diario del Congreso de los Diputados* (parliamentary record), session of 2 March 2022.
17 The data on the evolution of temporary employment in both countries indicate that the decline was more pronounced in Spain than in Portugal (see Figure I.1 in the introduction).

References

Afonso A., Dorigatti L., Molina O. and Tassinari A. (2022) Labour market (de)regulation and wage-setting institutions in Mediterranean capitalism. In: Burroni L., Pavolini E. and Regini M. (eds) Mediterranean Capitalism Revisited: One Model, Different Trajectories. 115–148. New York/London: Cornell University Press.

Andreotti A., Garcia S. M., Gómez A., Hespanha P., Kazepov Y. and Mingione E. (2001) Does a Southern European model exist? *Journal of European Area Studies* 9(1): 43–62.

Branco R. (2022) *Proteção Social no Portugal Democrático. Trajetórias de Reforma.* Lisbon: Fundação Francisco Manuel dos Santos.

Campos Lima M. da P. (2019) Portugal: Reforms and the turn to neoliberal austerity. In: Müller T., Vandaele K. and Waddington J. (eds) *Collective Bargaining in Europe: Towards an Endgame?* Vol. III, 483–504. Brussels: European Trade Union Institute.

Campos Lima M. da P. and Naumann R. (2011) Portugal: From broad strategic pacts to policy-specific agreements. In: Avdagic S., Rhodes M. and Visser J. (eds) Social Pacts in Europe: Emergence, Evolution, and Institutionalization. 147–173. Oxford: Oxford University Press.

Court of Justice of the European Union (2016) *Case C-16/15, María Elena Pérez López v Servicio Madrileño de Salud (Comunidad de Madrid).* Judgment of 14 September 2016. ECLI:EU:C:2016:679.

Court of Justice of the European Union (2020) *Joined Cases C-103/18 and C-429/18, Domingo Sánchez Ruiz v Comunidad de Madrid (Servicio Madrileño de Salud); Berta Fernández Álvarez and Others v Comunidad de Madrid (Servicio Madrileño de Salud).* Judgment of 19 March 2020. ECLI: EU:C:2020:219.

CPCS [Comissão Permanente de Concertação Social] (2018) Combater a precariedade e reduzir a segmentação laboral e promover um maior dinamismo da negociação coletiva, Lisboa: Conselho Económico e Social. Available at: https://ces.pt/wp-content/uploads/2022/03/acordo-2018-2.pdf.

Crouch C. (1993) *Industrial Relations and European State Traditions.* Oxford: Clarendon Press.

Dray G., Lopes F. R., Albuquerque J. L., Guerra R., Ministro A. and Feliciano T. (2016) *Livro Verde Sobre As Relações Laborais.* Lisbon: Gabinete de Estratégia e Planeamento do Ministério do Trabalho, Solidariedade e Segurança Social.

Ebbinghaus B. and Hassel A. (2000) Striking deals: Concertation in the reform of continental European welfare states. *Journal of European Public Policy* 7(1): 44–62.

Emmenegger P. (2014) *The Power to Dismiss: Trade Unions and the Regulation of Job Security in Western Europe.* Oxford: Oxford University Press.

Eurofound (1999) *Employers' organisations in Spain examined*, Eurofound. Available at: www.eurofound.europa.eu/en/publications/all/employers-organisations-spain-examined.

Europa Press (2020) Garamendi dice que ahora es "el peor momento" para plantear una reforma laboral, 29 May. Madrid: Europa Press. Available at: www.europapress.es/economia/laboral-00346/noticia-garamendi-dice-ahora-peor-momento-plantear-reforma-laboral-20200529123054.html.

European Commission (2017) *Commission Recommendation (EU) 2017/761 of 26 April 2017 on the European Pillar of Social Rights (C(2017) 2600; OJ L 113*, pp. 56–61).

European Commission (2021) *The European Pillar of Social Rights Action Plan* (COM(2021) 102 final).

European Union (2019) Directive 2019/1152 of 11 July 2019 concerning transparent and predictable working conditions in the European Union. *Official Journal of the European Communities*, L186, 11/07/2019, pp. 105–121.

European Union (2022) Directive 2022/2041 of 19 October 2022, concerning adequate minimum wages in the European Union. *Official Journal of the European Communities.* L275, 25/10/2022, pp. 33–47.

Hancké B. and Rhodes M. (2005) EMU and labour market institutions in Europe: The rise and fall of national social pacts. *Work and Occupations* 32(2): 196–228.

Kyriazi A. and Miró J. (2023) Towards a socially fair green transition in the EU? An analysis of the Just Transition Fund using the Multiple Streams Framework. *Comparative European Politics* 21(1): 112–132.

Lisi M. and Loureiro J. (2022) Interest groups, business associations, and unions. In: Fernandes J., Magalhães P. and Pinto A. C. (eds) *The Oxford Handbook of Portuguese Politics*. 423–439. Oxford: Oxford University Press.

Malo M. A. (2012) The February 2012 Spanish Labour Market Reform. *Spanish Economic and Financial Outlook* 2012(0): 50–59.

Marques P. and Fonseca D. (2022) Understanding the positions taken by moderate union confederations and centre-left parties during labour market reforms in Portugal and Spain: Why the configuration of left parties and trade union confederations matters. *European Journal of Industrial Relations* 28(1): 65–84.

Marques P. and Salavisa I. (2017) Young people and dualization in Europe: A fuzzy set analysis. *Socio-Economic Review* 15(1): 135–160.

Molina Ó. (2006) Trade union strategies and change in neo-corporatist concertation: A new century of political exchange? *West European Politics* 29(4): 640–664.

Molina Ó. (2014) Beyond de-centralization: The erosion of collective bargaining in Spain during the Great Recession. *Stato e Mercato* 34(3): 397–422.

Molina Ó. (2022) *Collective Bargaining and Social Dialogue – Back to Normal in 2021?* Dublin: Eurofound.

Molina Ó. and Rhodes M. (2007) The political economy of adjustment in mixed market economies: A study of Spain and Italy. In: Hancké B., Rhodes M. and Thatcher M. (eds) Beyond Varieties of Capitalism. 223–252. Oxford: Oxford University Press.

Perez S. A. and Matsaganis M. (2018) The political economy of austerity in Southern Europe. *New Political Economy* 23(2): 192–207.

Petmesidou M., Branco R., Pavolini E., González Begega S. and Guillén A. M. (2023) The EPSR and the Next Generation EU: Heralding a reconfiguration of social protection in South Europe? *Social Policy & Administration* 57(4): 497–512.

Scharpf F. W. (2016) Forced structural convergence in the eurozone: or a differentiated European monetary community. MPIfG Discussion Paper 16/15. Cologne: Max Planck Institute for the Study of Societies.

Sousa J. B., Díaz-Saavedra J. and Marimon R. (2022) Introducing an Austrian backpack in Spain. *SERIEs* 13(3): 513–556.

Appendix: Interview List and Technical Note

Interview list Portugal

- Interview 1: Portuguese Communist Party (PCP) member of parliament. Date: 16/05/2022. Site: Lisbon.
- Interview 2: Left Block (BE) member of parliament. Date: 17/05/2022. Site: via Zoom.
- Interview 3: Confederation of Commerce and Services of Portugal (CCP) representative. Date: 18/05/2022. Site: Lisbon.

- Interview 4: Former member of cabinet of the Portuguese Socialist government. Date: 20/05/2022. Site: Lisbon.
- Interview 5: Ecologist Party "The Greens" (PEV) member of parliament. Date: 01/06/2022. Site: via Zoom.
- Interview 6: Christian Democrats (CDS-PP) member of parliament. Date: 02/06/2022. Site: Lisbon.
- Interview 7: General Confederation of Portuguese Workers (CGTP) representative. Date: 09/06/2022. Site: Lisbon.
- Interview 8: General Union of Workers (UGT-P) representative. Date: 20/06/2022. Site: over Zoom.
- Interview 9: Confederation of Portuguese Industry (CIP) representative. Date: 01/07/2022. Site: via Zoom.
- Interview 10: Social Democratic Party (PSD) member of parliament. Date: 12/07/2022. Site: Lisbon.
- Interview 11: Socialist Party (PS) member of parliament. Date: 19/10/2022. Site: Lisbon.

Interview list Spain

- Interview 12: Trade Union Confederation of Workers' Committees (CCOO) representative. Date: 04/07/2022. Site: via Zoom.
- Interview 13: Member of cabinet of the Spanish Coalition government. Date: 04/11/2022. Site: via Zoom.
- Interview 14: Member of cabinet of the Spanish Coalition government. Date: 17/11/2022. Site: via Zoom.
- Interview 15: Spanish Confederation of Employers' Organizations (CEOE) representative. Date: 25/11/2022. Site: via Zoom.
- Interview 16: General Workers' Union (UGT-S) representative. Date: 02/03/2023. Site: over Zoom.
- Interview 17: Member of cabinet of the Spanish Coalition Government and Podemos member of parliament. Date: 11/04/2023. Site: via Zoom.

Technical Note MAXQDA

We used MAXQDA (version 2022) to conduct a content analysis of 18 parliamentary debates from 2016–2019 in Portugal, involving 32 relevant participants, and of 67 debates from 2020–2022 in Spain, involving 43 relevant participants.

4 Iberian Minimum Wages

Two Paths to Inclusive Solidarity

Paulo Marques, Nuno Rodrigues, and Óscar Molina

Introduction

This chapter analyses the evolution of national minimum-wage policies in Portugal and Spain during the years of progressive coalitions. Throughout the chapter, we analyse two equivalent six-year windows that coincide with the life span of the recent progressive coalitions in each country: 2016–2022 in Portugal and 2019–2025 in Spain.[1] Focussing on identical durations allows a cleaner comparison of political dynamics, policy sequencing, and distributive outcomes, while grounding the analysis firmly in the periods during which left governments held executive responsibility for wage policy. Building on the theoretical framework set out in Chapters 1 and 2, it explores how national minimum-wage policies were conceived and implemented in both countries, examining their relationship with the ideal-types of solidarity and the governing social blocs that supported such policies. It also reflects on the decision-making arenas, namely the roles of the European Union (EU) and social concertation.

The minimum wage is, by design, a policy instrument aligned with inclusive solidarity: it raises the wage floor for all workers, particularly benefiting outsiders, without directly challenging insiders' positions. Although minimum-wage increases are intrinsically inclusive, their scale and implementation are shaped by political alignments, the strength of supporting social blocs, and the institutional arenas in which decisions are taken. As this chapter demonstrates, Spain's coalition government relied less on the consensus-building logic of social concertation and instead legitimated the reform through public discourse and EU-level developments, pursuing an ambitious strategy of steep increases from the outset to align with EU criteria set in the European Pillar of Social Rights. In Portugal, by contrast, the Socialist Party (PS) sought to preserve its traditional alliances with employers and moderate unions, adopting a compromise-oriented, incremental approach that exposed the fragility of the parliamentary left coalition. Moreover, the Portuguese government could not frame its strategy around EU initiatives, as upratings began in 2015, before the EU's social turn that emphasised the need to raise national minimum wages.

DOI: 10.4324/9781003519874-5

From a methodological perspective, this chapter is founded upon an evidence base comprising four key pillars. First, we conducted a media analysis of the main national broadsheets – *Público, Expresso and Diário de Notícias* in Portugal and *El País, ABC and El Mundo* in Spain – capturing day-to-day framing by political elites, employers, and unions. Second, we coded parliamentary proceedings with MAXQDA, examining 97 debates in the *Assembleia da República* and 24 in the *Congreso de los Diputados*; these transcripts reveal how positions evolved in public, supply additional quotations when interviewees are reticent, and extend our reach to parties or MPs who declined to be interviewed. Third, we reviewed relevant official documents and reports (laws, Royal Decrees, social-dialogue minutes, EU recommendations), situating claims in their formal context. Fourth, we carried out 16 semi-structured interviews with key political and social actors. Using these four sources in tandem enables triangulation: the press and parliamentary records corroborate or challenge statements made in interviews, supplement gaps, and bring in voices absent from our sample, while the documentary corpus grounds all claims in the institutional record. Together, this strategy delivers a wide analytical lens that spans political parties, governments, and social partners and strengthens the arguments advanced in the chapter.

The chapter is organized as follows. First, it sets the scene by outlining the main characteristics of the Southern European minimum-wage regime and reviewing the policy legacies inherited by the two progressive coalitions, with particular emphasis on wage stagnation during the austerity years and the subsequent shift after the sovereign-debt crisis. The following two sections present the Portuguese and Spanish case studies, tracing how each government designed, negotiated, and implemented minimum-wage reform as the linchpin of its effort to reverse austerity-era wage restraint and rebuild social solidarity. The fourth section offers a systematic comparison of the two trajectories, contrasting their coalitional alignments, decision arenas, EU linkages, and distributive outcomes. The concluding section distils the broader lessons on how progressive governments can use wage policy to roll back austerity and re-embed solidarity in contemporary labour market governance.

Contextualising National Minimum-Wage Policy in Southern Europe

Over the past two decades, the minimum wage has transitioned from the periphery to the centre of labour market debates. Its capacity to fulfil broader ambitions depends crucially on the regulatory regime within which it is embedded, encompassing the web of legal rules, bargaining institutions, and enforcement practices that govern how the wage floor is established, adjusted, and enforced.

The literature analysing minimum wage-setting has paid particular attention to two aspects. First, the interaction between the minimum wage and collective bargaining. Secondly, the role of the state vis-à-vis social partners in setting minimum wages. Regarding the interaction between collective bargaining and minimum wages, Grimshaw and Bosch (2013) developed a first typology of interactions that was later refined by Dingeldey et al. (2021). According to this later work, national arrangements can be arrayed along a continuum that runs from purely collective to purely statutory regulation. At one pole are countries such as Denmark, where collective bargaining alone establishes the floor ('substitute for the minimum wage'); at the other are systems such as Greece, where a statutory minimum wage operates largely in isolation from weak collective bargaining. Between these extremes the authors identify three intermediate patterns –'distant coexistence,' 'distant interaction,' and 'close interaction' – that capture progressively tighter coupling between statutory and negotiated minima as union coverage recedes and state activism grows. Spain, with a legal minimum that benchmarks but does not tightly shadow sectoral agreements, is classified in their 'distant interaction' group: the statutory rate matters, yet substantial room remains for collective bargaining to set higher floors. Portugal, by contrast, is placed in the 'close interaction' category, where the statutory minimum and collectively agreed wages increasingly converge, reflecting the narrowing gap between the two. When it comes to the role of the state, Picot's (2023) typology organises the cases by the degree of "statization" of wage regulation. He distinguishes a purely "collective" model, where social partners define autonomously minimum wages; a "collective-plus-state" variant in which social partners define the minimum wage and the public authority routinely extends agreements; and a "state-plus-collective" configuration in which a statutory minimum coexists with broad bargaining coverage, and a predominantly "state" model where the legal floor substitutes for frail collective institutions. Spain appears here in the "state-plus-collective" category, grouped with France and Portugal: the state provides a binding national minimum, yet collective bargaining still covers the majority of workers and remains central to wage setting.

The fact that Spain occupies different slots in the two classifications underscores the conceptual nuances separating them. Dingeldey et al. (2021) concentrate on the empirical interaction between statutory and negotiated minima (how closely the two benchmarks track one another) whereas Picot foregrounds governance authority: who ultimately wields the power to impose, extend, or enforce wage floors. Because Spanish sectoral agreements generally lie above the legal minimum, Dingeldey's lens places the country in the distant interaction group. Picot, by contrast, highlights the decisive role the national government plays in setting and annually uprating the national floor, thereby coding Spain as "state-plus-collective." The divergence is instructive: it shows that identical institutional elements can be read differently depending on whether the analyst privileges functional wage-setting dynamics or the distribution of regulatory authority.

Taken together, the two typologies highlight three features that still set Southern Europe apart (Table 4.1). First, wage setting in the region remains

Table 4.1 Portugal and Spain's position within the Southern-European "state-plus-collective" minimum-wage cluster

Dimension	*Southern-European cluster*	*Portugal (2016–2022)*	*Spain (2019–2025)*
Regulatory template	"State-plus-collective" model: statutory floor coexists with high collective-bargaining coverage (Picot, 2023)	Conforms to the model; the statutory floor increasingly overlaps sectoral minima	Same template, but the statutory floor still below most sectoral rates (Dingeldey et al., 2021; Molina, 2021)
Statutory–bargained interaction	Typically distant, trending to closer as statutory floors rise	Shifted from distant to close interaction once the wage floor overtook negotiated minima in low-pay sectors	Remains distant interaction; sectoral minima still well above statutory minimum wage. But recent uprates point towards closer interaction (Eurofound, 2025)
State-steering capacity	High: governments determine both the level and the timing of upratings	Council of Ministers decrees, with the Council for Social Concertation acting as a gatekeeper	Royal Decrees; social dialogue engaged only when politically expedient
Indexation rule	None: upratings are entirely discretionary	No automatic indexation	No automatic indexation
Approach to minimum wage-setting	No pre-established formula	Loosely defined criteria (includes productivity, inflation etc.)	Loosely defined criteria (includes productivity, inflation etc.)

Source: Authors' elaboration.

conspicuously state-steered. Even in Italy, often cited as a "collective-plus-state" or "substitute" case, the state constitutionalises collectively bargained minima by extending them *erga omnes*, while Greece, Portugal, and Spain rely directly on a legal floor whose level is ultimately decided in cabinet (Afonso, 2019). Second, and most distinctive, the region lacks any form of automatic indexation (Molina, 2021: 68). Annual upratings are driven by partisan negotiation and, in crisis times, by European conditionality rather than by a pre-established formula. In short, Southern Europe illustrates how minimum-wage outcomes flow less from a fixed legal design than from the shifting balance of power between the state and collective bargaining within broadly state-dominant regimes.

Southern Europe has lived through three contrasting phases. Before the global crisis (mid-1990s to 2008) governments used nominal minimum wage increases to narrow gaps with EU peers while seeking business support through tripartite pacts, Portugal's 2006 Social Concertation Accord being emblematic (Campos Lima and Naumann, 2011). The austerity phase (2010–2014) reversed that trajectory. Under Troika conditionality, Portugal froze its minimum wage at €485, while Spain imposed a real term cut (Campos Lima, 2019; Afonso, 2019; Molina, 2021: 80–84). In Greece, the statutory wage was slashed by 22%, illustrating how hard conditionality can even drag a country towards the "isolated statutory" pole (Molina, 2021: 77–79). Italy, lacking a statutory minimum wage, relied mainly on decentralising pressures within collective bargaining; wage floors eroded more slowly, confirming that available policy levers condition the depth of adjustment (Afonso, 2019). From 2015 onwards a progressive re-regulation cycle opened. Portugal's left-wing parliamentary agreement restored annual minimum wage hikes (Campos Lima et al., 2021) whilst Spain's coalition government combined a cumulative 61% rise in the minimum wage in the period 2019–2025.

Two broader lessons follow from the Southern-European trajectory, albeit with a subtle Iberian twist. First, regime labels are fluid: within a single decade both countries moved from consensual, collectively oriented wage-setting to coercive statutory freezes under Troika pressure, and back to politically driven catch-up once progressive coalitions took office. Yet they did not land on exactly the same spot. In Dingeldey et al.'s (2021) continuum, Spain was coded as 'distant interaction,' because the statutory floor still lay some distance below most sectoral minima, though recent studies have placed the country in the close interaction group (Eurofound, 2025); the same applies to Portugal, where the legal minimum and collectively bargained rates increasingly converge. Regarding the governance of the minimum wage, Picot places both cases in the broader 'state-plus-collective' camp, underscoring their shared reliance on an active statutory wage rooted in high bargaining coverage. Secondly, state capacity played a decisive role on two occasions: first in enforcing rapid standstills, and later in coordinating equally swift restorations. Its influence was further strengthened by the lack of indexation rules, which would have otherwise triggered automatic adjustments.

Taken together, the typological overview and the Iberian evidence presented above provide essential context for the next stage of analysis. Portugal and Spain entered the period of progressive governments with broadly similar ambitions and institutional characteristics, both fitting into the hybrid "state-plus-collective" regime category (Picot, 2023), albeit with some variations in how statutory floors interact with collective bargaining (Dingeldey et al., 2021; Eurofound, 2025). As will be explained below, both countries are positioned closer to the ideal type of inclusive solidarity, although some noteworthy differences remain. To clarify these differences, the analysis will focus primarily on the role of social concertation, the influence exerted by the EU, and the behaviour of key actors (political parties and social partners). The latter dimension is particularly important for understanding the composition of the governing social blocs underpinning the strategies adopted by each government.

Case Studies

The Politics of Minimum Wage Reform in Portugal: Inclusive Solidarity under Institutional Constraint

The evolution of the minimum wage in Portugal between 2016 and 2022 illustrates the complex interplay between progressive distributive goals, institutional negotiation, and multi-level constraints. Situated within the broader dynamics of inclusive solidarity, minimum wage policy became a key symbolic and material arena in the post-austerity governance of the Socialist Party (PS). While wage floor increases were consistent and politically visible, the means through which they were implemented – grounded in tripartite concertation and accompanied by compensatory measures – exposed the fragility of consensus and the limits of redistribution under constraint.

Following the 2015 elections, the PS formed a minority government supported in parliament by the Left Bloc (BE), the Portuguese Communist Party (PCP), and the Greens (PEV). This arrangement, often referred to as the "*Geringonça*," was built around a programme to reverse austerity and raise living standards and lasted between 2015 and 2021. Minimum wage reform was among the clearest commitments of the new governing alignment. As one cabinet member recalled, "[t]he minimum wage was a crucial pillar of the 2015 government, an explicit commitment we negotiated with the Left Bloc for a predetermined time frame" (Interview 8). The agreement between PS and the BE explicitly committed to increasing the national minimum wage to €600 by 2019, with minimum annual increases of 5% in the first two years. The agreements with PCP and PEV were less specific, referring broadly to the need to improve workers' purchasing power. These differences shaped the policy's implementation and the legitimacy disputes that emerged along the way. BE leaders would later accuse the government of insufficient ambition and of prioritising employer appeasement over distributive urgency.

As shown in Figure 4.1, the minimum wage remained frozen between 2011 and 2014, at €485 (14 months). Starting in 2015, it rose steadily each year, reaching €705 by 2022. This represented a nominal increase of nearly 40% between 2016 and 2022. These figures placed Portugal among the EU countries with the highest cumulative national minimum wage increases over the period.

By grounding minimum-wage policy in tripartite social concertation, the PS drew on its historic role as a centrist broker to offset parliamentary fragility and EU scrutiny while upholding Portugal's tradition of pact-based labour reform (Campos Lima and Naumann, 2011). Yet the enterprise was fraught from the outset: the PS had already pledged to the BE a fixed schedule of upratings through 2019, thereby hollowing out the scope for genuine negotiation. Still, the Government secured a concertation pact for the 2016 increase, persuading employers to accept €530 in exchange for a 0.75-percentage-point cut in their Social-Security contribution for minimum-wage workers, valid for 12 months (the same relief the previous PSD–CDS-PP cabinet had promised in 2014–2015). Even so, the General Confederation of Portuguese Workers (CGTP) stayed outside the deal, and BE and the PCP condemned it as a threat to Social-Security solvency.[2] For 2017 the minority PS cabinet struck a second pact with employers and the

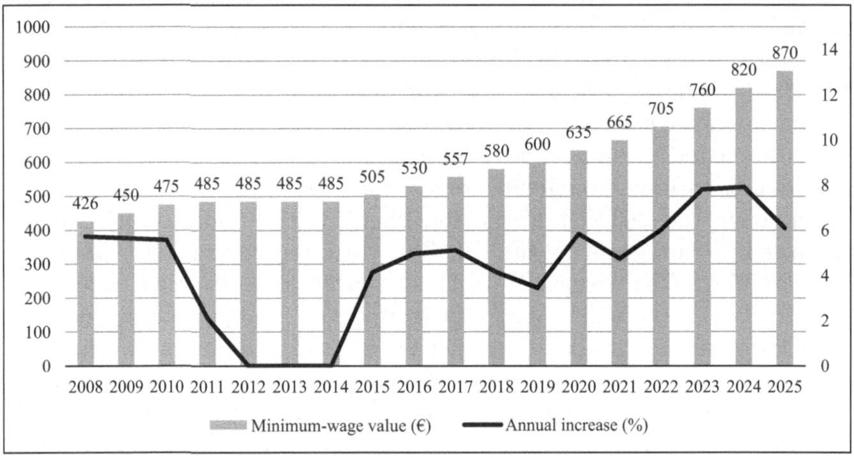

Figure 4.1 Portuguese national minimum wage and rate of change in each year (2008–2025).

Note: The left-hand y-axis shows the minimum wage value, while the right-hand y-axis indicates the annual increase.

Source: Direção-Geral do Emprego e das Relações Laborais, accessed at: www.dgert.gov.pt/evolucao-da-remuneracao-minima-mensal-garantida-rmmg

General Union of Workers (UGT-P), this time offering a 1.25-percentage-point reduction; CGTP and the left-wing allies again objected, and parliament passed a resolution that quashed the cut, nullifying the concertation agreement. The Government responded by substituting targeted tax relief, but no further tripartite pacts were signed during the years in which the PS did not hold an absolute majority (2015-2022), largely because the 2017 episode had shown that deals could be overturned on the floor of the National Parliament. Nonetheless, from 2018 to 2022 every uprating was still paired with direct financial subsidies to firms, signalling the PS's continuing effort to keep employer confederations on board (Table 4.2).

Employer organisations insisted each proposal be justified by 'measurable' offsets: when the €530 rate was floated for 2016, CIP president António Saraiva demanded that it first be 'tested against the country's economic and business reality' (DN, 2015); a year later he declared the confederation 'unwilling to raise the minimum wage to €600' without payroll-tax relief (DN, 2017), and all four organisations accepted €540 only after securing the agreed contribution cut (Expresso, 2016). Saraiva later condemned the December 2020 rise to €665 as 'untimely,' warning that firms 'cannot be pawns in the political game' and calculating that every €30 added to the floor

Table 4.2 Minimum wage increases and social concertation agreements in Portugal

Year (government in office)	*Social Concertation Agreement?*	*Type of agreement (where agreement exists)*
2015 (PSD-CDS-PP)	Yes	Government + Employers' confederations + UGT-P (CGTP did not sign)
2016 (PS)	Yes	Government + Employers' confederations + UGT-P (CGTP did not sign)
2017 (PS)	Yes	Government + Employers' confederations + UGT-P (CGTP did not sign)
2018 (PS)	No	–
2019 (PS)	No	–
2020 (PS)	No	–
2021 (PS)	No	–
2022 (PS)	No	–
2023 (PS)	Yes	Government + Employers' confederations + UGT-P (CGTP did not sign)
2024 (PS)	Yes	Government + Employers' confederations + UGT-P (CGTP did not sign)
2025 (PSD-CDS-PP)	Yes	Government + Employers' confederations + UGT-P (CGTP did not sign)

Source: Author's compilation from official protocols of the Standing Council for Social Concertation, Council of Ministers' resolutions, and *Diário da República* decrees.

Note: From 2016 to 2022, the PS minority government relied on parliamentary support from the PCP, BE, and PEV ("*geringonça*"). Between 2023 and 2024, the PS held an absolute majority in the National Parliament.

costs employers €43.40 once ancillary charges are included (DN, 2020). The Confederation of Commerce and Services of Portugal (CCP) likewise voiced persistent reservations and ultimately protested the cumulative increase (Interview 1).

Union responses diverged: CGTP rejected every compensation deal, arguing that such trade-offs 'encourage firms to cling to the minimum wage, undermine wider pay rises and paralyse collective bargaining' (Interview 3); whereas UGT-P accepted the logic, provided upratings were annual and tax credits temporary (Interview 10).

Thus, concertation simultaneously legitimised PS wage policy and exposed enduring cleavages, as government, business, and labour each contested the path of Portugal's post-2015 minimum-wage trajectory. Read through Chapter 2's arena logic, the Portuguese strategy placed minimum-wage policy inside a joint-decision setting in which employer assent operates as a de facto veto. In the post-austerity settlement – marked by eroded union leverage and strengthened employer outside options – this 'consent constraint' systematically trims redistributive ambition unless the executive credibly threatens non-concertation. The compensation packages attached to upratings thus served both as side-payments that softened employer resistance and as signals of fiscal prudence under the European Semester's 'liberal' tilt in 2016–2017.

Although the PS sought to frame each uprating as a concertation outcome, right-wing parties repeatedly objected that there was no 'real' negotiation because the annual targets had been pre-agreed with the BE. Hence, they argued, any responsible increase had to (*i*) emerge from a fresh tripartite pact and (*ii*) relate clearly to productivity and firms' sustainability. A CDS-PP MP warned that "any rise must be agreed in social concertation, not imposed from above, because exceeding productivity can doom the firms that pay it" (Interview 2), while a PSD MP, "in principle favourable" to raising what she viewed as a low floor, condemned preset horizons that "impose rather than negotiate," squeeze intermediate wages, and might force future freezes, insisting that any relief for employers must be "hammered out at the table, not decreed from above" (Interview 4). These grievances converged dramatically in January 2017. The PS–employer–UGT-P accord that paired the rise to €557 with a 1.25-percentage-point reduction in the employers' Social-Security rate was already anathema to the CGTP, PCP, BE, and PEV, all of whom had denounced compensation as a threat to the solvency of Social Security. Spotting an opportunity to expose fissures inside the *Geringonça*, PSD and CDS-PP, despite having backed a similar rebate in 2014, joined the far-left parties to pass a parliamentary resolution that struck down the contribution cut. The move dealt the PS a rare legislative defeat and, as a BE MP later celebrated, "annulled, destroyed, blown up" the government's manoeuvre (Interview 7); UGT-P called the cross-bench alliance "a huge shock" (Interview 10). From that moment, the PS abandoned contribution relief and turned to one-off subsidies and tax credits, while the right continued to insist that future upratings be tied to productivity and endorsed in a genuine tripartite pact. Thus, the political battlefield crystallised: the left split over employer offsets, the PS tried to balance wage solidarity with business competitiveness, and the right made its support conditional on productivity, fiscal prudence, and concertation, turning Portugal's 'inclusive solidarity' into a fragile, continually renegotiated compromise.

In Portugal, the EU exerted a constraining influence during the early phase of minimum-wage reform. After the troika bailout, the country remained under enhanced surveillance through the European Semester, and successive Country-Specific Recommendations from the European Commission (2015, 2016) warned that further increases could endanger employment and competitiveness.[3] This external pressure shaped the Socialist Party's strategy: despite pledges to its left-wing allies, it paired each rise with compensatory measures for employers and sought tripartite endorsement in the Social Concertation Council. As a senior official recalled, "the Commission raised many doubts about employment impacts" (Interview 8). The PS therefore pursued incrementalism: the minimum wage climbed every January, but never by more than €40, reaching €705 by 2022, a notable nominal gain, yet consistently framed as 'predictable' and 'accompanied' by fiscal cushions for small firms. Brussels' stance became more supportive only later, explaining both the initial caution and the importance of securing concertation agreements in the first two years of the cycle. Although the EU's pivot towards a 'Social Europe,' embodied in the European Pillar of Social Rights and the draft Adequate Minimum-Wage Directive, might have furnished political cover, neither the Government, nor the unions, nor the left parties highlighted it. The Directive's 60% of median-wage benchmark had already been met in 2016 (60.2%) and stood at roughly 67.4% by 2022 (OECD, 2025), and overemphasis on that fact risked giving employers and the right fresh ammunition to argue that the wage floor was converging too quickly on the median and that collective bargaining was losing its central role.

The MAXQDA code map (Figure 4.2) offers a thematic visualisation of the parliamentary debates and corroborates the interpretation advanced above.[4] Two antagonistic clusters dominate. In the upper-left quadrant, the PCP, BE, and PEV converge with the codes 'Tension on the Left,' 'Solidarity,' and, above all, 'Against Social Concertation' and 'Against Compensation Measures.' This cluster reflects their parliamentary stance: they advocated a higher minimum wage yet rejected employer rebates and condemned concertation as a neoliberal trap. Opposite them, the PS and the 'PS Government' form a dense nexus with 'For Social Concertation,' 'For Compensation Measures,' 'Parliament,' and the coalition codes 'Left' and 'Centrist.' The thickness of these connections visualises the party's bridging strategy: annual increases were routed through the tripartite council to reassure employers, moderate unions, and Brussels, even at the cost of recurrent skirmishes with its left allies (most notably the 2017 defeat over a proposed cut to employers' social-security contributions). A looser constellation comprising the PSD, CDS-PP, and the former PSD–CDS-PP government links to 'Troika,' 'European

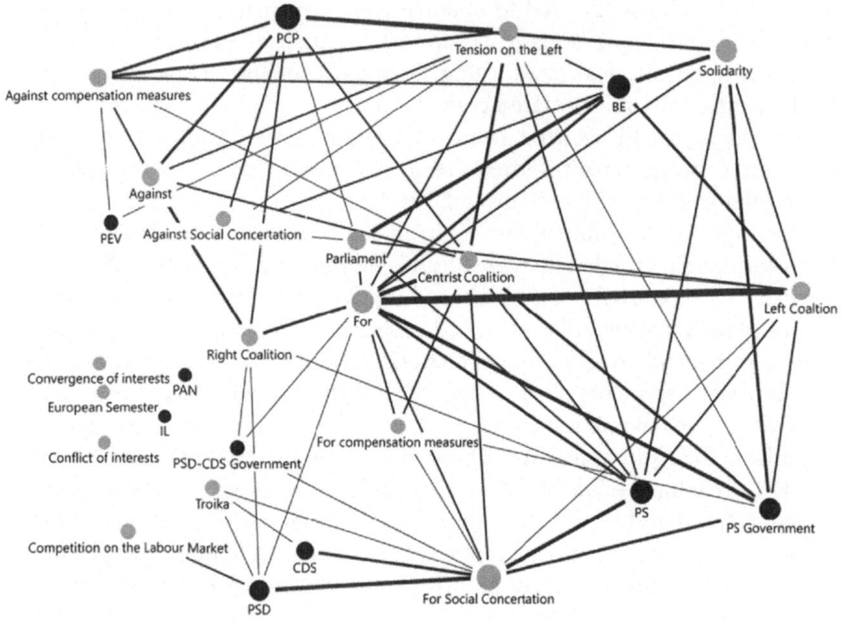

Figure 4.2 Actor coalitions and thematic clusters in Portuguese parliamentary debates on the minimum wage.

Notes: Chord thickness reflects the weighted frequency with which two codes co-occur in the parliamentary-debate corpus. The thicker and darker the chord, the stronger the association.

Sources: Authors' elaboration; MAXQDA Code Map.

Semester,' and 'Labour-Market Competition,' indicating that austerity-era competitiveness narratives persisted but rapidly lost agenda-setting influence once the left gained parliamentary leverage. Overall, the map underscores the centrality, and contestation, of social concertation: 'For Social Concertation' emerges as the single most connected grey node, bridging otherwise polarised camps and confirming the argument that concertation functioned simultaneously as procedural ritual, distributive buffer, and political lightning rod within Portugal's fragile architecture of inclusive solidarity. It also reveals that this issue united the PSD, CDS-PP, and PS. In short, the visual evidence validates the chapter's characterisation of Portuguese wage politics as negotiated yet brittle egalitarianism.

To sum up, Portugal exemplifies 'negotiated inclusive solidarity under constraint': parliament, concertation, and the EU formed a triangle of authorisation. Incremental but continuous upratings delivered tangible redistribution, yet the policy remained brittle because its procedural foundation (social dialogue) doubled as a distributive side-payment to employers, provoking cyclical clashes with the very forces that had made the reform possible.

Spain: A More Cohesive but Polarised Form of Inclusive Solidarity

The Spanish experience of minimum wage reform constitutes a paradigmatic case of inclusive solidarity characterised by strong governmental cohesion but limited institutional embedding. While the policy delivered significant distributive outcomes, it was politically polarised and implemented with minimal reliance on traditional social dialogue mechanisms. In contrast to Portugal, where concertation remained a structuring element, the Spanish policies were primarily driven by political coalition-building, executive initiative with technical legitimation, and support from the EU. This section examines the political and institutional dynamics underlying this process.

Functionally, the Government's recourse to Royal Decrees placed minimum-wage setting on the *state-majoritarian track*. For our purposes this channel is equivalent to Chapter 2's 'parliamentary' arena insofar as it contains no institutional employer veto; it allowed a cohesive Left–Union bloc to legislate closer to its inclusive ideal point while using expert benchmarking and EU norms for external validation.

In contrast to the Portuguese case, the minimum wage in Spain became a distinctly political instrument of coalition-building. The first major increase occurred under the minority Socialist (PSOE) government of Pedro Sánchez, following the no-confidence motion that ousted Mariano Rajoy in 2018. The subsequent general election of 2019 produced a fragmented parliament but enabled the formation of the first coalition government in modern Spanish democracy, between PSOE and *Unidas Podemos*. As part of the coalition agreement, both parties committed to raising the statutory minimum wage to €1,200 over the course of the legislature. Several interviewees highlighted that this increase was part of the political price of coalition-making. In this sense, the policy was not only an economic measure, but a form of distributive signalling meant to consolidate the new executive's left-wing credentials. Indeed, the dramatic increase in the statutory minimum wage, from €736 in 2018 to €1,185 in 2025 (14 payments), was framed not only as a measure of social justice, but also as a symbol of progressive governance (Figure 4.3).

There are two distinctive traits of the Spanish experience in minimum-wage setting over this period. First, unlike Portugal's routinised corporatism, Spanish minimum-wage politics treated social concertation as a dispensable add-on rather than a binding gatekeeper (Table 4.3). Second, for the first time, the government relied on a technical committee tasked with drafting a report that provides recommendations regarding the minimum wage increase. This report takes into account the objective of achieving 60% of the median wage, as stipulated in the European Pillar of Social Rights, alongside the prevailing economic context.

Regarding the first aspect, the Sánchez–Díaz cabinet convened the *mesas de diálogo social*, yet made clear that the destination, 60% of the median wage, was politically pre-set. Hence, despite the government convening social partners every year to negotiate the minimum wage, agreements alternated

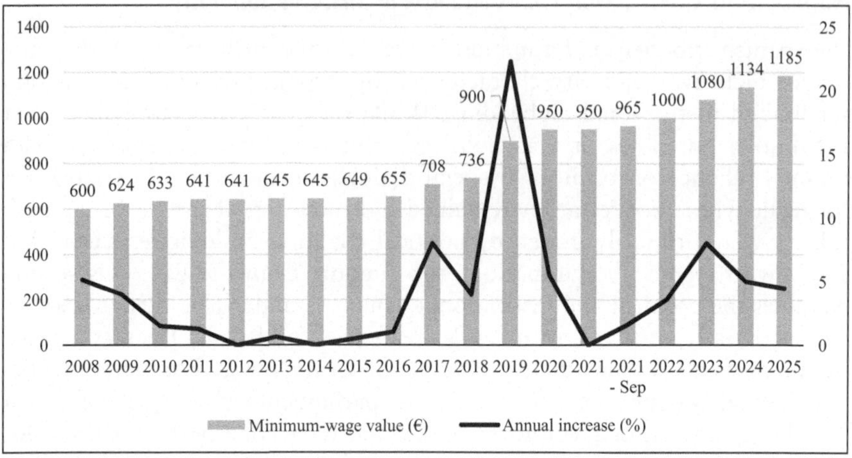

Figure 4.3 Spanish national minimum wage and rate of change in each year (2008–2025).

Note: The left-hand y-axis shows the minimum wage value, while the right-hand y-axis indicates the annual increase.

Sources: Authors' elaboration; Ministerio de Trabajo y Economía Social, accessed at: www.mites.gob.es/es/guia/texto/guia_6/contenidos/guia_6_13_2.htm

Table 4.3 Minimum wage increases and social concertation agreements in Spain

Year (government in office)	*Social Concertation Agreement?*	*Type of agreement (where agreement exists)*
2015 (PP)	No	–
2016 (PP)	No	–
2017 (PP)	No	–
2018 (PP)	Yes	Government + Employers' confederations + Unions
2019 (PSOE)	No	–
2020 (PSOE – *Unidas Podemos*)	Yes	Government + Employers' confederations + Unions
2021 (Jan.) (PSOE – *Unidas Podemos*)	No	–
2021 (Sept.) (PSOE – *Unidas Podemos*)	Yes	Government + Unions (employers did not sign)
2022 (PSOE – *Unidas Podemos*)	Yes	Government + Unions (employers did not sign)
2023 (PSOE – *Unidas Podemos*)	Yes	Government + Unions (employers did not sign)
2024 (PSOE – *Sumar*)	Yes	Government + Unions (employers did not sign)
2025 (PSOE – *Sumar*)	Yes	Government + Unions (employers did not sign)

Source: Author's compilation from minutes of the Spanish Economic and Social Council, Ministry of Labour press releases, and Boletín Oficial del Estado (BOE) Royal Decrees.

with unilateral decrees. An initial tripartite pact produced the €900 objective in 2018, but the record 22% leap of January 2019 was enacted by Royal Decree without any accord, prompting CEOE to warn, in statements to *El País*, that such unilateralism "questioned the legitimacy of social dialogue" and risked blocking the negotiated wage path it had just endorsed (El País, 2018). COVID briefly revived tripartite discipline, the 2020 rise to €950 carried the three signatures, yet employers again walked out in 2021, a move unions judged "more electoral than economic" (Interview 14). CEOE's core grievance was the "unexpected drag effect" that steep statutory hikes could exert on sectoral pay scales and autonomy; although it acknowledged the EU's 60% benchmark as "a valid criterion," it argued further jumps should await productivity gains (Interview 13). By contrast, CCOO and UGT-S embraced the benchmark as a minimum. CCOO leader Unai Sordo lauded the "autonomy and maturity of the social partners" behind the €1,000 agreement (ABC, 2020a), while UGT-S's Pepe Álvarez praised the government's "speed" in sealing the €950 rise (ABC, 2020b). Both confederations then pressed the cabinet to reopen talks to reach 60%, endorsing experts' scenarios of €1,012–1,047 by 2023 (ABC, 2021a). When negotiations stalled they coupled bargaining with street pressure: Álvarez vowed to "step up mobilisations" (ABC, 2021b) and later declared the jump to €1,000 from 1 January 2022 "non-negotiable" (ABC, 2022). Interviews confirm that union leaders view the 50% leap already achieved, from €735 to €1,080, only as the first stage towards restoring wage dignity (Interviews 14 and 16). For the government, concertation remained desirable but expendable: it welcomed employer signatures when attainable yet relied on executive decree to keep its redistributive timetable on track. The resulting hybrid governance model uses expert reports and euro-legal benchmarks for procedural veneer, Royal Decrees for delivery, and social dialogue for an episodic seal of approval.

The second distinctive feature of the Spanish experience has been the pivotal role of technocratic legitimation in complementing both social dialogue and unilateral executive action. Since 2021, a committee convened by the Ministry of Labour, comprising academics and social partners, has issued three reports. The committee's mandate was to provide technical support and offer advisory input to the government and social partners regarding the trajectory of the minimum wage, aiming to achieve 60% of the median wage. Subsequent reports were published in 2022 and 2025 (Comisión Asesora para el Análisis del Salario Mínimo Interprofesional, 2021, 2022, 2024). In each instance, the government fully endorsed the recommendations presented in the reports, integrating them into the social dialogue processes with social partners. Thus, the government strategically employed technocratic legitimacy in minimum wage-setting, in conjunction with social dialogue.

Spain's conservative Popular Party (PP) adopted a two-track narrative on the minimum wage: it accepted increases negotiated in social dialogue but denounced unilateral 'brusque' jumps. Party leader Pablo Casado told the Financial Times in 2018 that raising the statutory minimum wage "so abruptly would be an economic suicide" (ABC, 2018). At home he nevertheless promised to "abide by the agreement to raise the minimum wage to €850 in 2020," adding that "not a single social-policy lesson for the Partido Popular is needed" because collective bargaining already provides a responsible path (ABC, 2019). Meeting trade unions in January 2020, Casado reiterated that the PP "will support any agreement reached within social dialogue" while pairing this with calls for tax relief and reforms to spur productivity (El País, 2020).

Framed not as an external constraint but as a multi-layered source of legitimation, the EU supplied Spain's minimum-wage surge with political momentum, legal authority, and financial leverage. Politically, senior officials hailed what a PSOE labour adviser called a "Copernican turn" inside the Commission: "from 2011 the good practice was wage moderation; today the Directive tells us 60 per cent of the median is the benchmark" (Interview 12). A cabinet member and *Unidas Podemos* MP was blunter still: "[i]n the last two years the wind from Brussels blows in favour of decent minimum wages" (Interview 15). A key reason why government and unions embraced that wind is numerical: the Spanish statutory minimum wage equalled only about 41% of the median wage in 2018 and, even after the 2023 hikes, had reached roughly 52% (OECD, 2025) – still well short of the Directive's 60% yardstick, in stark contrast to Portugal, which surpassed the 60% threshold as early as 2016. Legally, each Royal Decree was cast as a step towards compliance with the forthcoming Directive on Adequate Minimum Wages and with the European Social Charter, neutralising the charge that large hikes were a parochial left-wing whim.[5] The advisory committee's reports on minimum wage-setting aimed to guide the government towards a sustainable approach in achieving the 60% target. For trade union confederations, this EU benchmark served as a unifying goal: CCOO's negotiator stated, "[o]ur objective is exactly what the European Social Charter says: reaching 60% of the median wage" (Interview 16). Similarly, UGT-S connected this threshold to the "*Componente 23*" milestones in Spain's Recovery and Resilience Plan, asserting that progress on wages, job security, and collective bargaining was essential for accessing Next Generation EU funds (Interview 14). Employers, too, invoked Europe, though to urge caution. A CEOE official conceded that "these international indicators are now valid criteria" but insisted that, having already chased the 60% banner for several years, Spain should pause further jumps until productivity catches up (Interview 13). In effect, Brussels offered a protective umbrella: the Directive, the Social Charter, and the promise of recovery funding armed the Sánchez–Díaz cabinet and the unions with a rights-based narrative and a fiscal carrot, while giving employers a common reference point, even if interpreted as minimum obligation by labour and government, and maximum ceiling by business. The EU thus shifted from watchdog to booster, becoming central to the politics of inclusive solidarity that powered the fastest statutory-wage climb in Spain's democratic history.

This fits Chapter 2's expectation that, during the EU's 'social turn,' legal templates and fiscal instruments lower the political cost of unilateral re-regulation in majoritarian channels by widening statutory floors and supplying normative cover.

The MAXQDA code map for the Spanish minimum wage reform visualises the actor coalitions and thematic framings that shaped minimum wage-setting (Figure 4.4).[6] The Spanish MAXQDA code map crystallises a markedly different geometry from its Portuguese counterpart. 'Solidarity' dominates the diagram as a grey hub drawing thick ties from PSOE, *Unidas Podemos*, and several regional parties. Its gravitational pull visually encodes the narrative made above: the Sánchez–Díaz coalition cast the minimum-wage hike as a unifying emblem of social justice, mobilising support across the left while sidelining procedural dialogue throughout the reform cycle. Immediately behind this hub sits 'Left Coalition,' linked by dense edges to PSOE and the hybrid code 'For,' underscoring how executive cohesion, not concertation, anchored the reform. Thick strokes on these central spokes further signal the salience of distributive language in debate. By contrast, 'For Social Concertation' is relegated to the upper-left periphery, connected only by thin lines to the former PP government and national right-wing parties. Its marginality confirms that Spain's wage policy advanced largely outside tripartite bargaining. A secondary cluster in the lower-left features the PP, *Ciudadanos*, and the grey issues 'Competition on the Labour Market' and 'Conflict of interests,' forming a triangular lattice of thick lines. This embodies the opposition's competitiveness frame and its warnings about small and medium enterprises costs. Yet their lack of direct connection to 'Solidarity' highlights rhetorical isolation and limited agenda-setting power. Finally, the bottom-right alliance between 'European Social Charter,' regional left parties, and 'Solidarity' channels the EU-level normative wind discussed in the chapter, bridging supranational mandates and domestic progressive actors. Overall, the map depicts a Spanish variant of inclusive solidarity that is politically cohesive yet procedurally unilateral.[7]

To sum up, Spain exemplifies 'programmatic inclusive solidarity via executive initiative.' A cohesive left coalition leveraged electoral legitimacy, expert authority, and European norms to deliver a rapid, high-profile wage floor, consciously bypassing employer vetoes. The result was a politically coherent and potent reform, but one whose long-term institutional embedding depends on whether social dialogue structures can be re-knitted after years of marginalisation.

Comparison and Discussion: Varieties of Inclusive Solidarity in Iberian Wage Politics

The Portuguese and Spanish minimum wage-setting processes exemplify two analytically distinct variants of inclusive solidarity, each shaped by domestic coalition politics, inherited institutions, and evolving EU incentives. Both

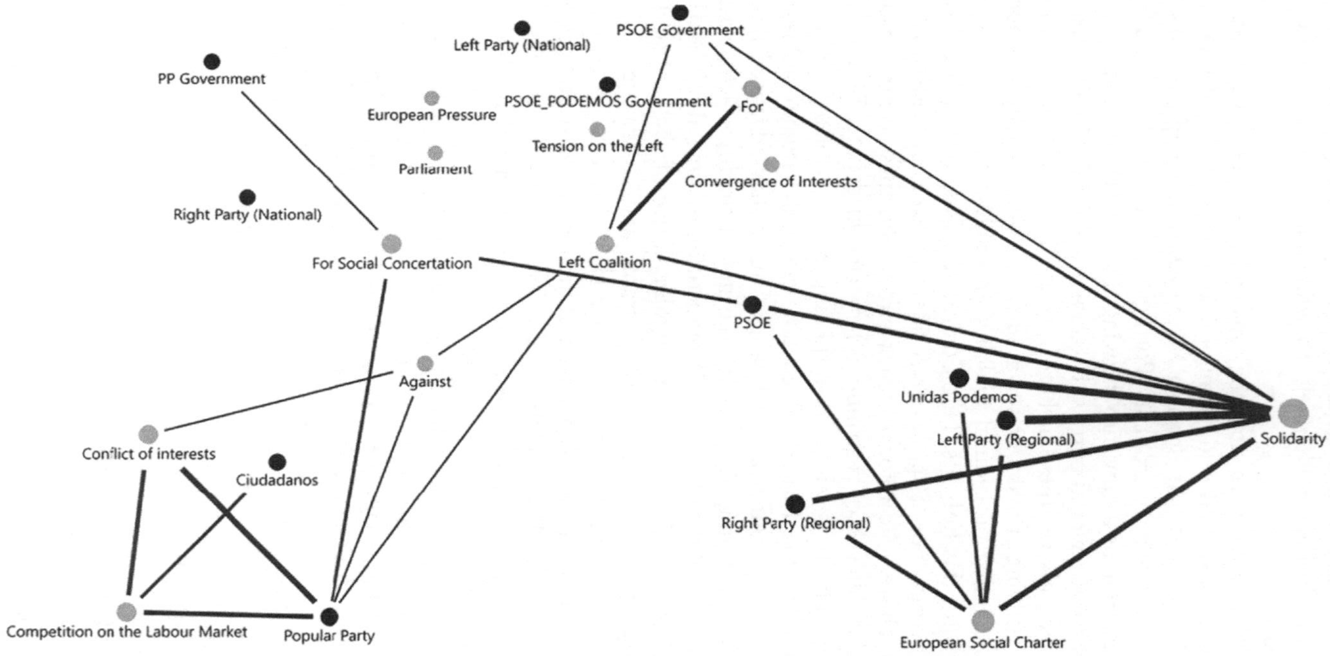

Figure 4.4 Actor coalitions and thematic clusters in Spanish parliamentary debates on the minimum wage.

Notes: Chord thickness reflects the weighted frequency with which two codes co-occur in the parliamentary-debate corpus. The thicker and darker the chord, the stronger the association.

Sources: Authors' elaboration; MAXQDA Code Map.

countries delivered sizeable upratings with clear redistributive intent, yet the coalitional constellations, decision arenas, and legitimation logics that sustained those increases diverged in fundamental ways.

We situate both trajectories within the eight-fold typology advanced in Chapter 2. In Portugal, a Left–Union governing social bloc operated predominantly through tripartite concertation under a liberal-tilted EU stance in 2016–2017, yielding low-to-medium inclusive outcomes; as the EU entered its social turn after 2018, the same bloc–arena configuration produced medium-intensity inclusive change. By contrast, Spain combined a Left–Union governing social bloc with the parliamentary arena during the EU's social turn, delivering maximal inclusive reform. This mapping underscores our core claim: bloc composition is the necessary determinant of reform orientation, while arena choice and EU leverage act as conditional amplifiers (or brakes) shaping the scope and durability of change. In both cases, arena choice is endogenous to bloc priorities, as argued in Chapter 2.

Pace and scale. As Table 4.4 shows, Spain front-loaded its reform: the statutory minimum wage leapt by 22% in 2019 and reached €1,185 in 2025, a cumulative rise of about 61% over the 2019–2025 window. Portugal, by contrast, adopted negotiated annual increments of roughly €20–€40, generating a more gradual, though still substantial, about 40% increase between 2016 and 2022. Madrid's left coalition showcased the statutory minimum wage as a high-visibility emblem of progressive ambition; Lisbon integrated smaller, predictable hikes into a broader bargain designed to reassure employers, moderate unions, and Brussels.

Legitimation mechanisms. Portugal embedded each yearly decision in the Permanent Council for Social Concertation. Although only a minority of increases won full tripartite endorsement, the ritual supplied procedural legitimacy, enabled compensatory side-payments to employers and signalled fiscal prudence to the EU. Spain relied chiefly on executive authority, technical support, and ad-hoc parliamentary bargaining: tripartite pacts were welcomed when attainable, but Royal Decrees were issued whenever the timetable was threatened. Portuguese solidarity was therefore institutionally embedded but frequently contested; Spanish solidarity was politically cohesive, fostered social dialogue, but this often failed, and the government acted unilaterally.

The EU dimension. Consistent with Chapter 2's argument, the Union acted as a conditional selector rather than a unidirectional booster. In Portugal, the lingering shadow of the Troika and European-Semester surveillance initially acted as a brake, nudging the PS to pair each rise with employer offsets and to keep increases 'predictable.' In Spain, the same templates provided political momentum, legal authority, and fiscal room to advance rapid uprates.

Governing social blocs and bargaining institutions. Portugal's path reflects a Left–Union governing social bloc operating in the concertation arena during a phase that shifted from a liberal-tilted to a social-turn EU. This configuration generated incremental but fragile progress: employer confederations

Table 4.4 Minimum wage increases under progressive coalitions: Portugal and Spain

	Portugal (2016–2022)	*Spain (2019–2025)*
Baseline at the start of the progressive cycle	€505 (2015)	€736 (2018)
Statutory rate in the latest year of the period	€705 in 2022	€1,185 in 2025
Cumulative nominal increase	40% (2016–2022)	61% (2019–2025)
Largest single-year rise within the period	+6% in Jan 2022 (from €665 to €705)	+22% in Jan 2019 (Royal-Decree increase from €736 to €900)
Typical yearly pattern	Negotiated annual increments of €20–€40 each January; no freezes (pace determined in the tripartite council)	Front-loaded 'shock,' then gradual steps: sharp 2019 rise followed by smaller annual top-ups
Political logic	*Negotiated inclusive solidarity under a consent constraint:* the PS exchanged annual increases for tax or social-security offsets, reassuring small and medium enterprises, Brussels, and centrist allies	*State-majoritarian convergence (no institutional employer veto):* the PSOE–Unidas Podemos/Sumar coalition framed rapid increases as necessary to reach the EU "60 per cent of median wage" benchmark relying on technical advice, legislating by decree when negotiations stalled
Headline narrative	Predictable convergence within EU-Semester parameters; gradualism presented as small and medium enterprises friendly and fiscally prudent	Rapid convergence towards the EU adequacy directive; the minimum wage became a flagship measure of the progressive coalition, despite employer walkouts

Source: Author's elaboration.

Note: Statutory minimum-wage figures are expressed on a 14-payment basis in both countries.

wielded veto power inside concertation, moderate unions traded wage gains for offsets, and the PS balanced wage solidarity with business competitiveness. Spain's configuration, a Left–Union governing social bloc plus parliament in a social-turn EU, produced a more cohesive bloc and faster redistribution by marginalising employer vetoes. The result was a politically coherent but more polarised process, with thinner corporatist channels.

Implications for collective bargaining. In Portugal, anchoring wage policy in social concertation helped protect sectoral bargaining, albeit only partially, by keeping employers at the table. The caution shown by the PS is understandable: the statutory minimum has long stood very close to bargained rates, equalling about 67% of the median wage by 2022, which places Portugal in Dingeldey et al.'s (2021) "close interaction" category.[8] Because any abrupt uplift risked compressing pay ladders and crowding out negotiation space, the government opted for gradual increments and compensations to employers. In Spain, by contrast, the statutory minimum wage represented roughly 52% of the median in 2023, still some distance from the 60% benchmark; however, very recent uprates have allowed to reach the 60% goal, hence transitioning from distant to close interaction (Eurofound, 2025). This structural gap gave the Sánchez–Díaz cabinet far more room to legislate sharp increases without destabilising collective bargaining, though at the cost of bypassing employers and relying on executive decree. Thus, while both countries pursued inclusive solidarity, Portugal had to temper redistribution to safeguard a bargaining system in which the statutory wage already shadows negotiated scales, whereas Spain could advance more aggressively precisely because collective agreements still sit above the legal floor.

Ideal types of solidarity. The Portuguese use of employer compensations also signals a residual strand of competitive solidarity (Chapter 1) running beneath the dominant inclusive narrative. By reimbursing firms – first via temporary Social-Security rebates, later through direct subsidies – the PS implicitly accepted that in parts of the economy, individual productivity sits close to the old wage floor and that rapid, unfunded increases could erode cost-competitiveness. The State therefore stepped in to bridge the gap, treating higher wages as a public good but treating their financing as a shared responsibility. In Spain, by contrast, the coalition assumed that most firms could absorb sizeable hikes and that wage compression reflected an asymmetry of power rather than a hard productivity ceiling; hence no systematic offsets were offered. Both countries thus pursued inclusive solidarity, yet Portugal's reliance on compensations reveals a mercantile undercurrent that Spain's executive-led strategy deliberately rejected.

In sum, inclusive solidarity in wage policy can crystallise through negotiated incrementalism under external constraint (Portugal) or through programmatic executive initiative (Spain). Each path carries distinct trade-offs between distributive ambition, institutional durability, and social-partner inclusion.

Conclusions

This chapter has shown that Portugal and Spain have pursued the shared goal of raising the minimum wage through two contrasting, but equally 'inclusive,' pathways. Portugal relied on incremental, concerted upratings: annual increases were packaged with fiscal offsets, vetted in the social concertation arena, and calibrated to placate both EU surveillance and employer concerns. Spain instead adopted a front-loaded, executive-driven strategy: the PSOE-led coalition leveraged electoral authority, EU norms and expert advice to legislate record hikes, inviting unions into the spotlight while accepting the risk of employer walkouts. The comparison demonstrates that inclusive solidarity is not a single institutional recipe but a repertoire that can be assembled either through corporatist brokerage under external constraint or through programmatic state initiative under a favourable European tailwind. The trade-offs are clear: Portugal's model offers procedural durability but limited distributive reach; Spain's delivers rapid redistribution but leaves the institutional moorings of social dialogue thinner.

Two wider implications follow. First, EU integration has moved from 'watchdog' to 'booster.' Where the Troika once froze Iberian wage floors, the Adequate Minimum Wage Directive and Recovery Plan now provide normative and fiscal cover for ambitious upratings. Yet the chapter also shows that Brussels' leverage is mediated by domestic politics: the same Directive that empowers Spanish unions to demand a 60% benchmark furnishes Portuguese employers with a discursive ceiling. Second, employment relations institutions still matter, but in different ways. In Portugal, concertation remained a veto arena that both legitimised and constrained wage policy; in Spain, its marginalisation raised questions about the long-term balance between statutory action and collective bargaining.

By mapping the political pathways through which two neighbouring states reversed a decade of wage austerity, the chapter underlines a broader lesson: inclusive solidarity is as much a question of political agency and institutional choice as of macroeconomic room for manoeuvre. Recognising those choices, and their limits, remains essential for understanding how progressive governments can harness wage policy to rebuild solidarity in a post-crisis Europe.

Notes

1 In the case of this chapter, in Portugal, we utilise the time span 2016–2022, as decisions regarding minimum wage increases have consistently taken effect in the January following the decision. Accordingly, rather than the period 2015–2021, as employed in all other empirical chapters, we analyse the period 2016–2022.
2 On this point, see CGTP (2016).
3 It is worth noting that EU institutions were not alone in opposing higher minimum wages; other international organisations raised similar concerns. When the PSD–CDS-PP government announced an increase in 2014, the IMF warned that the measure could hinder job creation and economic growth (Observador, 2014). In July 2015 the OECD echoed this view (Expresso, 2015).
4 The study covers 97 parliamentary debates held between 2015 and 2022, using the same coding grid applied in the Spanish analysis. The grid comprises eight thematic dimensions. "Actor" identifies the principal stakeholders, while "Compensation measures for employers" codes arguments for and against such offsets. "Levels of decision-making" captures references to the arenas in which influence is exerted – social concertation, the national parliament, and supranational bodies such as the

Troika and the European Semester – again distinguishing supportive from critical views. "Positions on reform" records each party's stance (support, opposition, or neutrality), and "Solidarity references" flag explicit invocations of solidarity. "Labour-market competition" documents perceived challenges within the employment sphere. "Coalition supporting the reform" classifies the political location of backers (left, centre, or right), whereas "Tension on the left" traces intra-left disagreements over the minimum-wage package. Taken together, this coding scheme provides a nuanced lens through which to interpret Portuguese parliamentary discourse on minimum-wage policy.

5 Notably, each Royal Decree (1462/2018, 231/2020, 817/2021, and 152/2022) that raised the minimum wage invokes the European Social Charter and its 60% benchmark.

6 In Spain, we analysed 24 parliamentary debates; details of the coding grid employed are provided in endnote 4.

7 Note, however, that every year the government convened social partners to negotiate the minimum wage. Procedurally, there was always social dialogue, but an agreement was only occasionally reached.

8 Consistent with this trend, the proportion of workers paid the minimum wage rose markedly between 2015 and 2022, increasing from 18% to 24%. These figures refer to individuals aged 30–64 (Youth Employment Observatory, 2025).

References

ABC (2018) (23 October 2018) Casado denuncia en el "Financial Times" que los Presupuestos de Sánchez son un "suicidio económico", ABC, Madrid. Available at: www.abc.es/espana/abci-casado-denuncia-financial-times-presupuestos-sanchez-suicidio-economico-201810231102_noticia.html.

ABC (2019) (10 April 2019) Casado dice que cumplirá con el acuerdo alcanzado con sindicatos y patronal para "subir el SMI a 850 euros en 2020", ABC, Madrid. Available at: www.abc.es/espana/abci-casado-dice-cumplira-acuerdo-alcanzado-sindicatos-y-patronal-para-subir-850-euros-2020-201904101427_video.html.

ABC (2020a) (22 January 2020) CC.OO. pone en valor la autonomía de los agentes sociales, ABC, Economía section. Available at: www.abc.es/economia/abci-ccoo-pone-valor-autonomia-agentes-sociales-202001222127_video.html.

ABC (2020b) (30 January 2020) UGT felicita al Gobierno por la "rapidez" del acuerdo sobre el SMI, ABC, Economía section. Available at: www.abc.es/economia/abci-felicita-gobierno-rapidez-acuerdo-sobre-202001301436_video.html.

ABC (2021a) (15 June 2021) CC.OO. y UGT piden reabrir la mesa de diálogo social para debatir la subida del salario mínimo, ABC, Economía section. Available at: www.abc.es/economia/abci-ccoo-y-piden-reabrir-mesa-dialogo-social-para-debatir-subida-salario-minimo-202106151507_noticia.html.

ABC (2021b) (8 June 2021) Los sindicatos avanzan más movilizaciones para exigir la subida del salario mínimo, ABC, Zaragoza/Madrid. Available at: www.abc.es/economia/abci-sindicatos-avanzan-mas-movilizaciones-para-exigir-subida-salario-minimo-202102151336_noticia.html.

ABC (2022) (12 January 2022) UGT amenaza con movilizaciones si no se sube el salario mínimo a mil euros desde el 1 de enero, ABC, Madrid. Available at: www.abc.es/economia/abci-amenaza-movilizaciones-si-no-sube-salario-minimo-euros-desde-1-enero-202201121221_noticia.html.

Afonso A. (2019) State-led wage devaluation in Southern Europe in the wake of the Eurozone crisis. *European Journal of Political Research* 58(3): 938–959.

Campos Lima M. da P. (2019) Portugal: Reforms and the turn to neoliberal austerity. In: Müller T., Vandaele K. and Waddington J. (eds) *Collective Bargaining in Europe: Towards an Endgame?* Vol. III, 483–504. Brussels: European Trade Union Institute.

Campos Lima M. da P., Martins D., Costa A. C. and Velez A. (2021) Internal devaluation and economic inequality in Portugal: Challenges to industrial relations in times of crisis and recovery. *Transfer: European Review of Labour and Research* 27(1): 47–73.

Campos Lima M. da P. and Naumann R. (2011) Portugal: From broad strategic pacts to policy-specific agreements. In: Avdagic S., Rhodes M. and Visser J. (eds) *Social Pacts in Europe: Emergence, Evolution, and Institutionalization.* 147–173. Oxford: Oxford University Press.

CGTP (2016) *Posição da CGTP-IN sobre a revisão do Salário Mínimo Nacional em 2017.* Lisbon: CGTP-IN. Available at: www.cgtp.pt/images/images/2016/12/revisao_smn.pdf.

Comisión Asesora para el Análisis del Salario Mínimo Interprofesional (2021) *I Informe de la Comisión Asesora para el Análisis del Salario Mínimo Interprofesional.* Madrid: Gobierno de España. Available at: www.lamoncloa.gob.es/serviciosdeprensa/notasprensa/trabajo14/Documents/2021/80621-%20Resumen_ejecutivo_comision_smi.pdf.

Comisión Asesora para el Análisis del Salario Mínimo Interprofesional (2022) *II Informe de la Comisión Asesora para el Análisis del Salario Mínimo Interprofesional.* Madrid: Gobierno de España. Available at: www.lamoncloa.gob.es/serviciosdeprensa/notasprensa/trabajo14/Documents/2022/191222-Informe-SMI-2023.pdf.

Comisión Asesora para el Análisis del Salario Mínimo Interprofesional (2024) *III Informe de la Comisión Asesora para el Análisis del Salario Mínimo Interprofesional.* Madrid: Gobierno de España. Available at: www.lamoncloa.gob.es/serviciosdeprensa/notasprensa/trabajo14/Documents/2025/150125-III-Informe-Expertos-SMI.pdf.

Dingeldey I., Schulten T. and Grimshaw D. (2021) Introduction: Minimum wage regimes in Europe and selected developing countries. In: Dingeldey I., Grimshaw D. and Schulten T. (eds) *Minimum Wage Regimes: Statutory Regulation, Collective Bargaining and Adequate Levels.* 1–16. London/New York: Routledge.

DN (2015) (4 December 2015) Patrões têm reservas sobre salário mínimo de 530 euros em 2016, Diário de Notícias. Available at: www.dn.pt/portugal/patroes-tem-reservas-sobre-salario-minimo-de-530-euros-em-2016-4914939.html.

DN (2017) (19 November 2017) CIP indisponível para aumentar salário mínimo para 600 euros, Diário de Notícias. Available at: www.dn.pt/dinheiro/cip-indisponivel-para-aumentar-salario-minimo-para-600-euros-8928149.html.

DN (2020) (9 December 2020) CIP considera aumento do salário mínimo para 665 euros "extemporâneo", Diário de Notícias. Available at: www.dn.pt/dinheiro/cip-considera-aumento-do-salario-minimo-para-665-euros-extemporaneo-13122642.html.

El País (2018) (11 October 2018) CEOE avisa de que la subida del salario mínimo frenará el alza del resto de sueldos, El País, Madrid. Available at: https://elpais.com/politica/2018/10/11/actualidad/1539263180_883248.html.

El País (2020) (27 January 2020) Casado apoyará la subida del salario mínimo, El País, Madrid. Available at: https://elpais.com/economia/2020/01/27/actualidad/1580162997_585488.html.

Eurofound (2025) *Impact of National Minimum Wages on Collective Bargaining and Wages for Low-Paid Workers.* Luxembourg: Publications Office of the European Union.

European Commission (2015) *Council Recommendation on the 2015 National Reform Programme of Portugal and Delivering a Council Opinion on the 2015 Stability Programme of Portugal.* Brussels: European Commission. Available at: https://commission.europa.eu/system/files/2017-02/csr2015_portugal_en_0.pdf.

European Commission (2016) *Council Recommendation on the 2016 National Reform Programme of Portugal and delivering a Council opinion on the 2016 Stability Programme of Portugal.* Brussels: European Commission. Available at: https://eur-lex.europa.eu/legal-content/EN/TXT/PDF/?uri=CELEX:52016DC0342.

Expresso (2015) (9 July 2015) OCDE sugere crédito fiscal em Portugal em vez da subida do salário mínimo, Expresso, Lisboa. Available at: https://expresso.pt/economia/2015-07-09-OCDE-sugere-credito-fiscal-em-Portugal-em-vez-da-subida-do-salario-minimo.

Expresso (2016) (19 December 2016) Confederações patronais admitem salário mínimo de 540 euros com redução da TSU, Expresso. Available at: https://expresso.pt/politica/2016-12-19-Confederacoes-patronais-admitem-salario-minimo-de-540-euros-com-reducao-da-TSU.

Grimshaw D. and Bosch G. (2013) The intersection between minimum wage and collective bargaining institutions. In: Grimshaw D. (ed.) *Minimum Wages, Pay Equity and Comparative Industrial Relations.* 50–80. New York/London: Routledge.

Molina Ó. (2021) Minimum wages in Southern Europe: Regulation and reconfiguration under the shadow of hierarchy. In: Dingeldey I., Grimshaw D. and Schulten T. (eds) *Minimum Wage Regimes: Statutory Regulation, Collective Bargaining and Adequate Levels.* 64–85. London/New York: Routledge.

Observador (2014) (5 November 2014) FMI: decisão de aumentar salário mínimo foi prematura e pode ter consequências negativas, Observador, Lisboa. Available at: https://observador.pt/2014/11/05/fmi-decisao-de-aumentar-salario-minimo-foi-prematura-e-pode-ter-consequencias-negativas/.

OECD (2025) *Minimum Relative to Average Wages of Full-time Workers.* Paris: OECD Publishing. Available at: https://data-explorer.oecd.org/vis?fs[0]=Topic%2C1%7CJobs%23JOB%23%7CEarnings%20and%20wages%23JOB_EW%23&pg=0&fc=Topic&bp=true&snb=10&vw=tb&df[ds]=dsDisseminateFinalDMZ&df[id]=DSD_EARNINGS%40MIN2AVE&df[ag]=OECD.ELS.SAE&df[vs]=1.0&pd=2000%2C&dq=... ..MEDIAN.&ly[rw]=REF_AREA&ly[cl]=TIME_PERIOD&to[TIME_PERIOD]=false.

Picot G. (2023) Minimum wages: By collective bargaining and by law. In: Clegg D. and Durazzi N. (eds) *Handbook of Labour Market Policy in Advanced Democracies.* 234–248. Cheltenham: Edward Elgar.

Youth Employment Observatory (2025) *Key Data.* Lisbon: DINÂMIA'CET-Iscte. Available at: https://obsempregojovem.com/indicadores.

Appendix: Interview List and Technical Note

Interview list – Portugal

- Interview 1: Confederation of Commerce and Services of Portugal (CCP) representative. Date: 18/05/2022. Site: Lisbon.
- Interview 2: Christian Democrats (CDS-PP) member of parliament. Date: 02/06/2022. Site: Lisbon.
- Interview 3: General Confederation of Portuguese Workers (CGTP) representative. Date: 09/06/2022. Site: Lisbon.
- Interview 4: Social Democratic Party (PSD) member of parliament. Date: 12/07/2022. Site: Lisbon.
- Interview 5: Confederation of Portuguese Industry (CIP) representative. Date: 01/07/2022. Site: via Zoom.
- Interview 6: Ecologist Party "The Greens" (PEV) member of parliament. Date: 01/06/2022. Site: via Zoom.
- Interview 7: Left Block (BE) member of parliament. Date: 17/05/2022. Site: via Zoom.
- Interview 8: Former member of cabinet of the Portuguese Socialist government. Date: 20/05/2022. Site: Lisbon.
- Interview 9: Portuguese Communist Party (PCP) member of parliament. Date: 16/05/2022. Site: Lisbon.
- Interview 10: General Union of Workers (UGT-P) representative. Date: 20/06/2022. Site: via Zoom.
- Interview 11: Socialist Party (PS) member of parliament. Date: 19/10/2022. Site: Lisbon.

Interview list – Spain

- Interview 12: Cabinet Member of the Spanish Coalition government. Date: 04/11/2022. Site: via Zoom.
- Interview 13: Spanish Confederation of Employers' Organizations (CEOE). Date: 25/11/2022. Site: via Zoom.
- Interview 14: General Workers' Union (UGT-S) representative. Date: 02/03/2023. Site: via Zoom.
- Interview 15: Member of cabinet and Podemos member of parliament. Date: 11/04/2023. Site: via Zoom.
- Interview 16: Trade Union Confederation of Workers' Committees (CCOO) representative. Date: 04/07/2022. Site: via Zoom.

Technical note: Parliamentary debates were analysed using MAXQDA 2022. The dataset comprised 97 debates from Portugal and 24 from Spain.

5 Regulating Platform-Mediated Passenger Transport in Portugal and Spain

Luís Guerreiro, Paulo Marques, and Víctor Riesgo Gómez

Introduction

Portugal and Spain were severely affected by the global financial and European sovereign-debt crises. Between 2008 and 2014, economic growth stalled, real incomes fell, and unemployment, particularly among young labour-market participants, soared (Marques and Horisch, 2020). To address this situation, both economies undertook major reforms from 2011 onwards with the aim of liberalising their labour and product markets. The key objective was to promote what at the time were termed 'internal devaluation policies,' that is, policies that reduced labour costs to restore external competitiveness and thereby boost foreign direct investment (Armingeon and Baccaro, 2012; Campos Lima et al., 2021). This was seen as essential to reduce unemployment and promote economic growth.[1] Unsurprisingly, the private passenger-transport sector stagnated in both countries during this period, as austerity policies and high unemployment constrained domestic demand. For instance, the number of taxi rides in Madrid fell to 561,627 in 2008 – 200,000 fewer than in 2007 (Vectio, 2017). Consequently, the issue of new taxi licences stagnated, and investment in new vehicles declined.

It was in this context that digital platforms, led by Uber, entered the market in 2014. It is well documented in the academic literature that these companies adopt lean business models with low fixed costs (Rahman and Thelen, 2019; Culpepper and Thelen, 2020). As digital platforms entered the Portuguese and Spanish markets in large numbers, bringing new vehicles while incurring no regulatory costs, taxi drivers protested, as app-based transport services were perceived as a threat. This was particularly problematic because taxi drivers were already experiencing economic difficulties. Taxi associations argued that, unlike their own services, those of the digital platforms were unregulated and therefore did not comply with the rules in force. In contrast with other countries (Funke and Picot, 2021; Thelen, 2018), the Iberian governments moved to regulate digital platforms in 2018. Nonetheless, they did so in markedly different ways, as explained below. Whereas the Portuguese government facilitated the entry of digital platforms

DOI: 10.4324/9781003519874-6

into the passenger-transport sector, the Spanish government moved in the opposite direction.

This chapter adopts a qualitative methodological approach. We conduct a comparative case study analysis of the two laws that sought to regulate platform work in the passenger-transport sector (the Portuguese Law No. 45/2018 and the Spanish Royal Decree No. 13/2018). The chapter triangulates multiple sources of empirical evidence. We collected and analysed media statements from three leading newspapers in each country: *Público*, *Expresso*, and *Diário de Notícias* in Portugal; and *El País*, *ABC*, and *El Mundo* in Spain. The main objective was to identify the actors involved in the political negotiations and the key issues under discussion. We also selected and analysed relevant parliamentary debates to identify the principal issues addressed and the relationships among actors.[2] Further documentary sources, such as official documents and reports, were collected and analysed. Finally, we conducted 13 semi-structured interviews with key informants (10 in Portugal; 3 in Spain). The interviews probed their positions and views regarding the negotiation process and the content of each reform. These actors – members of parliament, trade-union officials, taxi-association leaders, and company representatives – were identified through prior analysis of media statements and parliamentary debates. The selection of interviewees was therefore based on their involvement in policy negotiations and decision-making processes.

The chapter is structured into four main sections. Sections 1 and 2 set out the Portuguese and Spanish cases; Section 3 compares their trajectories; and the conclusion relates the findings to Chapters 1 and 2 by explicitly mobilising the ideal types of solidarity, the governing social blocs, the decision-making arenas, and the role played by the European Union (EU).

Portugal

Sectoral and Regulatory Background

The Portuguese taxi sector is regulated by Law No. 10/1990. Decree-Law No. 297/1992 regulates fares, which must be agreed with taxi associations and municipalities.[3] Subsequent Decree-Law No. 251/1998 conferred licensing and regulatory powers on municipalities. When the new law on digital platforms was approved in 2018, the taxi sector was heavily regulated (AMT, 2016) and atomised; the average number of licences per taxi company stood at just 1.4 in 2017 (AMT, 2020).

Digital platforms entered the Portuguese market in 2014. Soon after, taxi associations claimed that platform services were illegal and filed a legal complaint with the court. In April 2015, the Lisbon District Court upheld the complaint and issued an order halting the operation of digital platforms (Lisbon District Court, 2015); however, the platforms disregarded the order. Taxi associations then demanded government intervention and organised strikes and demonstrations in the largest cities (RTP1, 2016). The issue

Table 5.1 Taxi licences in Portugal, 2013–2021

Year	*Taxi licences*
2013	13,790
2014	13,786
2015	13,766
2016	13,766
2017	13,717
2018	12,326
2019	12,323
2020	12,316
2021	12,293

Source: Portuguese Mobility and Transport Authority (AMT, 2023).

Note: Data for the Autonomous Regions of Madeira and the Azores are available only up to 2017.

of taxi licences, which had already stagnated following the global financial crisis, declined slightly after the entry of digital platforms (Table 5.1). In 2021, there were 23,167 drivers working for platform companies and 25,677 taxi drivers (IMT, 2021). At that time, platform-company drivers outnumbered taxi drivers in both Lisbon (12,436 vs 9,427) and Porto (3,927 vs 3,322). The most recent information, from 2024, shows that the number of authorised platform drivers has risen to 69,814 (Público, 2024),[4] while the number of authorised taxi drivers fell from 26,984 in 2020 to 21,217 in 2023 (Executive Digest, 2024).

Law No. 45/2018: Core Provisions

Law No. 45/2018 regulates the individual transport of passengers in uncharacterised vehicles (TVDEs) operating via digital platforms. It identifies three entities responsible for service provision: digital platforms, TVDE operators, and drivers (Amado and Moreira, 2019;Figure 5.1). *Digital platforms* must ensure that accurate information is available and displayed to consumers (who are protected against service disruptions and substandard provision) and must pay a 5% tax on their intermediation margin. A *TVDE operator* must be a licensed Portuguese company and is responsible for managing the business (recruiting drivers, owning the vehicles, and providing the service). *Drivers* must be registered and certified, and their vehicles must be certified by the Institute for Mobility and Transport. Training certificates are valid for five years (taxi drivers are exempt from the training programme if they wish to drive a TVDE vehicle). Drivers who are not self-employed must have a written contract with the TVDE operator, in accordance with the Portuguese Labour Code. Working hours are limited to 10 hours per day, but this limit may be further reduced where cumulative hours would exceed the limits set by the Labour Code. For contracted drivers, the Labour Code

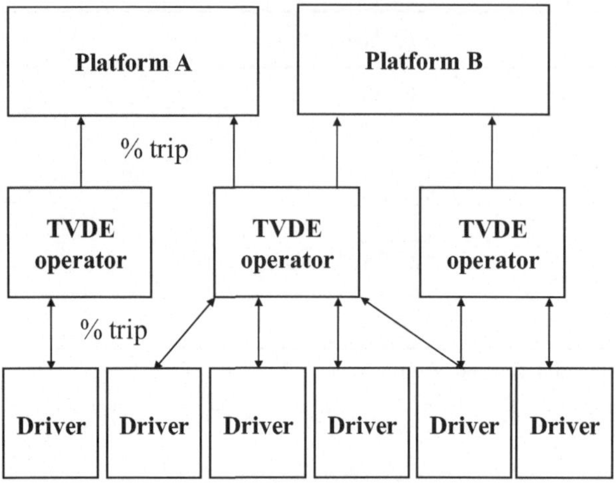

Figure 5.1 Business model of platform-mediated passenger transport in Portugal.

Source: Own elaboration.

requires employers to provide regular and fair remuneration in compensation for work performed. Finally, all such workers must be registered with the social security system.

The law frames the TVDE service as a legitimate competitor to the traditional taxi service. TVDEs face fewer restrictions than taxis, no price controls, and no vehicle quotas, but public hailing and parking at taxi ranks are prohibited. The law explicitly addresses TVDE drivers and seeks to guarantee minimum protections and regulate working conditions.

Legislative Politics and Coalitions

In May 2016, the Secretary of State for the Environment convened a working group to discuss possible reforms. After consulting key actors, the Socialist Party (PS) government released the first draft law, which was sent to Parliament in January 2017 (Portuguese Government, 2017). At the time, the Socialist Minister for the Environment, João Matos Fernandes, argued that this draft law aimed to regulate drivers' working conditions and was aligned with consumer needs. In his view, it was a balanced proposal. By legalising the activities of digital platforms, the government sought agreement with the centre-right Social Democratic Party (PSD), which strongly favoured allowing digital platforms to expand their activities. Conversely, it sought the support of the radical-left parties by strengthening platform workers' rights regarding contracts, working time, training (see previous section), and access to social security. Minister João Matos Fernandes also argued in favour of regulatory differences between TVDEs and taxis.[5] Finally, the government explicitly excluded the implementation of TVDE quotas, 'that is, a limited number of vehicles, because it is a private business' (Observador, 2017).

The radical-left parties opposed this proposal (Interviews 2 and 10). The Left Block (BE) presented an alternative draft law (BE, 2017) aimed at harmonising the regulations governing TVDEs and taxis. This alternative proposed a maximum quota of 25% for TVDEs relative to the total number of taxis in each municipality.[6] In addition, it proposed that municipalities be responsible for licensing TVDEs. The Portuguese Communist Party (PCP) aligned with the BE and argued that TVDEs provided the same service as taxis (Interview 10), citing the Court of Justice of the European Union's (CJEU) ruling on this matter to substantiate its position (CJEU, 2017). In the PCP's view, digital-platform vehicles should follow traditional taxi regulations. At the time, the PCP proposed that platform and taxi drivers receive the same training and have the same employment contracts, that TVDEs be subject to quotas relative to the total number of taxis, that TVDE fares be regulated, and that digital platforms maintain offices in Portugal.[7] Instead of presenting its own draft law, the PCP tabled amendments to the government's proposal (PCP, 2017; 2018).

The centre-right PSD presented its own draft law, supporting digital platforms and their innovative business model, while including measures concerning drivers' working conditions. As a PSD Member of Parliament told us:

> [...] [the new regulation was needed because] digital platforms would give work to thousands of people ... but it was necessary to do something because these jobs would be performed by young people who would work almost like slaves.
>
> (Interview 1)

The PSD argued that the PS government's draft law was excessively deregulatory.[8] The centre-right Popular Party (CDS-PP) proposed amendments to the PS draft (CDS-PP, 2018). It argued in favour of regulating TVDEs in line with consumer preferences, with the aim of enabling a competitive market in the private individual-transport sector (Interview 3). CDS-PP disagreed with the government's proposal to establish national TVDE operators, doubting that this would benefit drivers' working conditions, and it opposed the introduction of TVDE quotas demanded by the left.[9]

The PS parliamentary group concurred that digital platforms were innovative and that their activities should be legalised. However, PS MPs suggested revising the government's draft to better safeguard drivers' working conditions.[10] They put forward several changes; most notably, they included an employment-contract clause in the final draft (PS, 2018a; 2018b; 2018c). As one PS MP explained:

> [...] digital-platform drivers now have a set of labour protection laws and there are regulations for consumers that did not previously exist.
>
> (Interview 4)

This was also an attempt to better accommodate the positions of other parties – namely, the radical-left parties supporting the government in Parliament on crucial matters such as the national budget (Interview 4).[11]

By late January 2018, the parties had presented either their final list of changes to the government proposal or their own draft laws; these were to be voted on in the 'speciality' discussion in mid-March 2018. The PSD and the PS both submitted a new list of modifications less than two weeks before the speciality discussion. In the vote, the PS and the PSD agreed on the final draft and, together, passed all but five amendments. All PS amendments were accepted; several PSD amendments were also approved. One proposal from CDS-PP and another from the PCP were approved. None of the BE proposals was accepted. After some delays, the final vote was held in March 2018. Ultimately, the PSD, the PS, and the CDS-PP voted in favour of the final version of the law, while the PCP and the BE voted against.

However, the law was subsequently vetoed by the President of the Portuguese Republic. The PS and PSD therefore revised the previous version; the most important change was an increase in the intermediation tax that digital platforms were required to pay. As before, the PSD, the PS, and the CDS-PP voted in favour, and the PCP and the BE voted against. The amended law was approved.

In terms of coalitions, the parliamentary majority that supported Law No. 45/2018 corresponds to a Centrist–Employer governing social bloc: the PS joined forces with centre-right parties and business actors to legalise the platform model while calibrating a limited set of labour protections. This mapping follows the framework in Chapter 2, where bloc composition is the necessary determinant of reform orientation.

Before moving on to the Spanish case, we briefly describe the positions of the taxi associations and platform companies. The National Association of Road Transportation in Lightweight Vehicles (ANTRAL) and the Portuguese Taxi Federation (FPT) are Portugal's two major taxi associations. Both opposed the government's draft law and aligned with the radical-left parties (Interviews 8 and 9). Taxi associations demanded that TVDEs be subject to the same rules as taxis (ANTRAL, 2016). As an ANTRAL representative told us:

> [...] the key difference is that there is no limit on the number of TVDE vehicles. TVDE operators may inject as many vehicles into the market as they need to sideline the competition.
>
> (Interview 9)

They considered the PS government's proposal 'unconstitutional, illegal and immoral' (FPT, 2016). Taxi associations organised three strikes between 2015 and 2017, causing disruption in the major cities (Lisbon, Porto, and Faro). During this process, there were several episodes of violence against platform workers and their vehicles, as well as journalists (Expresso, 2018). In 2018, the taxi associations protested again following the approval of Law No. 45/2018 (Público, 2018).

Digital platforms favoured the new law but made several suggestions. Cabify called for some price regulation; the inclusion of existing taxis and taxi drivers in the digital platform market; fleet limits (a minimum of seven cars per TVDE operator and a maximum vehicle age of seven years); extended driver training (partially funded by digital platforms); and driver exclusivity (Cabify, 2016). Uber criticised certain operational details – namely, the ban on TVDEs using taxi lanes and the duration of driver training, which, it argued, should have been set at 30 hours (Uber, 2016).

In December 2016, TVDE operators established two associations: the National Association of Transport Using Digital Platforms (ANTUPE) and the National Association of the Partners of Alternative Transportation Platforms (ANPPAT). Their affiliates were TVDE operators and the companies responsible for hiring drivers, acquiring vehicles, and negotiating and contracting services with digital platforms. These employer associations opposed a maximum working time of 10 hours per day and demanded an increase to 12 hours. They also called for a cap on the number of TVDE vehicles and for higher prices. ANTUPE considered that the new law gave taxis an advantage over TVDEs, since it required newer fleets for TVDEs, imposed stringent driver sanctions, and mandated transparent invoicing (Interview 6). ANPPAT expressed concerns about revenue, noting that digital platforms retained large commissions that left TVDE operators and drivers with insufficient margins to cover costs (Observador, 2017).

Spain

Sectoral and Regulatory Background

Transport in Spain was historically regulated by two laws: Law No. 16/1987 and Royal Decree No. 1211/1990, which distinguished two private individual-transport services: taxis and private hire vehicles (VTCs). VTCs provided premium transport services for weddings, funerals, and private events. Royal Decree No. 1211/1990 limited the number of VTCs to a fraction of the number of taxis (Guillén, 2018). To provide these services, operators had to obtain administrative authorisation from both municipalities and the Autonomous Communities.

Law No. 25/2009, passed by the Socialist Party (PSOE) government, amended these laws, including by removing restrictions on VTC authorisations. Subsequently, the Popular Party (PP) government passed

Law No. 9/2013, later consolidated by Royal Decree No. 1057/2015, which reinstated the proportionality criterion whereby there could be no more than one VTC licence for every 30 taxi licences. It also effectively excluded small companies from operating by setting a minimum fleet size of seven vehicles per company and restricted VTC operations to local transport: at least 80% of journeys were required to take place within the Autonomous Community that had granted the licence.

Before Royal Decree No. 1057/2015 was passed, the PP government consulted key public authorities,[12] the Autonomous Communities,[13] and other stakeholders.[14] Nonetheless, these changes were contested by the National Markets and Competition Commission (CNMC), Unauto VTCs (one of the largest VTC operators), Uber, and Maxi Mobility Spain (another VTC operator). In early 2016, the CNMC initiated administrative litigation against Royal Decree No. 1057/2015. In 2018, the Spanish Supreme Court ruled that the paragraphs of Article 181.2 requiring operating companies to own at least seven vehicles should be annulled (Spanish Supreme Court, 2018).

Platforms criticised Law No. 9/2013 and Royal Decree No. 1057/2015 because VTC authorisations were crucial to their operations. Uber launched its first UberPop service in Barcelona in 2014, and later in Valencia and Madrid. The regulated, traditional taxi sector organised several protests in these cities in what became known as *la Guerra del taxi* (de-Miguel-Molina et al., 2021). Taxi associations filed legal complaints in the commercial courts of Barcelona (El País, 2014b) and Madrid, accusing Uber of providing an illegal service.[15] In December 2014, the Commercial Court of Madrid ordered the precautionary suspension of Uber operations throughout the country (El País, 2014c), leading Uber to cease operations in Spain (El País, 2014d). To overcome this obstacle, digital platforms took advantage of a regulatory loophole that existed until Royal Decree No. 1057/2015 was passed. This loophole, VTC authorisations, was used to enter the private transport market and stabilise operations (Baño León, 2017; Guillén, 2018). Local investors, partly supported by digital platforms, submitted a wave of applications in 2014 and 2015 across Spain (El Confidencial, 2017a; 2017b). The CNMC also opposed attempts to tighten government regulation. Cabify, a small Spanish platform company in the private individual-transport sector founded in 2011 that used VTC authorisations, pursued an 'innovation without permission' strategy by launching a low-cost service with fares below those of taxis in summer 2014 (Muy Pymes, 2015; Langlois and Elmer, 2019). In March 2016, 15 months after being forced out of the Spanish market, Uber launched a new service, UberX, also using VTC authorisations. Although the new regulations precluded the granting of additional VTC authorisations (in line with the 1:30 rule), the Supreme Court ruled in favour of the applicants in 2017 (El Confidencial, 2017b), and digital platforms continued the litigation.[16]

To address this situation, the PP government annulled previous changes and passed a new transport law. Royal Decree No. 3/2018 set a minimum of

Table 5.2 VTC and taxi licences in Spain, 2013–2020

Year	*VTC licences*	*Taxi licences*
2013	2,754	67,280
2014	2,703	63,853
2015	3,474	65,539
2016	4,296	66,395
2017	5,473	66,938
2018	6,687	63,656
2019	13,115	65,653
2020	16,549	63,295

Source: Ministry of Transportation, Mobility and Urban Agenda (MTMAU, 2023).

seven vehicles per VTC company, limited VTC licences to one for every 30 taxi licences (allowing the Autonomous Communities to set less restrictive limits), and required that 80% of VTC operations be local. This Royal Decree was submitted by the PP government and approved in the Spanish Parliament following negotiations with taxi associations and VTC associations. The PSOE, *Podemos*, and other minority parties voted in favour. One PSOE MP, one *Podemos* MP, and all *Ciudadanos* MPs (which supported the PP government) abstained.

Finally, the taxi sector in Spain is highly atomised. Most city councils limit the number of licences owned by a single entity, and more than 90% of companies have only one licence (MTMAU, 2023). Moreover, while the number of taxi licences remained stable (Table 5.2), VTC licences increased significantly in densely populated regions, producing regional concentration: Madrid accounts for 48% of VTC licences, Andalusia 18%, Catalonia 16%, and Valencia 4%. Other Autonomous Communities hold smaller shares, in contrast to the traditional taxi service, which is more evenly distributed. Nonetheless, the number of VTC licences remains far lower than the number of taxi licences.

Royal Decree-Law 13/2018: Core Provisions

In September 2018, the PSOE government led by Pedro Sánchez issued Royal Decree No. 13/2018. In line with Royal Decree No. 3/2018, it maintained quotas for VTCs (the 1:30 rule). Nevertheless, VTCs were permitted to operate only locally: journeys had to start within the Autonomous Community that issued the VTC licence. Furthermore, the Autonomous Communities became responsible for issuing VTC licences and could amend VTC regulations within their jurisdictions (El País, 2018). Platform companies were granted a four-year transition period to adapt to the new regulations, and December 2022 was set as the expiry date for all authorisations exceeding the 1:30 rule.

Royal Decree No. 13/2018 was the outcome of a lengthy process that began with the entry of these companies into the Spanish market in 2014. The law set out the business model for the digital-platform transport service in Spain, in which there is a direct relationship between platforms/entrepreneurs and drivers (Figure 5.2). VTCs play a crucial role in this model.

Finally, it should be noted that this legislation empowered holders of VTC authorisations, since digital platforms chose to enter the Spanish market by acquiring authorisations. Small owners are thus incentivised to sell their authorisations on the secondary market. Two large digital-platform companies, Uber and Cabify, dominate the market, and three large business groups control a significant share of authorisations (La Información, 2020). These business groups provide the vehicles used in the transport service and sign employment contracts with drivers. The employment contracts are not signed with the digital platforms, which seek to avoid direct labour responsibilities. By contrast, taxi drivers retain their licences and mostly work independently, producing a segmented private transport labour market.

Legislative Politics and Coalitions

The PSOE government took office in summer 2018. Its initial stance was that taxis and VTCs provided a similar service; further legislative changes should therefore be implemented to align the regulation of the two services. The law also needed revision because the national ratio of VTCs to taxis had recently

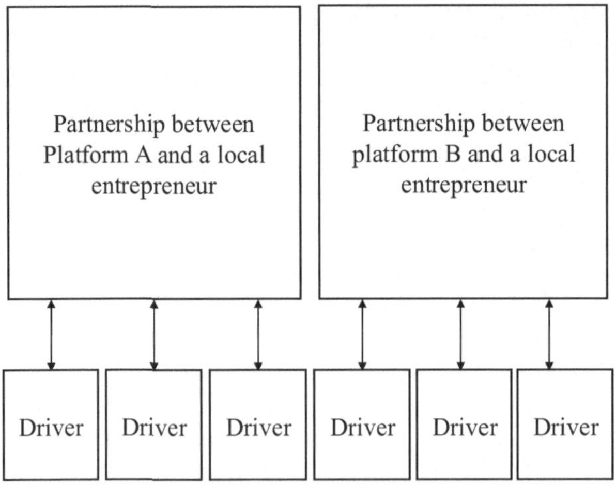

Figure 5.2 Business model of platform-mediated passenger transport in Spain (VTC-based).

Source: Own elaboration.

risen from 1:9 to 1:6. In contrast to the position taken by the PP government, the PSOE proposed that VTCs should be regulated by the Autonomous Communities like any other transport service. Similarly, it proposed that VTCs should operate within the Autonomous Community that issued the authorisation (see previous section), arguing that the proposal aligned with recommendations by EU institutions to 'promote integrated mobility policies,' to be pursued by 'local, autonomous or regional bodies.' Although left-wing parties backed the law, some differences are worth noting. *Podemos*' opposition to precariousness and offshore companies was very much in line with Royal Decree No. 13/2018. The party argued that the position taken by taxi associations safeguarded the sector's interests, workers' rights, and the public service.[17] A *Podemos* MP stated:

> Obviously, the fact that we were part of the process changed the situation a lot [...] We played a central role in obtaining a favourable agreement for taxi drivers and also achieved an advanced sanctioning regime for VTCs. (Interview 12)

By contrast, PSOE MPs argued that VTCs and taxis should be subject to similar regulation, while also noting the benefits to consumers from new technologies. They emphasised the importance of reaching parliamentary agreements before the law was approved and of involving the Autonomous Communities in the process. It should be noted that, at the time of the parliamentary debates, the Autonomous Communities had not yet supported this legislative change.[18] PSOE MPs also maintained that, while VTC regulation should protect workers' rights, such protection should not impede technological progress.[19]

PP and *Ciudadanos* opposed Royal Decree No. 13/2018. The PP argued that Royal Decree No. 3/2018 already protected the taxi sector and blamed the Zapatero government for deregulating individual transport licences in 2009, which VTC operators had subsequently used to enter the Spanish market. PP MPs claimed that Royal Decree No. 13/2018 was an attempt to transfer government responsibility to the Autonomous Communities, which was particularly unacceptable as they had not been sufficiently involved in the decision-making process. They argued that the PSOE was considering only *Podemos*' position and ignoring the other parties. *Ciudadanos* was the party most supportive of liberalising the sector. It argued that the new law limited the development of VTCs and thus hindered market competition. *Ciudadanos* favoured less regulation – namely, lower licensing costs, flexible fares, and consumer choice – and opposed VTC quotas and geographic restrictions. The party believed that VTCs and traditional taxis alike would benefit from competition because this would improve the services provided. However, it supported new rules to protect VTC drivers.

Royal Decree No. 13/2018 was approved by the PSOE, *Podemos*, and other minority parties (whose support was crucial for final approval). The

PP and *Ciudadanos* voted against. This coalition configuration maps onto a Left–Union governing social bloc: the PSOE–*Podemos* partnership aligned with taxi organisations and union allies to reassert public control over market access, accepting a more restrictive settlement for platforms. As conjectured in Chapter 2, this bloc alignment pushed the reform towards a more inclusive orientation.

Before moving on to the comparison between the two case studies, the positions taken by taxi associations and platform companies are briefly set out below. As explained in previous sections, taxi associations opposed the activities of digital platforms in the passenger-transport sector. As a Taxi Union of Catalunya (STC) representative explained to us:

> [...] we condemned them on the grounds that an authorisation was required for this transport service. And they [the digital platforms] disagreed.
> (Interview 11)

Taxi associations organised protests and strikes in cities such as Barcelona, Madrid, and Valencia (ABC, 2018; El Mundo, 2014) to demand a ban on digital platforms (El País, 2014a). They also submitted a complaint to the Court of Justice of the European Union (CJEU), which led to a ruling that considered digital platforms to be providers of a transport service, not a digital service. The ruling strengthened taxi associations' demands for stricter regulation of digital platforms (Interview 12). Not surprisingly, taxi associations agreed with the content of Royal Decree No. 13/2018 and acted at the regional level to impose further restrictions on the operations of digital platforms (Interview 11). Platform companies, by contrast, opposed Royal Decree No. 13/2018, as it constrained their activities.

Comparative Analysis

Having described the positions taken by the different political parties in the previous two sections, we now summarise the dimensions that were most salient in the parliamentary debates and interviews. From our perspective, the following four dimensions are the most important for comparative purposes:

a) *Training and employment contracts*: the training, certification, and hiring of drivers for digital-platform vehicles.
b) *Licensing and operating costs*: operational constraints on digital-platform business models (e.g., operating fees, vehicle licensing, and authorisations).
c) *Quotas*: limits on the number of vehicles operating for digital platforms.
d) *Price regulation:* minimum and maximum fares charged by digital platforms.

In the Portuguese case, the PS, PSD, and CDS-PP agreed to avoid interference with the core of the digital-platform business model (quotas and

Table 5.3 Portuguese parties' positions by regulatory dimension

Regulatory dimensions	*Training and employment contracts*	*Licensing and operating costs*	*Quotas*	*Price regulation*
PS	Medium	Low	No	No
PSD	Medium	Low	No	No
CDS-PP	Medium	Low	No	No
PCP	High	High	Yes	Yes
BE	High	High	Yes	Yes

Source: Own elaboration based on analysis of parliamentary debates, media reporting, and interviews.

Notes: Dimensions are rated according to how political actors framed them in debates and interviews. A three-level intensity scale – low, medium, high – is used for the first two dimensions; a binary yes–no scale is used for the other two.

price regulation) and to impose low operating charges, alongside certain obligations regarding employment contracts and access to social security (Table 5.3). The radical left opposed this position and called for tighter regulation of digital-platform operations. Thus, a clash emerged between the centre-left/centre-right and the radical left. The creation of TVDE operators as intermediaries ensured that digital platforms could operate as intended (Tomassoni and Pirina, 2022). The law approved in 2018 adopted a market-opening template, tempered by a baseline protective floor for drivers. This approach is characteristic of competitive solidarity and has led to a substantial increase in the number of vehicles operated by platforms. By 2022, the number of TVDE drivers outnumbered traditional taxi drivers in Lisbon, Porto, and Faro. Hence, the private transport labour market became more mixed, more competitive, and less regulated, with many more drivers. The parties that supported this legislative change in Parliament believed that opening the private transport sector to digital platforms would introduce technological innovation and competition, create new jobs, and provide better service to end users; it would also force the incumbent taxi sector to modernise. Nonetheless, platform workers' rights needed to be respected.

In Spain, all political parties except *Ciudadanos* agreed on imposing VTC quotas relative to the number of taxis (Table 5.4). Apart from *Podemos*, there was also agreement that prices should not be regulated. What set the PSOE–*Podemos* apart from the centre-right was the issue, validity, and scope of authorisations. While the centre-right wanted licences to be valid at the national level, the PSOE and *Podemos* agreed that licences should be issued by each Autonomous Community and that VTCs should be regulated and integrated into the transport networks of the Autonomous Communities. Thus, in Spain, regulation aimed to balance the new VTC service with the incumbent taxi sector. While the new VTC service was accepted, it was not viewed as a new technological service but rather as a transport service that

Table 5.4 Spanish parties' positions by regulatory dimension

Regulatory dimensions	*Training and employment contracts*	*Licensing and operating costs*	*Quotas*	*Price regulation*
PP	-	Medium	Yes	No
PSOE	-	High	Yes	No
Podemos	-	High	Yes	Yes
Ciudadanos	-	Low	No	No
Other small parties	-	Medium	Yes	No

Source: Own elaboration based on analysis of parliamentary debates, media reporting, and interviews.

should be overseen by the regulator of the transport network, the Autonomous Community. The PSOE–*Podemos* agreement restricted VTC licences and their operation to contain expansion and preserve the traditional taxi service. The *numerus clausus* of authorisations prevented growth and fragmented the Spanish market into 17 regional markets, some of which became unprofitable for digital platforms. Although the number of companies with more than 60 authorised vehicles surged and authorisations increased six-fold, this growth was concentrated in Madrid (8,420, 47% of the total), Andalusia (3,280, 18%), and Catalonia (2,956, 16%), which together account for 81% of all authorisations.

While Royal Decree No. 13/2018 did not explicitly address working conditions, the employment situation of VTC drivers had to comply with the Spanish labour code. Moreover, there was a more favourable climate for workers' rights. Although no public policy was specifically aimed at safeguarding platform workers' rights, measures such as increases in the minimum wage, the Rider Law (Vieira and Mendonça, 2025), the obligation to register working hours, and labour market reforms to reduce temporary employment all acknowledged the growing importance of algorithms in the control of the work process (Lee et al., 2015; Rosenblat and Stark, 2016).[20] It should also be noted that drivers formed works councils with union support and obtained judicial rulings recognising the working day as the time drivers spent at the wheel, whether or not they had a client (El País, 2021; Riesgo Gómez, 2023). In the Madrid region, drivers and employers signed a collective agreement in 2021 that acknowledged the importance of digital platforms in the organisation of work in the VTC sector (Business Insider, 2021).

This section shows that the key differences between the two cases relate to quotas, licensing procedures, and the regulation of employment contracts. These three dimensions are crucial because they help to explain why the two markets evolved differently. While the Portuguese law did not include quotas and had straightforward licensing procedures, it contained specific rules on employment contracts. By contrast, Spain imposed quotas and strict licensing procedures, but no specific rules on employment contracts. Consequently, the number of vehicles operated through digital platforms in Portugal increased sharply. That is, the PS government allowed the expansion of services provided by digital platforms while seeking to regulate this by extending workers' rights. This was not the case in Spain, where the main goal of the PSOE government was to contain the expansion of this market in order to safeguard workers' labour market position.

Discussion and Conclusions

In 2018, centre-left governments in Portugal and Spain were compelled to respond to the distributive and regulatory tensions generated by the rapid entry of digital platforms into urban passenger transport. Read through the lens of Chapters 1 and 2, these policy episodes are best understood as attempts to rebuild solidarity in a domain where liberalisation had advanced quickly and informally. The ideal-typical distinction between inclusive and competitive solidarity helps to clarify the design choices. Inclusive solidarity strengthens universal floors without trading insider protections for outsider gains; competitive solidarity couples protections for outsiders with greater managerial discretion elsewhere (see Chapter 1). Applied to our cases, the Spanish reforms moved more clearly in an inclusive direction, whereas the Portuguese law retained important competitive features. Specifically, we argue that the Portuguese TVDE statute aligns more closely with competitive solidarity. It regularised the operation of platforms and introduced minimum safeguards for drivers, but it did so through a market-opening template that preserved managerial discretion and eschewed robust, collectively enforceable labour standards. By contrast, the Spanish trajectory, combining the tightening of operating rules for VTC services with measures to curtail bogus self-employment in adjacent platform labour markets, leans towards inclusive solidarity. Figure 5.3 summarises these linkages between ideal types and the two legal frameworks.

These twin paths also expose common challenges. A credible protective floor is difficult to build in segments where entry barriers are low and enforcement capacity is thin; at the same time, excessively restrictive operating rules risk serving either as a barrier to the entry of vulnerable workers or as a protectionist shield for incumbents.

These divergent conceptions of solidarity rested on distinct *governing social blocs*. In Portugal, a Centrist–Employer bloc coalesced around the PS with centre-right support, backed by platform firms and moderate actors willing to accept light-touch labour standards in exchange for market access. In Spain, a Left–Union bloc, anchored in the PSOE-led coalition and allied with unions and taxi organisations, pushed for tighter operating limits and curbs on bogus self-employment, while the PP, historically closer to taxi interests, opposed elements of this agenda. Turning to *decision arenas*, neither case was driven by robust tripartite social concertation. Decisions were

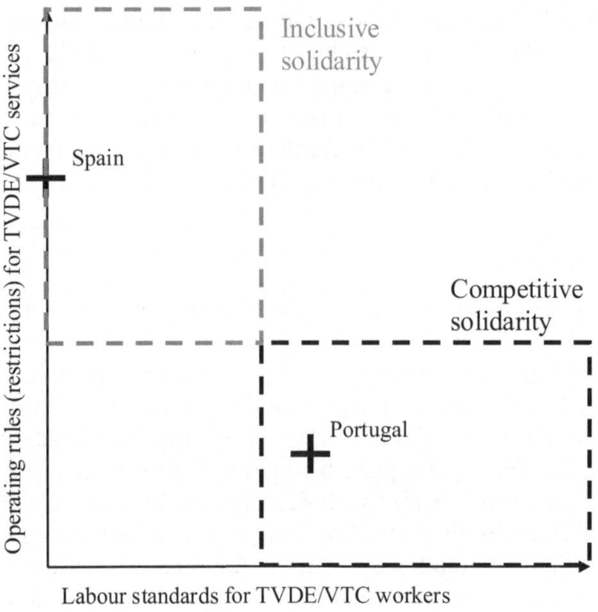

Figure 5.3 Linking operating rules and labour standards to the competitive–inclusive solidarity continuum.

Source: Own elaboration.

largely executive–parliamentary, with social dialogue only intermittent. Finally, *the EU* operated as a conditional and comparatively weak selector in this policy field. Consistent with the post-Maastricht liberalising tilt of integration, there was little binding EU guidance when the Iberian laws were crafted; this limited Brussels' capacity either to constrain or to underwrite ambitious re-regulation. Only with the EU's more recent 'social turn,' including initiatives on platform work, did normative resources emerge that governments could invoke. In our cases, however, EU leverage served chiefly to amplify domestic choices at the margin rather than to determine them.

Situating the two cases of platform regulation within the framework summarised in Chapter 2 (Table 2.2) helps to clarify the sources of divergence. In Portugal (Law No. 45/2018 on TVDE), a Centrist–Employer governing social bloc legislated through Parliament at a time when EU leverage tilted towards liberalisation. In the typology, this maps onto constellation 5 (Centrist–Employer + Parliament + Liberal EU), which predicts a competitive-solidarity outcome marked by maximal liberalisation and only limited compensatory measures. This is consistent with the reform's core features: light entry barriers, no numerical caps, and a market-opening orientation tempered solely by baseline protections for drivers. By contrast, Spain's path corresponds to constellation 2 (Left–Union + Parliament + Liberal EU), in which the EU does not provide normative cover for more protective regulation. The expected outcome would be inclusive solidarity at a high level, albeit with some limits. Nonetheless, that is not what transpired: the Spanish reform was highly restrictive towards platforms. This suggests that, even with limited EU support, high-impact inclusive reforms may still occur; indeed, a Left–Union bloc combined with parliamentary decision-making was sufficient for a maximal-intensity inclusive reform.

Notes

1 These reforms also sought to reshape these economies' growth models. The prevailing consumption-led model was deemed unsustainable in view of high public-debt levels. The objective was to increase the share of exports in GDP (Hall, 2018).
2 We analysed one parliamentary debate in Portugal and two in Spain.
3 This Decree-Law was revised several times, specifically by Law No. 156/1999, Law No. 106/2001, Decree-Law No. 41/2003, Decree-Law No. 4/2004, Law No. 5/2013, and Law No. 35/2016.
4 It is difficult to gauge the growth of the digital-platform service from these figures, as driver authorisations are valid for five years and the number of authorised but inactive drivers is unknown. Moreover, because Portugal has no licensing/authorisation mechanism for vehicles operating via digital platforms, the true scale of the service is hard to ascertain.
5 See speeches by the PS Minister José Matos Fernandes (parliamentary debate 2017-03-18).
6 See speeches by BE member of parliament Heitor Sousa (parliamentary debate 2017-03-18).
7 See several speeches by PCP member of parliament Bruno Dias (parliamentary debate 2017-03-18).
8 See speeches by PSD member of parliament Paulo Neves (parliamentary debate 2017-03-18).
9 See speeches by CDS-PP member of parliament Helder Amaral (parliamentary debate 2017-03-18).
10 See speeches by PS member of parliament Hugo Costa (parliamentary debate 2017-03-18).
11 At the time, the PS did not hold an absolute majority in Parliament. The PS government was made possible by support from the PCP and BE in 2015.
12 National Land Transport Council (Passenger Transport Section); National Road Transport Committee (Passenger Transport Department: Public Transport of Passengers in Tourist Vehicles and Hirers of Vehicles with Driver sections).
13 Autonomous Communities: Castilla-La Mancha, Catalonia, Cantabria, Andalusia, La Rioja, and Madrid; Navarre missed the deadline.
14 Ministry of Economy and Competitiveness (29 June); Comisión Nacional de los Mercados y de la Competencia (25 June); Informe de la Secretaría General Técnica del Ministerio de Fomento (art. 24.2 Ley 50/1997 del Gobierno).

15 In addition, taxi associations from Catalonia submitted a complaint to the CJEU, which ruled that digital platforms were providing a transport service rather than a digital service (CJEU, 2017).

16 Conversely, consolidation of the quota system created a secondary market in which VTC authorisations were traded at far higher values than their initial licence cost. In Spain, platforms partnered and co-invested with local entrepreneurs to acquire VTC licences, as more licences meant higher revenue. The secondary market for VTC authorisations surged; the price rose from €36 to over €40,000 per licence (El Confidencial, 2017a). This mirrors dynamics in the traditional taxi-service market. Platforms also shared ownership of vehicles and the costs of operation and driver recruitment; this led to market concentration, with up to 60% of VTC licences owned by three large investment groups.

17 See speeches by *Podemos* member of parliament Mayoral Perales (parliamentary debates 2018-05-10 and 2018-10-25).

18 See speeches by PSOE member of parliament Estebán Ramos (parliamentary debate 2018-05-10).

19 See speeches by PSOE member of parliament Estebán Ramos (parliamentary debate 2018-10-25).

20 See Chapters 3 and 4 of this book on revisions to labour law aimed at reducing the share of temporary employment and, respectively, on government decisions to increase the minimum wage.

References

ABC (2018) (30 July 2018) *Los taxistas colapsan el centro de Barcelona con sus reivindicaciones*, ABC, Madrid. Available at: www.abc.es/espana/catalunya/abci-taxistas-colapsan-centro-barcelona-reivindicaciones-201807302033_noticia.html.

Amado J. L. and Moreira T. C. (2019) A lei portuguesa sobre o transporte de passageiros a partir de plataforma eletrónica: sujeitos, relações e presunções. *LaBoUR & Law Issues* 5(1): 47–81.

AMT (2016) *Relatório Estatístico dos Serviços de Transporte em Táxi — A Realidade Atual e a Evolução na Última Década.* Lisbon: Autoridade da Mobilidade e dos Transportes — Observatório dos Mercados da Mobilidade, Preços e Estratégias Empresariais. Available at: https://taxis.amt-autoridade.pt.

AMT (2020) *O Transporte em Táxi em Portugal.* Lisbon: Autoridade da Mobilidade e dos Transportes. Available at: www.amt-autoridade.pt/media/2558/sintese-mercado-taxi-portugal-junho2020.pdf.

AMT (2023) *Táxis – Licenças e Contingentes.* Lisbon: Autoridade da Mobilidade e dos Transportes — Observatório. Available at: https://observatorio.amt-autoridade.pt/publicacao/Taxis-Licencas-Contingentes.

ANTRAL (2016) *Análise e Parecer da ANTRAL.* Lisbon, 6 October 2016. Available at: www.parlamento.pt/ActividadeParlamentar/Paginas/DetalheIniciativa.aspx?BID=40897.

Armingeon K. and Baccaro L. (2012) Political economy of the sovereign debt crisis: The limits of internal devaluation. *Industrial Law Journal* 41(3): 254–275.

Baño León J. M. (2017) *Informe sobre la regulación jurídica de las VTC en relación al taxi.* Available at: www.taxi-companys.com/wp-content/uploads/2021/03/bano-leon-Informe-regulacion-juridica-VTC.pdf.

BE (2017) *Projeto de Lei No. 450/XIII/2.ª — Estabelece um novo regime jurídico para a atividade de transporte de passageiros em veículos automóveis ligeiros descaracterizados*. Lisbon: Assembleia da República. Available at: www.parlamento.pt/ActividadeParlamentar/Paginas/DetalheIniciativa.aspx?BID=41420.

Business Insider (2021) (19 November 2021) Sindicatos y patronales de la VTC acuerdan su primer convenio en Madrid con un salario bruto de 14.720 euros anuales, a menos de un año de que acabe el plazo que les permite operar en ciudades, Business Insider. Available at: www.businessinsider.es/sector-vtc-acuerda-primer-convenio-colectivo-madrid-967489.

Cabify (2016) *Petição*. Lisbon: Cabify. Available at: www.parlamento.pt/ActividadeParlamentar/Paginas/DetalheIniciativa.aspx?BID=40897.

Campos Lima M. P., Martins D., Costa A. and Velez A. (2021) Internal devaluation and economic inequality in Portugal: Challenges to industrial relations in times of crisis and recovery. *Transfer: European Review of Labour and Research* 27(1): 47–73.

CDS-PP (2018) *Propostas de Alteração à Proposta de Lei No. 50/XIII*. Lisbon: Assembleia da República. Available at: www.parlamento.pt/ActividadeParlamentar/Paginas/DetalheIniciativa.aspx?BID=40897.

CJEU (2017) *The Service Provided by Uber Connecting Individuals with Non-professional Drivers is Covered by Services in the Field of Transport*. Press Release No. 136/17. Luxembourg: Court of Justice of the European Union. Available at: www.politico.eu/wp-content/uploads/2017/12/uber-ecj-press-release.pdf.

Culpepper P. D. and Thelen K. (2020) Are we all amazon primed? Consumers and the politics of platform power. *Comparative Political Studies* 53(2): 288–318.

Decree-Law No. 297/92 of 31 December. Regime de Preços Convencionados (1992).

de-Miguel-Molina M., de-Miguel-Molina B., and Catalá-Pérez D. (2021). The collaborative economy and taxi services: Moving towards new business models in Spain. *Research in Transportation Business & Management* 39, 100503.

El Confidencial (2017a) (15 February 2017) El TS inflama la guerra del taxi en Madrid con 3.000 nuevos permisos de Uber y Cabify, El Confidencial. Available at: www.elconfidencial.com/espana/madrid/2017-02-15/supremo-taxi-madrid-licencias-vtc_1331985/.

El Confidencial (2017b) (15 November 2017) El TS tumba al taxi: concede nuevas licencias de Uber y Cabify (y vienen miles más), El Confidencial. Available at: www.elconfidencial.com/tecnologia/2017-11-15/uber-cabify-taxi-supremo-licencias-vtc_1477937/.

El Mundo (2014) (13 October 2014) Los taxistas protestan contra Uber, El Mundo. Available at: www.elmundo.es/madrid/2014/10/13/543b7c8fe2704e21238b456e.html.

El País (2014a) (31 October 2014) Los taxistas denuncian a Uber ante consumo por competencia desleal, El País. Available at: https://elpais.com/ccaa/2014/10/31/catalunya/1414756567_420943.html.

El País (2014b) (7 November 2014) Los taxistas demandan a Uber por "venderse" como consumo colaborativo, El País. Available at: https://elpais.com/ccaa/2014/11/06/catalunya/1415309786_229019.html.

El País (2014c) (9 December 2014) Un juez ordena el cierre cautelar de las actividades de Uber en España, El País. Available at: https://elpais.com/economia/2014/12/09/actualidad/1418132663_205298.html.

El País (2014d) (31 December 2014) Uber cierra su servicio en España, El País. Available at: https://elpais.com/economia/2014/12/31/actualidad/1419993561_752162.html.

El País (2018) (25 October 2018) El Congreso aprueba el decreto de los VTC pero abre la vía para suavizarlo, El País. Available at: https://elpais.com/economia/2018/10/25/actualidad/1540472606_988927.html.

El País (2021) (5 March 2021) Conductores VTC: la pausa entre dos trayectos computa como tiempo de trabajo, Cinco Días, El País. Available at: https://cincodias.elpais.com/cincodias/2021/03/01/legal/1614599818_627367.html.

Executive Digest (2024) (17 July 2024) Portugal perdeu quase 6.000 taxistas em três anos. Pandemia, TVDE e salários são os sinais vermelhos do setor, Executive Digest, Lisbon. Available at: https://executivedigest.sapo.pt/noticias/portugal-perdeu-quase-6-000-taxistas-em-tres-anos-pandemia-tvde-e-salarios-sao-os-sinais-vermelhos-do-setor/.

Expresso (2018) (19 September 2018) Táxis. Três grandes protestos desde 2015, Expresso. Available at: https://expresso.pt/sociedade/2018-09-19-Taxis.-Tres-grandes-protestos-desde-2015.

FPT (2016) *Pronúncia da Federação Portuguesa do Táxi sobre o projecto de diploma emanado do Governo... regime jurídico das plataformas eletrónicas...* Lisbon, 6 October 2016. Available at: www.parlamento.pt/ActividadeParlamentar/Paginas/DetalheIniciativa.aspx?BID=40897.

Funke C. and Picot G. (2021) Platform work in a coordinated market economy. *Industrial Relations Journal* 52(4): 348–363.

Guillén A. L. (2018) El arrendamiento de vehículos con conductor (VTC) y su entramado jurídico: el avance de Uber, Cabify y la economía colaborativa. *REALA. Nueva Época* 9: 128–147.

Hall, P. (2018). Varieties of capitalism in light of the euro crisis. *Journal of European Public Policy* 25(1): 7–30.

IMT (2021) *Avaliação do regime TVDE — Relatório final.* Lisbon: Instituto da Mobilidade e dos Transportes, I. P.

La Información (2020) (17 April 2020) El mayor jefe de VTC choca con Trabajo: luz roja para tres de sus ERTE en Madrid, La Información. Available at: www.lainformacion.com/empresas/moove-cars-vtc-choca-trabajo-rechaza-tres-erte/6559807/.

Langlois G. and Elmer G. (2019) Impersonal subjectivation from platforms to infrastructures. *Media, Culture & Society* 41(2): 236–251.

Law No. 10/90 of 17 March (1990) Lei de Bases do Sistema de Transportes Terrestres.

Law No. 25/2009 of 22 December (2009) Ley 25/2009, de modificación de diversas leyes para su adaptación a la Ley sobre el libre acceso a las actividades de servicios y su ejercicio. Boletín Oficial del Estado No. 308, 23 December 2009, pp. 108507–108578 (72 pp.). BOE-A-2009-20725. Available at: www.boe.es/eli/es/l/2009/12/22/25.

Law No. 9/2013 of 4 July (2013) Ley 9/2013. Boletín Oficial del Estado No. 160. Jefatura del Estado.

Law No. 45/2018 of 10 August (2018) Lei No. 45/2018. Diário da República No. 154/2018 — Série I, 10 August 2018. Assembleia da República, Lisbon.

Lee M. K., Kusbit D., Metsky E. and Dabbish L. (2015) Working with machines: The impact of algorithmic and data-driven management on human workers. In: *Proceedings of the 33rd Annual ACM Conference on Human Factors in Computing Systems (CHI'15)*. 1603–1612. New York: ACM Press (conference location: Seoul).

Lisbon District Court (2015) Judgment of the Lisbon District Court (Tribunal Judicial da Comarca de Lisboa) — first civil section, 23 April 2015, Case No. 7730/15.OT8LSB — J13. Available at: https://s3.observador.pt/wp-content/uploads/2015/04/decisao-comarca-de-lisboa-uber.pdf.

Marques P. and Hörisch F. (2020) Understanding massive youth unemployment during the EU sovereign debt crisis: A configurational study. *Comparative European Politics* 18(2): 233–255.

MTMAU (2023) *Observatorio del Transporte de Viajeros por Carretera: Oferta y Demanda*. Madrid: Ministerio de Transportes, Movilidad y Agenda Urbana. Available at: https://cvp.mitma.gob.es/observatorio-del-transporte-de-viajeros-por-carretera-oferta-y-demanda-enero-2023.

Muy Pymes (2015) (9 December 2015) Cabify: "somos de las empresas más inspeccionadas de España", Muy Pymes. Available at: www.muypymes.com/2015/12/09/somso-empresas-inspeccionadas-espana.

Observador (2017) (20 January 2017) ANPPAT e ANTUPE — Os parceiros da Uber e Cabify já têm quem os defenda, Observador. Available at: https://observador.pt/2017/01/20/anppat-e-antupe-os-parceiros-da-uber-e-cabify-ja-tem-quem-os-defenda/.

PCP (2017) *Propostas de Alteração à Proposta de Lei No. 50/XIII*. Lisbon: Assembleia da República. Available at: www.parlamento.pt/ActividadeParlamentar/Paginas/DetalheIniciativa.aspx?BID=40897.

PCP (2018) *Propostas de Alteração à Proposta de Lei No. 50/XIII (2)*. Lisbon: Assembleia da República. Available at: www.parlamento.pt/ActividadeParlamentar/Paginas/DetalheIniciativa.aspx?BID=40897.

Portuguese Government (2017) *Cria o regime jurídico do transporte em veículo a partir de plataforma eletrónica*. Proposta de Lei No. 50/XIII (2.ª) — II Série A. Lisbon: Assembleia da República.

PS (2018a) *Propostas de Alteração à Proposta de Lei No. 50/XIII/2*. Lisbon: Assembleia da República. Available at: www.parlamento.pt/ActividadeParlamentar/Paginas/DetalheIniciativa.aspx?BID=40897.

PS (2018b) *Propostas de Alteração à Proposta de Lei No. 50/XIII/2 (2)*. Lisbon: Assembleia da República. Available at: www.parlamento.pt/ActividadeParlamentar/Paginas/DetalheIniciativa.aspx?BID=40897.

PS (2018c) *Propostas de Alteração à Proposta de Lei No. 50/XIII/2 (3)*. Lisbon: Assembleia da República. Available at: www.parlamento.pt/ActividadeParlamentar/Paginas/DetalheIniciativa.aspx?BID=40897.

Público (2018) (22 September 2018) Taxistas mantêm protesto e querem intervenção de Costa, Público. Available at: www.publico.pt/2018/09/22/sociedade/noticia/taxis-associacoes-mantem-protesto-e-querem-intervencao-de-costa-1844967.

Público (2024) (13 July 2024) Há 69 mil licenças de motoristas de TVDE activas em Portugal, Público. Available at: www.publico.pt/2024/07/13/economia/noticia/ha-69-mil-licencas-motoristas-tvde-activas-portugal-2097397.

Rahman S. and Thelen K. (2019) The rise of the platform business model and the transformation of twenty-first-century capitalism. *Politics and Society* 47(2): 177–204.

Royal Decree No. 1057/2015 of 20 November (2015). Boletín Oficial del Estado No. 279. Ministerio de Fomento.

Royal Decree-Law No. 3/2018 of 20 April (2018). Boletín Oficial del Estado No. 97. Jefatura del Estado.
Royal Decree-Law No. 13/2018 of 28 September (2018). Boletín Oficial del Estado No. 236. Jefatura del Estado.
Riesgo Gómez V. (2023) Worker Resistance Strategies and Union Action in Platform Work: The Case of Uber in Spain. *Employee Relations* 45(4): 823–839.
Rosenblat A. and Stark L. (2016) Algorithmic labor and information asymmetries: A case study of uber's drivers. SSRN Scholarly Paper 2686227. Rochester, NY: Social Science Research Network.
RTP1 (2016) (10 October 2016) Prós e Contras, ep. 25, season 14 — "Os táxis e as novas plataformas de transportes". Available at: www.rtp.pt/play/p2233/e253898/Pros-e-Contras.
Spanish Supreme Court (2018) Sentencia de 4 de junio de 2018, de la Sala Tercera del Tribunal Supremo, que estima en parte el recurso interpuesto contra el Real Decreto 1057/2015, de 20 de noviembre. *Boletín Oficial del Estado* No. 174, 19 July 2018, p. 72571. BOE-A-2018-10126.
Thelen K. (2018) Regulating Uber: The politics of the platform economy in Europe and the United States. *Perspectives on Politics* 16(4): 938–953.
Tomassoni F. and Pirina G. (2022) Portugal, um laboratório para a Uber. In: Pavoni A. and Tomassoni F. (eds) *A produção do mundo. Problemas logísticos e sítios críticos*. 249–260. Lisbon: Outro Modo.
Uber (2016) *Posição da Uber sobre o diploma que estabelece o regime jurídico TVDE*. 6 October 2016. Available at: www.parlamento.pt/ActividadeParlamentar/Paginas/DetalheIniciativa.aspx?BID=40897.
Vectio (2017) *Estudio del Servicio del Taxi*. Madrid: Ayuntamiento de Madrid. Available at: www.madrid.es/UnidadesDescentralizadas/UDCMovilidadTransportes/TAXI/Ficheros/Otros/Ayto%20Madrid%20%C2%B7%20Estudio%20del%20Servicio%20del%20Taxi.pdf.
Vieira T. and Mendonça P. (2025) The times, are they changing? Examining platform companies' chameleonic labour process as a response to the Spanish Ley Rider. *Socio-Economic Review* 23(2): 877–898.

Appendix: Interview List and Technical Note

Interview list – Portugal

Interview 1: Social Democratic Party (PSD) member of parliament. Date: 06/05/2022. Site: Lisbon, Portugal.
Interview 2: Left Block (BE) member of parliament. Date: 09/05/2022. Site: Lisbon, Portugal.
Interview 3: Popular Party (CDS-PP) member of parliament. Date: 09/05/2022. Site: via Zoom.
Interview 4: Socialist Party (PS) member of parliament. Date: 24/05/2022. Site: Lisbon, Portugal.
Interview 5: Federation of Transport and Communications Unions (FECTRANS-CGTP) representative. Date: 31/05/2022. Site: Lisbon, Portugal.
Interview 6: Business Association for TVDE Operators (AEO-TVDE) representative. Date: 07/06/2022. Site: Lisbon, Portugal.

Interview 7: Independent Trade Union for TVDE Drivers (SIMTVDE) representative. Date: 07/06/2022. Site: Lisbon, Portugal.
Interview 8: Portuguese Taxi Federation (FPT) representative. Date: 01/07/2022. Site: Lisbon, Portugal.
Interview 9: National Association of Road Transportation in Lightweight Vehicles (ANTRAL) representative. Date: 15/07/2022. Site: Lisbon, Portugal.
Interview 10: Portuguese Communist Party (PCP) member of parliament. Date: 01/08/2022. Site: via Zoom.

Interview list – Spain

Interview 11: Taxi Union of Catalunya (STC) representative. Date: 29/09/2022. Site: via telephone.
Interview 12: *Podemos* member of parliament. Date: 10/11/2022. Site: via Zoom.
Interview 13: General Director of Transports and Mobility Cataluña (DTER) representative. Date: 26/10/2023. Site: via Zoom.

6 Regularising Precarious Public Employment in Portugal and Spain

A Comparative Analysis

Nuno Rodrigues, Paulo Marques, Renato Miguel Carmo, and Maria Asensio

Introduction

The main goal of this chapter is to analyse and compare the Programme for the Extraordinary Regularisation of Precarious Contracts in the Portuguese Public Administration (PREVPAP), launched in 2017 (Law No. 112/2017), and the Spanish *Ley de Interinos*, launched in 2021 (Ley de Interinos, 2021). Both programmes sought to address high levels of precariousness in public administration by regularising and integrating workers on non-permanent contracts. Both national governments negotiated these programmes with public-sector unions and other political parties. In the Spanish case, the European Union (EU) also played an important role.

We adopt a qualitative methodological approach, conducting a comparative case study of the two programmes. We triangulate multiple sources of empirical evidence. Media statements were collected from three leading newspapers in each country – *Público*, *Expresso*, and *Diário de Notícias* for Portugal; *El País*, *ABC* and *El Mundo* for Spain – and analysed to identify the actors involved in the political negotiations and the key issues under discussion. In addition, parliamentary debates – 28 in Portugal and 7 in Spain – were collected and analysed using MAXQDA software, with the aim of identifying the main issues addressed and the relationships between actors. We also collected and analysed other relevant documents and reports, particularly those relating to the design of the two programmes. Finally, we conducted 17 semi-structured interviews with key informants (12 in Portugal, 5 in Spain) to explore their positions on the negotiation processes and the content of each programme. These actors – members of government, members of parliament, and trade-union representatives – were identified through prior analysis of media statements and parliamentary debates. The selection of interviewees was therefore based on their involvement in policy negotiation and decision-making processes.

The chapter proceeds in four sections. First, we analyse Portugal; second, we examine the Spanish case. Third, we compare instruments and outcomes. Finally, we draw out the implications for the theoretical debate, explicitly

DOI: 10.4324/9781003519874-7

linking the findings to ideal types of solidarity, governing social blocs, decision-making arenas, and EU leverage.

Portugal

Background and Actors

The Portuguese public administration underwent a corporatisation process beginning in the 1990s, characterised by the incorporation of New Public Management principles (Madureira, 2015). This process transformed labour relations in public administration. Gonçalves (2013) categorises this as the entrepreneurialisation of public administration, encompassing the diffusion of private-law logics in the recruitment of public employees, the broadening of grounds for dismissal, and, finally, greater restrictions on recruitment. Subsequently, internal devaluation during the austerity years accelerated these changes and included several measures aimed at transforming labour relations in public administration (Caldas, 2012; Campos Lima and Caldas, 2023; Campos Lima et al., 2021). Among other measures adopted in Portugal during this period, the following were pivotal: (*i*) a comprehensive plan to promote the flexibility, adaptability, and mobility of human resources; (*ii*) limits on hiring to achieve annual staffing reductions of 1% in central government and 2% in local and regional government between 2012 and 2014; (*iii*) a nominal freeze of public-sector wages in 2012 and 2013; and (*iv*) restrictions on promotions (Madureira, 2015: 553–554).

PREVPAP was launched following the signing of parliamentary agreements between the Socialist Party (PS) and each of its left-wing partners. Three separate agreements were concluded: the first with the Left Bloc (BE), the second with the Portuguese Communist Party (PCP), and the third with the Ecologist Party "The Greens" (PEV). The agreements included the following measures related to public administration:

- The end of the requalification/special-mobility regime (mentioned in the agreements with BE, PCP, and PEV).
- The right to collective bargaining in public administration (mentioned in the agreements with BE, PCP, and PEV).
- The gradual restoration of public-administration salaries starting in January 2016: 25% in the first quarter, 50% in the second, 75% in the third, and 100% in the fourth (mentioned in the agreement with BE).
- The restoration of public-administration workers' salaries in 2016 (mentioned in the agreements with PCP and PEV).
- The restoration of the 35-hour week in public administration (mentioned in the agreements with PCP and PEV).
- The elimination of hiring restrictions in central, regional, and local public administration (mentioned in the agreements with PCP and PEV).

PREVPAP was among the most emblematic measures of this political period: it was approved at the outset of the political cycle and was the only labour market reform passed in parliament with the support of all left-wing parties. The programme was negotiated between the government, public-administration unions, and parliamentary parties. There was particular emphasis on government–parliament relations. The following unions were involved in the negotiations: the Federation of Public Administration Unions (FESAP), linked to the General Union of Workers (UGT-P); the Common Front of Public Administration Unions (Common Front), linked to the General Confederation of Portuguese Workers (CGTP); and the State Technical Staff Union (STE), which operates as an independent union. The Common Front is the most representative union in the Portuguese public administration (Marques Alves, 2017). For context, it is also important to note that PREVPAP was not the first programme to address high levels of precariousness in the Portuguese public administration (Gonçalves, 2013). In 1998, a similar programme was implemented, based on the automatic identification of precarious workers. Moreover, regularisation did not depend on whether a worker met a permanent need. As explained below, PREVPAP adopted a different approach. Finally, official data help to place PREVPAP in context. As shown in Table 6.1, there was a significant decline in the number of public-sector workers during the austerity period, from 727,701 in 2011 to 659,138 in 2015 (a reduction of 9.4%). The figures then rose steadily in the post-austerity period, reaching 742,194 in 2022 (an increase of 12.6%

Table 6.1 Portuguese public administration: Workers and types of contracts (2011–2022)

	Total number of workers	*Rate of change in the total number of workers*	*Total number of fixed-term contracts*	*Share of fixed-term contracts*
2011	727,701	:	82,985	11.40
2012	699,947	–3.8	83,594	11.94
2013	674,896	–3.6	72,790	10.79
2014	656,363	–2.7	68,602	10.45
2015	659,138	0.4	71,487	10.85
2016	664,162	0.8	75,649	11.39
2017	669,365	0.8	75,567	11.29
2018	683,162	2.1	71,713	10.50
2019	698,924	2.3	74,324	10.63
2020	718,761	2.8	89,726	12.48
2021	733,447	2.0	90,845	12.39
2022	742,194	1.2	89,759	12.09

Source: Directorate-General for Administration and Public Employment (DGAEP), "Estatísticas do Emprego Público" database, 2024.

Methodological note: Data refer to 31 December of each year.

between 2015 and 2022). The same table shows there were 82,985 workers on fixed-term contracts (12% of the total) in 2011; the number fell to 71,487 in 2015 (11%) before rising again to 89,759 (12%) in 2022. In sum, the total number of workers decreased during the austerity years (2011–2015) but increased after 2015, when the PS took office. However, the share of workers with atypical contracts remained broadly stable over 2011–2022. Thus, despite the regularisation undertaken through PREVPAP, there was no structural change in the incidence of precariousness in public administration.

Programme Design

The programme focused on precarious contracts in public administration in 2017. Two main criteria had to be met for individual regularisation to begin: (*i*) the worker had to have a non-permanent contract; and (*ii*) they had to be performing a function constituting a permanent need in the service in which they worked. The programme applied to workers who had been in a precarious situation for at least one year and who were in such a situation between 1 January and 4 May 2017 (Law No. 112/2017). Decisions were taken by committees, the Bipartite Evaluation Commissions, set up for this purpose in each ministry. Two complementary methods were used to identify precarious workers. First, heads of service were to identify permanent needs being met by precarious workers. Second, an online platform allowed precarious workers to submit applications for regularisation. Most requests analysed by the Bipartite Evaluation Commissions came via this platform; however, this route was the most controversial because it placed the onus on individual workers to initiate the process rather than relying on the automatic identification and regularisation of precarious situations.

The application phase began before the programme's final approval and unfolded in two windows: from 11 May to 30 June 2017 and from 6 to 17 November 2017. According to the government's final figures, 28,235 applications were submitted by individual workers, 1,772 workers were identified by heads of service,[1] and 1,950 workers with employment-insertion contracts were later added.[2] In total, 31,957 applications were submitted. The public-sector areas submitting the highest numbers of applications were: Health (8,516); Education (6,895); Science, Technology, and Higher Education (5,981); and Social Security (3,177).

Each case was evaluated by the Bipartite Evaluation Commissions on a case-by-case basis. Where a decision was positive, a tender was launched to regularise that worker. The Bipartite Evaluation Commissions comprised representatives of the Ministries of Finance and Labour; managers of the services responsible for the applications under review (i.e., the service to which the worker under review belonged); and union representatives. Unions were therefore in a minority. Some political parties contested this, arguing that there should have been parity between government and trade-union representatives. As noted by a BE Member of Parliament (MP):

> And that's what we proposed: an equal number of employers' representatives and workers' representatives and they must choose a president by consensus, that is, if the union says 'No, we don't trust this guy', he can't be president. This was a way of tying the president to both sides. This is not what happened, because the very composition of the Bipartite Evaluation Commissions was unbalanced in favour of the Government; the Government was always able to take the final decision.
>
> (Interview 2)

The evaluation process in the Bipartite Evaluation Commissions was marked by delays and by differing interpretations. Public-administration unions gave a negative assessment of how the Bipartite Evaluation Commissions conducted the processes (Público, 2017). Finally, it is important to note that regularisation applied only to workers who fulfilled a permanent need in public administration and who were in a precarious situation in 2017. It was therefore an exceptional response to precariousness in public administration. No new forms of recruitment or regularisation of precarious workers in public administration were introduced after this programme.

Negotiation Dynamics

The first step in the negotiation process was the establishment of a parliamentary working group to prepare the programme, after which contributions from public-administration unions were sought. The process concluded with approval of the law by the Council of Ministers on 29 June 2017 and by Parliament on 13 October 2017. The programme was approved with PS, BE, PCP, PEV, and the People–Animals–Nature Party (PAN) voting in favour, and the centre-right Social Democratic Party (PSD) and the Popular Party (CDS-PP) voting against. It should be noted, however, that some amendments proposed by PCP and BE during the parliamentary debate were rejected by PS. The following paragraphs detail how negotiations unfolded with unions and then with political parties.

Content analysis of the interviews indicates that FESAP was the union closest to the PS government's position, while the Common Front took a critical stance towards PREVPAP. The unions directly linked to public administration (FESAP and the Common Front) referred more frequently to tensions among left-wing partners. The Common Front was critical of the position of PCP (and other partners to the left of PS), arguing that the programme was too close to PS preferences (Interview 4) and that PCP conceded too much to PS demands. FESAP opposed the stance of the radical-left parties, especially their criticism of the programme (Interview 8). Moreover, FESAP was the only actor other than the government representatives we interviewed to consider PREVPAP a balanced programme (while acknowledging limitations and delays in the Bipartite Evaluation Commissions). In their view, it was the only feasible programme given the political context and the situation of public administration (Interview 8). Unions also criticised the central role given to parliament. The Common Front stated in an interview that its positions were not sufficiently considered (Interview 4); together with the CGTP confederation, it argued that unions lacked bargaining power because there was no mechanism for automatic identification and regularisation. According to a Common Front representative, this would have enabled the regularisation of more situations:

> The names of the people are there; the years are there. You don't have to say 'look, I've been there for four years.' It was just necessary to publish the list of people and then they [...] if it was a tool that had been discussed with us, we would have gone further [...] I'm not saying we would have solved the sixty thousand, but I reckon we would have reached fifty thousand.
>
> (Interview 4)

As mentioned above, PREVPAP was approved in parliament by PS and its left-wing partners but opposed by the right-wing parties. Nonetheless, differences existed even among those who voted in favour. On the left, debate centred on the definition of concepts such as precariousness and permanent need, the methods for identifying and regularising workers, and the functioning of the Bipartite Evaluation Commissions. During parliamentary negotiations, several important changes stemmed from these differences. In the first version, a worker in a precarious situation would have needed at least three years' service to access a tender for regularisation; this was subsequently reduced to one year following pressure from PS's left-wing partners (Interviews 1, 2, 5). Another significant change, again at the suggestion of the two radical-left parties, was the broadening of the profile of workers eligible for regularisation under PREVPAP. They succeeded in extending the programme to trainees and scholarship holders, workers with employment-insertion contracts, and to local public administration (Interviews 1, 2, 5). Radical-left parties also called for a change in the method of regularisation, opposing the permanent-need criterion (Interviews 1, 2, 3, 5, 12); PS rejected this change. The government and PS were therefore primarily responsible for the final design of the programme on this point. As one former cabinet member told us: "some government partners were in favour of a process of automatic regularisation and administrative identification of situations" (Interview 3). Even before final approval, the BE MP José Soeiro argued in parliament that the concept of 'permanent need' required greater clarification, anticipating the political struggle over its meaning and application in the Bipartite Evaluation Commissions:

> The [issue] I wanted to raise concerns the criterion for identifying a permanent need [...], because that criterion has to be substantial and not formal. For example, a teacher who has been at IEFP [Portuguese Public

> Employment Services] for 15 years is not self-employed. Even if you are paid on green receipts for 18 hours' teaching, [3] we know this is a full-time job because, in addition to the paid teaching hours, you have to attend meetings, prepare classes.
>
> (National Parliament, 2017a: 19)

Another point of controversy was the identification of precarious contracts. Here, PCP was particularly critical of the final version of the programme. As the PCP MP Rita Rato argued in parliament, automatic identification and regularisation were crucial:

> We propose the mandatory preparation by the services of the list of workers with precarious ties and its delivery to the representative structures of the workers who participated in the Bipartite Evaluation Commissions.
>
> (National Parliament, 2017b: 62)

In short, although the radical left acknowledged that PREVPAP enabled the regularisation of thousands of precarious workers, it criticised the government for the programme's design, scope, and delays. The central political debate concerned the appropriate method of regularisation, particularly the understanding and application of concepts such as precariousness and permanent need.

PS's position was shaped in part by the experience of a similar programme in 1998. In an interview, a government member involved in negotiating and implementing PREVPAP observed that the 1998 programme had not been well received by many public-administration workers and had followed a logic that PREVPAP sought to avoid (Interview 11). The problem was that workers who had built their careers through open competitions were dissatisfied to see others benefit from automatic regularisation.

Right-wing parties tended to reject the very existence of such a programme, as illustrated by the following statement from a CDS-PP MP:

> Regarding PREVPAP, there is a question of principle. The principle for contracting in public administration should be the tender. And PREVPAP, like all other processes of extraordinary regularisation of precarious workers in public administration, means trampling on what should be the basic principle of hiring for the public administration.
>
> (Interview 6)

Figure 6.1 shows a tri-polar configuration of frames and actors drawn from the parliamentary debates. On the left-hand side, PSD and CDS-PP cluster closely with the codes 'Against' and 'Poorly-designed reform,' signalling both a principled rejection of extraordinary regularisation and a technical critique of its architecture. On the opposite side, PCP, BE, and PEV gravitate towards 'Solidarity,' recognising the programme's

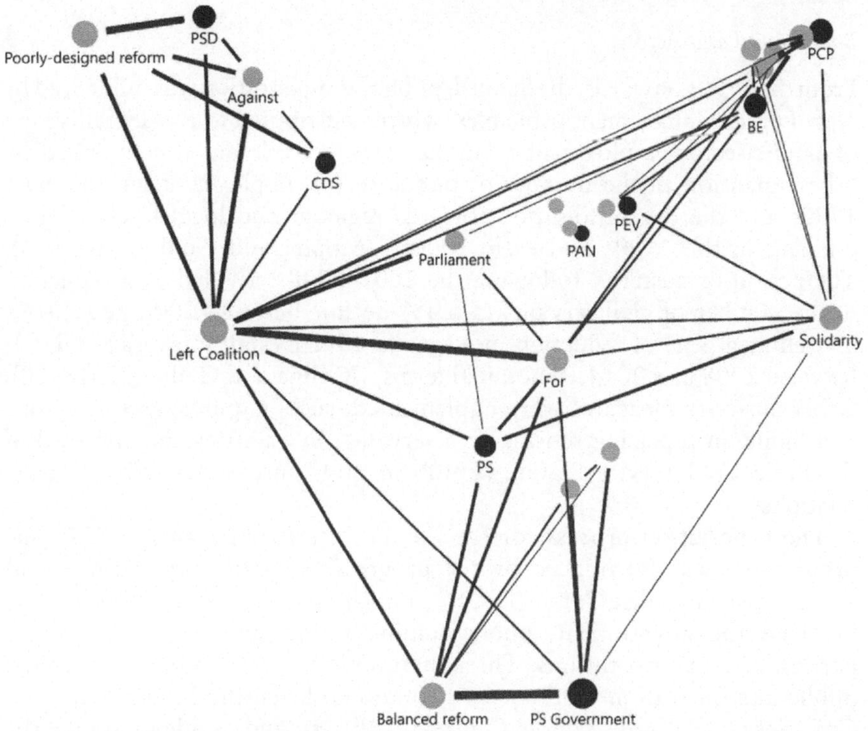

Figure 6.1 Connections between key themes in the legislative process and political actors in parliament (Portugal).

Note: Key: black: political actors (parties and the government); grey: dimensions of analysis.
Source: Authors' elaboration using the MAXMaps tool in MAXQDA.

inclusive intent while pressing to widen eligibility and curb discretion in the Bipartite Evaluation Commissions. PS and the Government hold the centre of the map, strongly connected to 'Balanced reform' and 'For,' defending the final compromise (permanent-need criterion and open competitions) as the feasible equilibrium under the prevailing constraints. The central position of 'Parliament,' bridging 'Left Coalition,' 'For,' and the executive, confirms that law-making, rather than social concertation, was the decisive arena, consistent with the changes negotiated during the legislative process. PAN aligns with 'For' but without a strong attachment to either normative frame. Overall, the code map captures both the three political camps and the distinct justificatory frames they deployed: PS/governmental balance; radical-left solidarity with demands for greater reach; and a right-wing blend of opposition in principle and criticism of design.

Spain

Background and Actors

From the 1990s onwards, the Spanish public administration was influenced by New Public Management principles, which contributed to the flexibilisation of public-sector employment relations. This process was accompanied by "the expansion in the number of public sector employees from the early 1980s and the decentralisation towards regional and local levels of government in the 1990s and early 2000s" (Molina and Godino, 2018: 4). The period of austerity following the 2007–2008 crisis led to a reduction in the number of civil servants (a 6.4% decline between 2008 and 2016), as well as a general reduction in wages (a 15–20% fall in average salaries between 2008 and 2014, in nominal terms) (Molina and Godino, 2018: 10). Other austerity measures were implemented, such as public-sector lay-offs and limits on replacing retiring civil servants. In addition, the approval of the Basic Civil Service Statute (EBEP) in 2007 further liberalised labour relations.

The negotiation process for the *Ley de Interinos* began in 2021. The programme was introduced by the progressive coalition government of the Spanish Socialist Party (PSOE) and *Unidas Podemos*. Negotiations involved the government, public-administration unions, parliamentary parties, and EU institutions. Three main union organisations represented public-administration workers at the national level: the Independent and Civil Servants' Trade Union Centre (CSIF), an independent union; the General State Administration Sector (FSC-CCOO), affiliated with the Trade Union Confederation of Workers' Committees (CCOO); and UGT – Public Administration (UGT-AP), linked to the General Workers' Union (UGT-S). Once an agreement had been reached with these unions, the programme was validated by the Council of Ministers. This was followed by negotiations in Parliament to secure final approval of the bill, essentially between PSOE, *Unidas Podemos*, and their preferred partners on the left. In parallel, negotiations also took place between the government and the EU.

Official data on the Spanish public administration highlight the importance of this programme. Data presented in Table 6.2 show that the number of workers in public administration declined during the austerity period but has recovered in recent years. The total number of civil servants in 2022 exceeded that in 2011 (3,526,200 compared with 3,234,700). Table 6.2 also indicates that this increase was accompanied by a rise in the proportion of workers in precarious situations, approximately three times that in Portugal. Precariousness is particularly high in the education and health sectors (Molina and Godino, 2018), which helped to legitimise the adoption of a programme of this kind in a post-pandemic context. Given its recent introduction, it is not yet possible to assess the programme's impact.

Table 6.2 Spanish public administration: Workers and types of contracts (2011–2022)

	Total number of workers	*Rate of change in the total number of workers*	*Total number of fixed-term contracts*	*Share of fixed-term contracts*
2011	3,234,700		769,859	23.8
2012	3,021,100	–6.6	592,136	19.6
2013	2,909,400	-3.7	578,971	19.9
2014	2,927,500	0.6	603,065	20.6
2015	3,000,700	2.5	657,153	21.9
2016	2,986,100	–0.5	680,831	22.8
2017	3,074,700	3.0	741,003	24.1
2018	3,211,000	4.4	844,493	26.3
2019	3,253,300	1.3	904,417	27.8
2020	3,379,100	3.9	1,010,351	29.9
2021	3,475,500	2.9	1,073,930	30.9
2022	3,526,200	1.5	1,064,912	30.2

Source: National Statistics Institute (INE, 2024), "Encuesta de Población Activa" database.
Methodological note: Data refer to 31 December of each year.

Programme Design

The programme stipulated that precarious contracts would be regularised through automatic identification. This meant that if a post had been occupied by a worker for more than three years without a permanent contract, a tender had to be held. As a result, regularisation did not require the specific post to be deemed a permanent need; the existence of a precarious situation for three or more years was sufficient for regularisation. Tenders were merit-based, with an evaluation process that included mechanisms recognising the experience of precarious workers who had held these posts. Given the diversity of cases, they were divided into two broad groups.

- In cases where the precarious situation had lasted between three and five years, the tender was open, i.e., external candidates could apply. Nevertheless, criteria weighted prior experience. If incumbent workers did not remain in public administration, they were entitled to compensation of 20 days' pay per year of service, capped at 12 months' salary.[4]
- If the precarious contract had been in place for more than five years, the tender was restricted, i.e., only the incumbent worker could apply. Nevertheless, the worker's competence was assessed. If they did not pass this assessment, they were compensated on termination.

The *Ley de Interinos* aimed not only to regularise the situation of workers who had been in a precarious situation for more than three years, but also to provide a structural response to precariousness in public administration. It did so by establishing procedures to prevent the recurrence of high levels of non-permanent contracts in the future. The programme therefore formed part of a broader strategy to reform public administration. Among these procedures, it is worth noting that any post that had been precarious for more than three years had to be regularised.[5] Penalties were introduced for administrations and autonomous communities that failed to comply with the established criteria for recruitment and regularisation. For example, if a precarious post was not regularised after three years, services were on notice that the post could be abolished. The programme aimed to reduce the share of atypical employment from 30% to 8%, with a view to modernising and organising human resources in public administration. It therefore established guidelines and measures to curb the use of precarious contracts (Font, 2022). The first phase of the programme was scheduled for completion by 31 December 2024. According to official data from the Spanish public administration, the programme could affect around 300,000 workers, i.e., all those who had been in a precarious situation since January 2016 (the point from which the three-year rule applied in the programme's first phase).

Negotiation Dynamics

Negotiations involved unions, political parties, and EU institutions. Final approval in Parliament was secured with 175 votes in favour, from PSOE, *Unidas Podemos*, the Republican Left of Catalonia (ERC), the Basque Nationalist Party (EAJ-PNV), and part of the Plural parliamentary group (a coalition of small left-wing parties). There were five abstentions: one member of the Popular Party (PP), one member of the *Unidas Podemos* parliamentary group, and three members of the Mixto parliamentary group. Votes against came from PP, VOX, *Ciudadanos*, part of the Plural parliamentary group, Basque Country Unity (EH-Bildu), and some members of the Mixto parliamentary group. Although EH-Bildu was one of the government's main negotiating partners, it did not support the programme because it believed it did not go far enough. Final approval was reached on 22 December 2021. Below, we detail how negotiations unfolded, first with unions and then with political parties and EU institutions.

The political negotiations between the government and the unions began in February 2021. An agreement was signed on 5 July 2021, the day before the programme was approved by the Council of Ministers. The trade unions sought to address two main issues (Interviews 14 and 17). The first concerned the legitimacy and legal certainty of the forms of regularisation, with a view to avoiding the judicialisation of tenders. This was one of the most debated aspects throughout the process, especially in relation to unopposed tenders, which were modified during the parliamentary negotiations (see below). Secondly, unions wanted to ensure that workers' previous experience would be recognised and valued despite the use of tenders, and that workers who did not retain their posts after a tender would be compensated for dismissal. The issue of legal certainty for unopposed tenders was frequently mentioned. In an interview, the CSIF representative expressed concern about changes made in Parliament:

> Unfortunately, the parliamentary process introduces new elements that, in our view, can be overturned by the Constitutional Court. [...] [T]he final result of the law raises doubts because it creates legal uncertainty.
>
> (Interview 14)

In the same vein, Unai Sordo, CCOO General Secretary, made clear that this change was the unions' main criticism of the process: '[S]ometimes you want to do things that you cannot do legally. I hope that this agreement will not be a problem in this respect' (El País, 2021). As explained below, there was lively debate on this amendment in Parliament, as several MPs questioned its legal basis (Font, 2022).

Parliamentary negotiations followed those with the unions. The parties supporting the PSOE–*Unidas Podemos* government demanded several changes before approving the decree in Parliament. The most significant was the introduction of an unopposed tender procedure for posts that had been precarious for more than five years. As a senior government member stated, these changes were 'a demand of the partners in Parliament,' i.e., a 'condition for the approval of the decree' (Interview 16). The interviewee also noted that the automatic regularisation of all precarious situations was demanded by the government's traditional parliamentary partners, but this was impossible due to legal constraints and even EU guidelines on contracting. What was agreed, therefore, was the introduction of a tender process that took into account workers' prior skills and experience:

> The parliamentary negotiation [...] meant that, depending on seniority [...] some would only have access to a merit-based competition, in which professional experience was valued, and other academic merits [...] It was a demand of the political bargaining of the government partners. They wanted an automatic process.
>
> (Interview 16)

This is consistent with what a PSOE MP involved in the negotiations told us. He stated that the final version of the law had to be negotiated with parliamentary partners, who pressed the government to broaden the possibilities for regularising precarious workers:

> The political forces did not want to validate the Royal Decree-Law because it did not include the possibility of a civil servant who had been working in the public administration for several years being given a permanent

> contract. Our Constitution [...] did not allow the regularisation and direct attribution of the status of public official to a person [...] In this agreement, together with other left-wing political parties, we were able to open up the possibility of seeking improvements in the processing of the bill and of finding a formula leading to a solution.
>
> (Interview 13)

EU influence was significant and evident throughout the negotiations in the Spanish case, for three reasons. First, a ruling by the European Court of Justice on the high level of precariousness in the Spanish public administration is cited in the preamble to the *Ley de Interinos*: "the doctrine established by the European Court of Justice in this matter provides that the Spanish authorities have to establish effective measures that dissuade and, where appropriate, clearly sanction the abuse of temporality" (Ley de Interinos, 2021: 165070). Second, the programme was shaped by Spain's Recovery and Resilience Plan, as approval of the programme was a precondition for receiving EU funding. Both reasons were noted in an interview with a senior member of government:

> It is related to the Recovery and Resilience Plan, because it is included in component 11 of the Plan [...] Component 11 [...] includes the reduction of temporary employment. What is also important is that [...] in addition to being a structural problem [...] there is an infringement procedure opened in the European Court against Spain, so the fact that it is included in the Plan is not a coincidence.
>
> (Interview 16)

The EU also influenced the programme's legal design (Interview 16). In particular, EU institutions made clear that certain public-procurement procedures had to be observed. The EU opposed the automatic regularisation of all workers, i.e., without tenders.

Figure 6.2 displays three distinct clusters of frames and actors. On the right-hand side, the PSOE–*Unidas Podemos* government and Unidas Podemos are tightly connected to 'Balanced reform' and 'For,' defending the final compromise as the legally secure way to stabilise long-term interim posts. By contrast, left regional parties gravitate towards 'Reform could go further,' using plenary debates to press for wider eligibility and simpler stabilisation routes; this also explains why some of them, notably EH-Bildu, ultimately voted against on grounds of insufficient ambition. The national right (PP and *Ciudadanos*) clusters around 'Poorly-designed reform' and 'Against,' criticising the regularisation tracks, especially the unopposed procedure for posts vacant for more than five years, as failing merit and transparency tests. 'European Pressure' occupies a bridging position: it is invoked across camps both to legitimise faster stabilisation in line with European Court of Justice doctrine and the Recovery and Resilience Plan milestones, and to demand

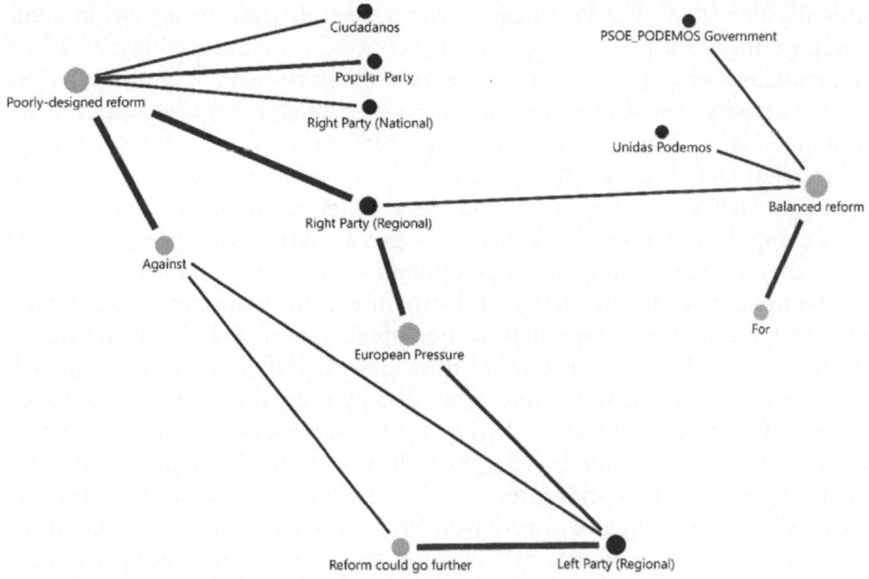

Figure 6.2 Connections between key themes in the legislative process and political actors in parliament (Spain).

Note: Key: black: political actors (parties and the government); grey: dimensions of analysis.

Source: Authors' elaboration using the MAXMaps tool in MAXQDA.

stricter competitive procedures. Overall, the map confirms our reading: government actors framed the law as a balanced fix; left regional parties sought deeper inclusion; and the right opposed it on grounds of design and legality.

Identifying the Key Differences between the Two Programmes

There are three fundamental differences between the two programmes. First, they were conceptualised differently, with divergent understandings of precariousness and of 'permanent need.' Second, distinct methods were used to identify the workers to be regularised. Third, the level of precariousness in public administration differed between the two countries.

In the Portuguese programme, a temporary contract can be converted into a permanent one only if the worker is performing an activity deemed a permanent need; this is not the case in the Spanish programme. As explained throughout the chapter, PREVPAP adopted a stricter conception of precariousness, in that it allowed regularisation only for workers meeting a permanent need, regardless of the duration of their precarious situation. The Bipartite Evaluation Commissions were responsible for defining and applying the concept of 'permanent need,' and difficulties of interpretation and application arose, helping to explain why the process took longer than initially expected. The Portuguese programme also assumed that, in some circumstances, the use of non-permanent contracts was acceptable even where individuals had worked for several years in the same post, because the nature of the activity was held to justify this stance. By contrast, the Spanish programme assumes that if a post has remained precarious for more than three years, that fact alone is sufficient to treat it as a permanent need and to regularise it. Hence, regularisation after three years is automatic, albeit subject to a compulsory tender. The concepts of precariousness and permanent need were therefore understood and operationalised differently in the two policies, with implications for the design and structure of the respective programmes. The programmes also differ in how individual workers are identified prior to regularisation. In Portugal, a more individualised and discretionary approach was followed: applications were submitted by individual workers, although heads of service could also identify cases for regularisation. In Spain, a more automatic and rule-based approach was adopted: the process did not depend on individual applications or on identification by heads of service, since all posts that had been precarious for more than three years had to be regularised. In other words, whereas the Portuguese model adopts a more conditional and case-contingent logic, the Spanish model is more unconditional and universalist in the way workers are regularised. Finally, the level of precariousness in the two countries' public administrations differed. As noted

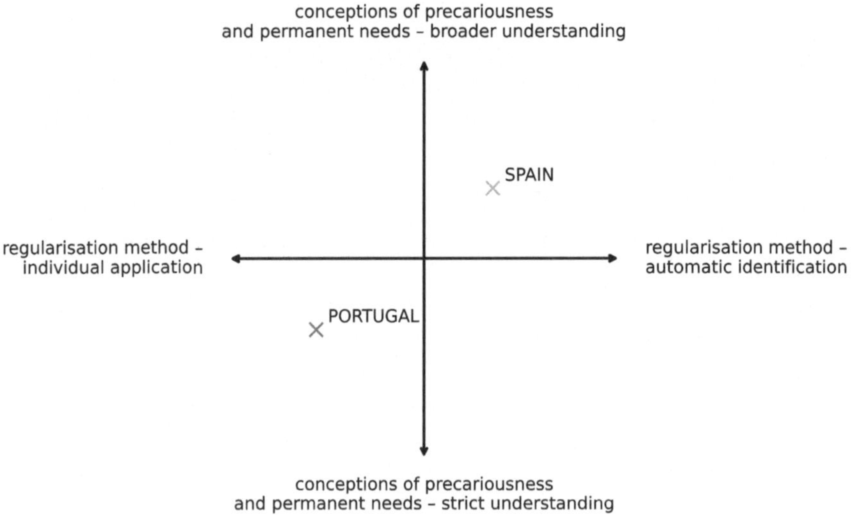

Figure 6.3 Regularisation method and conceptions of precariousness and permanent need in PREVPAP and the *Ley de Interinos*.

Source: Authors' elaboration.

above, the proportion of precarious workers in the Spanish public administration was approximately three times that in Portugal. In our view, this situation, together with the post-pandemic timing of the Spanish law, legitimised the design and adoption of a more ambitious programme in Spain.

Taking these differences as analytical axes and locating their respective end-points, Figure 6.3 categorises PREVPAP and the *Ley de Interinos*. The y-axis refers to conceptions of precariousness and permanent need (strict versus broad), and the x-axis refers to the regularisation method (individual application versus automatic identification). The figure shows that the two cases diverge markedly, lying in opposing quadrants.

Discussion and Conclusions

Portugal's PREVPAP and Spain's *Ley de Interinos* both sought to curb atypical employment in the public sector. Substantively, both amount to a public-sector variant of inclusive solidarity: they raise universal floors of employment security for outsiders without dismantling insiders' protections. Yet the two trajectories differ in ambition and institutional foundation, differences that our framework helps to explain.

Consistent with Chapter 1, we conceptualise competitive solidarity as reform packages that trade off selective gains for outsiders against continued flexibilisation elsewhere – typically by lightening protection for standard contracts and emphasising activation – whereas inclusive solidarity extends universal guarantees (stronger, uniform employment protection and non-contingent rights). Read through this lens, both programmes are predominantly inclusive: neither relied on labour-market liberalisation in the public sector, nor did they offset regularisation with deregulatory concessions.

Important nuances nonetheless allow us to gauge each programme's distance from the ideal types. Predominantly inclusive reforms can still contain competitive inflections, and the Portuguese programme exhibits several. First, regularisation required individual applications rather than automatic identification, privileging individualised over collective solutions. Second, precarious employment was deemed acceptable in certain functions, signalling a contingent tolerance of flexibility; by contrast, the Spanish programme treated precariousness lasting more than three years as unacceptable. Third, posts in Portugal remained subject to open competition, whereas in Spain tenders were unopposed where the incumbent had performed the role for more than five years. On these grounds, the Portuguese programme is less inclusive than its Spanish counterpart.

In terms of governing social blocs, both reforms were legislated by Left–Union configurations: in Portugal, a PS minority backed in parliament by BE and PCP, with active involvement from trade unions, including those affiliated with the CGTP, who, despite opposing certain aspects, maintained participation and engagement in the process; in Spain, a PSOE–*Unidas Podemos* coalition with strong union support. Differences in political architecture nonetheless mattered. In Portugal, parliamentary-support agreements instead of a coalition government enabled PS to reject amendments proposed by its left partners and trade-union confederations (particularly CGTP). In Spain, the governing bloc positioned itself further to the left and unions played a more significant role in shaping the programme; substantial changes were introduced in parliament to secure the backing of the government's left-wing partners. This configuration enabled a more ambitious reform in Spain.

Decision-making arenas also mattered. In a field where the state is the employer, tripartite concertation plays a limited role; outcomes hinged on bipartite negotiation with unions and, crucially, on parliamentary law-making. As anticipated in Chapter 2, legislating in parliament allowed governing blocs to move closer to their inclusive ideal points.

The EU–national interplay likewise differed. Portugal's programme dates to 2017, immediately after the Troika intervention – a phase marked by austerity and civil-service headcount restraint – rendering the environment less conducive to public-sector regularisation. Spain's reform unfolded in a more favourable European context. Inclusive-solidarity initiatives were more readily accommodated (Branco et al., 2024), facilitating approval of the *Ley de Interinos*, among others. Moreover, Spain legislated after the COVID-19 pandemic, which legitimised greater investment in the public sector (Di Carlo et al., 2024: 6). In this sense, the EU acted as a conditional amplifier: the post-Maastricht liberalising trajectory had long constrained public-sector stabilisation, but the pandemic-era 'social turn' – embodied in Recovery and Resilience Plan milestones and supportive jurisprudence – expanded the space for inclusive reform.

Table 2.2 in Chapter 2 formalises the contrast. PREVPAP maps onto Constellation 2 (Left–Union + Parliament + Liberal EU): an inclusive outcome that is high but bounded – visible in individualised applications, acceptance of 'structural' temporariness for some functions, and continued reliance on open competitions. Ley 20/2021 maps onto Constellation 1 (Left–Union + Parliament + Social EU): maximal inclusive intensity – automatic stabilisation tracks, sanction-backed deadlines, and a general presumption against long-duration temporariness. This chapter thus corroborates Chapter 2's claim that bloc composition is necessary for the solidaristic orientation of change, while arena structure and EU stance condition its intensity.

Notes

1 Data are available at: https://prevpap.gov.pt/ppap/javax.faces.resource/docs/PREVPAP_em_numeros_20180115.pdf

2 Employment-insertion contracts are active labour market policies aimed at reintegrating unemployed individuals through temporary work opportunities, often in the public or non-profit sectors. These are usually government-subsidised and include social security contributions.

3 "Green receipts" is the term used in Portugal for payments to self-employed workers.
4 Negotiations with the Autonomous Communities reduced compensation for dismissal from 33 to 20 days' pay per year of service where an employee did not secure the post following the tender. The unions opposed this (El Mundo, 2021).
5 As stated in the final wording of the law: "[t]he purpose of this Law, in full compliance with budgetary regulations, is to reinforce the temporary nature of interim personnel; to clarify the procedures for access to the status of interim personnel; to objectify the causes for termination of such personnel and to implement a system of responsibilities that constitutes a proportionate, effective and dissuasive mechanism for future non-compliance that also clarifies any gaps or interpretative doubts that the current regulations may have generated." (Ley de Interinos, 2021: 165071).

References

Branco R., Miró J. and Natili M. (2024) Back from the cold? Progressive politics and social policy paradigms in Southern Europe after the Great Recession. *Politics & Society* 52(4): 630–661.

Caldas J. C. (2012) *The Consequences of Austerity Policies in Portugal*. Friedrich-Ebert-Stiftung.

Campos Lima M. P. and Caldas J. C. (eds) (2023) *A persistência da Desvalorização do Trabalho e a Urgência da sua Revalorização*. Coimbra: Almedina.

Campos Lima M. P., Martins D., Costa A. and Velez A. (2021) Internal devaluation and economic inequality in Portugal: Challenges to industrial relations in times of crisis and recovery. *Transfer* 27(1): 47–73.

DGAEP [Directorate-General for Administration and Public Employment] (2024) Estatísticas do Emprego Público database. Available at: www.dgaep.gov.pt/index.cfm?OBJID=91dad2e4-245d-488f-a8e6-b6e83891e9ad (accessed 16 October 2024).

Di Carlo D., Ibsen C. L. and Molina O. (2024) The new political economy of public sector wage-setting in Europe: Introduction to the special issue. *European Journal of Industrial Relations* 30(1): 5–30.

El Mundo (2021) (30 June 2021) Iceta ofrece una indemnización de 20 días por año trabajado a todos los interinos que suspendan el examen y pierdan su puesto. Available at: www.elmundo.es/economia/macroeconomia/2021/06/30/60dc606afc6c83555a8b461a.html (accessed 16 October 2024).

El País (2021) (13 November 2021) Los sindicatos advierten sobre la inseguridad jurídica de dar una plaza fija a los interinos que lleven más de cinco años. Available at: https://elpais.com/economia/2021-11-13/los-sindicatos-advierten-sobre-la-inseguridad-juridica-de-dar-una-plaza-fija-a-los-interinos-que-lleven-mas-de-cinco-anos.html (accessed 16 October 2024).

Font J. G. (2022) The strategy to reduce temporary employment in public employment in Law 20/2021: A balm of beasts to definitively eradicate long-term interim relationships or a provisional solution to muddle through? *Revista de Estudios de la Administración Local y Autonómica* 18: 77–99.

Gonçalves N. (2013) *O progresso da ideia de gestão empresarial na administração pública portuguesa*. PhD thesis. Lisboa: ISCTE-IUL.

INE [National Statistics Institute] (2024) Encuesta de Población Activa database. Available at: www.ine.es/jaxiT3/Tabla.htm?t=4262&L=0 (accessed 16 October 2024).

Law No. 112/2017, de 29 de Dezembro. Estabelece o programa de regularização extraordinária dos vínculos precários. Diário da República. Available at: https://diariodarepublica.pt/dr/detalhe/lei/112-2017-114425584 (accessed 16 October 2024).

Ley de Interinos (2021) Ley 20/2021, de 28 de diciembre, de medidas urgentes para la reducción de la temporalidad en el empleo público. *Boletín Oficial del Estado*. Available at: www.boe.es/eli/es/l/2021/12/28/20 (accessed 16 October 2024).

Madureira C. (2015) A reforma da Administração Pública Central no Portugal democrático: do período pós-revolucionário à intervenção da troika. *Revista de Administração Pública* 49: 547–562.

Marques Alves P. (2017) A participação sindical na negociação coletiva na administração pública. In: Paula U., Maria M. S., Fátima A. (eds) Proceedings of the II International Meeting of ISSOW. 196–215. Almada, Portugal.

Molina Ó. and Godino A. (2018) *Bargaining for Social Rights in the Public Sector: Spain*. Amsterdam, Netherlands: University of Amsterdam.

National Parliament (2017a) Reunião Plenária de 16 de Fevereiro de 2017. Available at: https://debates.parlamento.pt/catalogo/r3/dar/01/13/02/052/2017-02-16 (accessed 16 October 2024).

National Parliament (2017b) Reunião Plenária de 13 de Outubro de 2017. Available at: https://debates.parlamento.pt/catalogo/r3/dar/01/13/03/008/2017-10-13/62 (accessed 16 October 2024).

Público (2017) (25 September 2017) CGTP desafia Governo a apresentar listas de precários. Available at: www.publico.pt/2017/09/25/economia/noticia/cgtp-desafia-governo-a-apresentar-listas-de-precarios-1786672 (accessed 16 October 2024).

Appendix: Interview List and Technical Note

Interview list – Portugal

- Interview 1: Portuguese Communist Party (PCP) member of parliament. Date: 16/05/2021. Site: Lisbon, Portugal.
- Interview 2: Left Bloc (BE) member of parliament. Date: 17/05/2021. Site: via Zoom.
- Interview 3: Cabinet member of the governing Portuguese Socialist Party (PS). Date: 20/05/2021. Site: Lisbon, Portugal.
- Interview 4: Common Front of Public Administration Unions (Common Front) representative. Date: 23/05/2021. Site: Barreiro, Portugal.
- Interview 5: Ecologist Party "The Greens" (PEV) member of parliament. Date: 01/06/2021. Site: via Zoom.
- Interview 6: Popular Party (CDS-PP) member of parliament. Date: 02/06/2021. Site: Lisbon, Portugal.
- Interview 7: General Confederation of the Portuguese Workers (CGTP) representative. Date: 09/06/2021. Site: Lisbon, Portugal.

- Interview 8: Federation of Public Administration Unions (FESAP) representative. Date: 09/06/2021. Site: Lisbon, Portugal.
- Interview 9: General Union of Workers (UGT-P) representative. Date: 20/06/2021. Site: via Zoom.
- Interview 10: Social Democratic Party (PSD) member of parliament. Date: 12/07/2021. Site: Lisbon, Portugal.
- Interview 11: Cabinet Member of the governing Portuguese Socialist Party (PS). Date: 06/08/2021. Site: via Zoom.
- Interview 12: Portuguese Socialist Party (PS) member of parliament. Date: 19/10/2022. Site: Lisbon, Portugal.

Interview list – Spain

- Interview 13: Spanish Socialist Party (PSOE) member of parliament. Date: 01/07/2022. Site: via Zoom.
- Interview 14: Independent and Civil Servants' Trade Union Centre (CSIF) representative. Date: 07/07/2022. Site: via Zoom.
- Interview 15: Popular Party (PP) member of parliament. Date: 31/08/2022. Site: via Zoom.
- Interview 16: Cabinet Member of the Spanish Socialist Party (PSOE)–*Unidas Podemos* coalition government. Date: 29/09/2022. Site: via Zoom.
- Interview 17: UGT – Public Administration (UGT-AP) representative. Date: 21/11/2022. Site: via Zoom.

Technical note: Parliamentary debates were analysed using MAXQDA 2022. The dataset comprised 28 debates from Portugal and seven from Spain.

7 Conclusion

Comparative Insights from a Decade of Iberian Labour Market Reforms

Rui Branco, Paulo Marques, and Renato Miguel Carmo

Introduction

Set against decades of liberalisation and dualisation (Rueda, 2005; Streeck, 2009; Palier and Thelen, 2010), this volume documents a significant countermovement over the past decade in Iberia, restoring elements of labour market solidarity and marking a decisive break from policies pursued before and during the European sovereign-debt crisis. Progressive coalition governments in both Portugal and Spain have, despite internal tensions and hesitations, enacted important reforms to enhance workers' protections and labour conditions across several domains. This "turn to solidarity" is carefully documented through detailed comparative analyses of reforms in four specific labour market policy arenas: (i) employment-protection legislation and collective bargaining (Chapter 3), (ii) statutory minimum-wage setting (Chapter 4), (iii) regulation of passenger-transport platforms (Chapter 5), and (iv) the conversion of atypical public-sector contracts into permanent positions (Chapter 6).

However, this resurgence of solidaristic reform is far from uniform: distinct strategic orientations emerge within the Iberian context. Spain's reform trajectory consistently aligns with the inclusive ideal type, characterised by broad re-regulation and de-commodification intended to benefit the workforce as a whole. Portugal, by contrast, presents a more heterogeneous profile. In two cases, the regularisation of precarious public-sector employment and statutory minimum-wage increases, the outcomes approximate the inclusive model, yet they incorporate competitive mechanisms (e.g., in public-sector recruitment processes) and offsets for employers (e.g., compensatory fiscal measures accompanying minimum-wage upratings). The remaining Portuguese reforms, employment protection legislation and platform-work regulation, fit squarely within the competitive ideal type, improving market conditions primarily for outsiders while maintaining, or even expanding, deregulation for insiders. Thus, Portugal exhibits a dual pattern, comprising both near-inclusive and straightforwardly competitive reforms, whereas Spain delivers predominantly inclusive outcomes across the four areas.

DOI: 10.4324/9781003519874-8

Chapters 1 and 2 set up the analytical framework required for interpreting the empirical variation documented in this volume. Chapter 1 elaborates the ideal-typical logics of competitive and inclusive solidarity. Chapter 2 advances an actor-centred account in which the composition of governing social blocs is the necessary, though not sufficient, determinant of reform orientation. It distinguishes a Left–Union bloc (emphasising inclusive solidarity) from a Centrist–Employer bloc (emphasising competitive solidarity) and specifies how arena-specific veto structures – the consent constraint and joint-decision logic in tripartite social concertation versus the absence of an institutional employer veto in parliamentary law-making – shape feasible outcomes. The European Union (EU) is theorised as a conditional external selector, whose 'liberal' and 'social' phases alternately constrain or enable solidaristic change.

Chapters 3–6 provide empirical evidence supporting these theoretical expectations, illustrating how the different compositions of governing social blocs in Portugal and Spain explain the divergent reform trajectories. Portuguese reforms aligned with competitive solidarity were enacted by centrist blocs that joined centre-left and centre-right parties, moderate unions, and employers' associations, prioritising social concertation to minimise parliamentary pressures. Conversely, Spain's uniformly inclusive reforms were driven by left blocs comprising centre-left and radical left parties with substantial incorporation of organised labour, achieved through political exchanges in both electoral and corporatist arenas. These inclusive reforms were compatible with, and sometimes propelled by, supportive European-level pressures. Notably, social concertation significantly influenced one major reform in Spain but played a limited or no role in other reforms, demonstrating variability in concertation's impact.

This chapter proceeds as follows. It first subjects our central argument regarding the primacy of governing social blocs to two empirical tests. Initially, we undertake a most-different comparison strategy, examining cases of divergent policy outcomes – specifically employment protection and collective bargaining reforms, as well as the regulation of platform work – to determine whether distinct configurations of governing social blocs explain Portugal's competitive and Spain's inclusive trajectories. Subsequently, we apply a most-similar comparison approach, analysing cases of statutory minimum-wage policies and the regularisation of precarious public-sector employment, which are both broadly inclusive in orientation, to assess whether similarly constituted left-wing blocs consistently underpin inclusive outcomes and to explore whether internal variations within these blocs account for differences in the extent of inclusivity. Moreover, we evaluate the role played by different decision-making arenas, specifically examining the strategic deployment or circumvention of social concertation mechanisms relative to parliamentary processes, alongside the varying degrees of EU support or constraint. In keeping with Chapter 2, we treat arena choice as endogenous to bloc priorities, a strategic variable that governments deploy in light of anticipated vetoes. After presenting these empirical analyses, we revisit the theoretical framework, highlight this book's contributions to comparative political economy and employment-relations scholarship, and conclude by drawing strategic lessons relevant for trade unions and progressive political parties.

Governing Social Blocs and the Spectrum of Solidarity in Iberian Labour Market Reforms

This section proceeds in two analytical steps. We begin with a contrasting pair of reforms where Portugal and Spain diverged to test whether differing governing social blocs, European orientations, and decision-making arenas account for competitive versus inclusive outcomes. We then turn to a couple of inclusive reforms to ask whether broadly similar left blocs are the precondition for inclusivity in both countries and to probe whether differences in other dimensions explain the varying depth of that inclusion. Consistent with Chapter 2, we use actor-centred bloc labels throughout: the Left–Union bloc (progressive centre-left plus radical left and class-oriented unions) and the Centrist–Employer bloc (centrist parties, employers' associations and moderate unions).

Inclusive vs Competitive Solidarity: Sectoral Contrasts in Iberian Labour Market Reform

As detailed in Chapter 3, Portugal's 2019 Labour Code reform strengthened outsiders by tightening the rules on fixed-term contracts and bogus self-employment. It nevertheless fell well short of a comprehensive re-regulation of the labour market. While it provided gains for precarious workers, the legislation simultaneously intensified the commodification of open-ended contracts (most visibly by lengthening trial periods) and left three cornerstones of the previous liberal settlement untouched: the end of ultra-activity in collective agreements, the abandonment of the *favor laboratoris* principle, and the curtailed severance pay for no-fault individual dismissal. The package therefore exemplifies competitive solidarity: advances for outsiders are offset by deregulatory concessions and the preservation of earlier cut-backs in labour law. Politically, the reform rested on a Centrist–Employer bloc formed by the Socialist Party (PS) with Social Democratic Party (PSD)/People's Party (CDS-PP), employers' confederations and the General Union of Workers (UGT-P), operating under concertation's consent constraint. The PS deliberately privileged social concertation, sidelining the more militant General Confederation of Portuguese Workers (CGTP) and avoiding a parliamentary arena in which the radical left enjoyed greater leverage – an archetypal deployment of arena choice as an endogenous strategy to limit the radical left's parliamentary leverage. The bill eventually passed only because the centre-right PSD and CDS-PP abstained. European economic governance, already edging towards a 'social turn' after the closure of the Excessive Deficit Procedure in 2017, further smoothed the path by repeatedly urging Portugal to address labour market segmentation.

Spain's 2021 reform improved the position of all salaried workers: it reinstated ultra-activity, curtailed temporary hiring, and re-established the primacy of sectoral agreements in collective bargaining. Some austerity-era changes, however, were left intact – most notably the lower severance pay for no-fault individual dismissal and, in certain domains, the precedence of company-level over sectoral collective agreements. The governing Left–Union bloc combined a PSOE–*Unidas Podemos* coalition with strong incorporation of the General Workers' Union (UGT-S) and the Trade Union Confederation of Workers' Committees (CCOO). Employers, internally divided and politically weakened, nevertheless endorsed the tripartite accord. The radical left's leverage was considerably greater than in Portugal: *Unidas Podemos* held cabinet portfolios and Yolanda Díaz served both as Minister of Labour and as Second Vice-President. European dynamics also differed. Negotiations took place after the pandemic, when Spain's Recovery and Resilience Plan made labour market reform, and above all the fight against *temporalidad* (excessive reliance on temporary contracts), a condition for substantial investment flows. This hierarchical European push, within the EU's social-turn configuration as a conditional external selector, combined with the stronger left presence in government, secured employer assent but provoked an unprecedented public clash between the Spanish Confederation of Business Organisations (CEOE) and the opposition Popular Party (PP), the latter accusing the government of allowing social dialogue to eclipse parliamentary scrutiny. Thus, social concertation played an important role in the making of the Spanish reform.

Viewed side by side, the two reforms occupy opposite ends of the solidarity spectrum, yet neither represents a "pure" ideal type. Portugal's 2019 Labour Code reform sits closer to competitive solidarity: while it afforded outsiders tighter limits on fixed-term contracts and bogus self-employment, it preserved Troika-era concessions to employers and even further commodified permanent contracts. By contrast, Spain's 2021 reform veers towards inclusive solidarity, reinstating ultra-activity, curbing temporary hiring, and restoring sectoral primacy. Even so, Madrid deliberately left in place the leaner severance pay for no-fault dismissals and, in some areas, the precedence of firm-level agreements. Such concessions temper the reform's redistributive reach and soften its impact on established insiders, thereby making a tripartite deal palatable to a divided employers' camp. Timing also matters. Lisbon legislated during the early "social turn" of EU governance, when Country-Specific Recommendations (CSRs) still counselled caution; Madrid acted in the post-pandemic phase, when Recovery and Resilience Plan milestones and the promise of sizeable EU transfers exerted a far stronger hierarchical push. These contrasting European contexts help explain why a centrist bloc sufficed in Portugal, whereas a left coalition underwritten by robust EU incentives was needed to secure employer assent in Spain.

As analysed in Chapter 5, the Portuguese Law 45/2018 legalised digital platforms in the passenger transport sector (TVDE), setting them as direct competitors to the highly regulated taxi trade. The measure massively expanded the supply of rides but did so on the basis of comparatively weakly protected driver jobs: TVDE operators face no caps on fleet size or pricing, and driver requirements are lighter than for taxis. Consequently, a two-tier driver market emerged in which an expanding cohort of outsiders constrains insiders through low-cost competition. In our typology, the orientation is one of competitive solidarity. Politically, the statute reflected a Centrist–Employer bloc (PS–PSD–CDS-PP aligned with platform firms), legislated via parliamentary law-making rather than concertation. Radical left parties – Left Bloc (BE) and the Portuguese Communist Party (PCP), taxi associations and the CGTP opposed the bill, demanding full alignment between TVDE and taxi regulation. Decision-making was confined to parliament; social concertation played no role. The European dimension proved facilitative, as the Court of Justice of the EU had recently affirmed that platform-mediated transport constitutes a transport service, rather than a digital, service.

In Spain, Royal Decree-Law 13/2018 charted a distinctly different course. Most notably, it retained the "1-to-30" rule (no more than one digital-platform (VTC) licence for every 30 taxi licences in a given Autonomous Community), thereby capping the potential size of the app-based fleet. The law also restricted the territorial scope of services: VTC journeys must both start and finish within the Autonomous Community that issued the licence, and any cross-border trip is counted against a stringent annual quota. A four-year transition period (2018–2022) allowed platforms and licence holders to adjust, after which all authorisations exceeding the 1-to-30 cap were set to lapse automatically. Crucially, the decree devolved regulatory authority to the Autonomous Communities, enabling them to impose even stricter conditions – such as local operating permits, minimum vehicle sizes, or environmental standards – and it introduced a more stringent sanctions regime for breaches. By limiting territorial expansion and aligning newcomer obligations with taxi regulations, the measure pursued fairer, rather than simply greater, competition, thus advancing an inclusive solidarity logic. The supporting coalition constituted a well-defined Left–Union bloc (PSOE, *Unidas Podemos*, UGT-S, CCOO, and taxi unions). Employers and the centre-right PP–*Ciudadanos* camp opposed the decree as excessive regulation. As in Portugal, the legislation was adopted in Parliament rather than negotiated through social concertation. EU-level influence was comparable to the Portuguese case: the same Court of Justice of the EU ruling on Uber provided legal backing for stricter national regulation, but the EU did not play a crucial role in this domain.

Both statutes were adopted in 2018, at the onset of the EU "social turn", and neither passed through the traditional corporatist channel. Crucially, the external constraints were almost identical: both Portugal and Spain faced the same Court of Justice judgement on Uber, broadly similar Semester recommendations, and no hard-law conditionality attaching EU funds to a particular regulatory design. Yet the policy outcomes diverged sharply. In Lisbon, a centrist bloc linking the PS to the main right-of-centre parties read the European signals as an endorsement of market opening: the reform pursued a competitive logic, privileging fleet expansion and lower consumer prices. In Madrid, a clear left bloc made up of PSOE, *Unidas Podemos*, and the two major union confederations interpreted the same EU cues as a permission to "level up": the decree curtailed platform growth to protect labour standards and mitigate dualisation. This contrast underscores a central claim of the book: European impulses are, in themselves, unable to account for cross-national variation. They provide a permission structure, not a deterministic script. What proves decisive is the domestic governing social bloc that filters, refracts, and ultimately translates Brussels' signals into concrete legislation. The Portuguese alliance selected the liberalising elements of the EU agenda, while the Spanish coalition foregrounded its social-protective potential. The upshot is clear: similar European incentives can be, and were, accommodated within radically different regulatory logics. Far from being epiphenomenal, the composition of the governing social bloc is the pivotal variable that determines whether EU guidance is harnessed for competitive liberalisation or for inclusive re-regulation.

Taken together, these parallel reforms reinforce our central claim: the make-up of the governing social bloc determines whether solidaristic regulation takes a competitive or an inclusive form. To probe this claim further, the ensuing section turns to statutory minimum-wage policy and the regularisation of precarious public-sector employment, arenas in which both Portugal and Spain adopted inclusive reforms. Examining these cases allows us to test whether inclusive outcomes invariably depend on the governing social blocs and, crucially, whether variation in the degree of inclusivity can be traced to differences in the composition of the governing social blocs.

Inclusive Solidarity: From Wage Floors to Employment Security

As analysed in Chapter 4, raising the statutory minimum wage is, in principle, a quintessentially inclusive reform: it raises the earnings of every employee, irrespective of contract status, without eroding anyone's existing rights.

In Portugal, the rise from €505 in 2015 to €705 in 2022 was steered by a Left-Union configuration centred on PS–BE in parliament and UGT-P in social concertation (in the early rounds), not by a centrist governing social bloc. The Socialist minority government had already pledged to the radical left BE a fixed path to €600 by 2019, which meant that only the first two upratings in 2016 and 2017 were actually negotiated in tripartite concertation; even those pacts, signed by employers and the moderate UGT-P, were boycotted by the CGTP and condemned by BE and the PCP because they coupled the higher floor with temporary payroll-tax rebates for firms. When the centre-right PSD and CDS-PP unexpectedly joined BE and the PCP in January 2017 to overturn the second rebate, tripartite bargaining collapsed. All subsequent increases were set unilaterally by the government, usually sweetened with one-off tax credits, without any formal pact with employers or endorsement from the parliamentary right, leaving an incomplete but decisive left bloc of PS plus BE (in parliament) and UGT-P (in social concertation) to carry the policy. European-Semester warnings about wage moderation encouraged this incremental, compensation-laden approach, yet the reform's orientation remained broadly inclusive: it raised the wage floor for all employees, even if fiscal offsets muted its redistributive bite.

Spain's trajectory was faster and less consensual, but it began with a moderate path negotiated by the centre-right. In late 2017 Mariano Rajoy's PP government signed a tripartite pact with CEOE, Spanish Confederation of Small and Medium-Sized Enterprises (CEPYME), UGT-S, and CCOO that set the statutory minimum wage at €735.9 for 2018 (a 4 per cent raise) and sketched a gradual route towards roughly €850 in 2020, conditional on GDP and employment targets. When the PSOE took office in mid-2018 and later formed a coalition with *Unidas Podemos*, it abandoned that timetable: by royal decree and bilateral deals with the unions it imposed a record 22 per cent leap to €900 from January 2019, a move denounced by the employers' association CEOE as a blow to social dialogue. Subsequent upratings, some endorsed by employers, others agreed only with the unions, pushed the floor to €1,184 by 2025, a cumulative rise of about 61 per cent. Throughout, no systematic fiscal offsets to employers were granted. Ministers presented the acceleration as both a social justice commitment and compliance with the EU goal of a minimum at 60 per cent of the median wage, citing the forthcoming Adequate Minimum Wage Directive and milestones in Spain's Recovery and Resilience Plan.

Taken together, the two cases show that an inclusive-solidarity measure can take sharply different shapes depending on who is inside the governing coalition. In Portugal an incomplete left alliance made up of PS and BE in parliament and UGT-P in social concertation kept employers nominally on board and tempered each uprating with targeted offsets, stretching the climb over six years. In Spain, a more cohesive political left under PSOE–*Unidas Podemos* brushed aside CEOE's veto and front-loaded the gains, lifting the floor by more than 60 per cent in six years with no compensatory sweeteners. The key variable, therefore, is the leverage secured by business: where employers retain a seat, the rise is gradual and cushioned; where they are sidelined, it is swift and openly redistributive.[1] With the wage-floor cases mapped, the analysis now turns to the regularisation of precarious public-sector jobs to test whether similar coalition logics shape inclusion there.

As discussed in Chapter 6, granting permanent status to fixed-term employees in the public administrations of Portugal and Spain constitutes an inclusive reform: it broadens employment security without eroding rights elsewhere. Nevertheless, the generosity of the two programmes diverges, and this divergence can be attributed to the composition of the governing social bloc.

Portugal's programme to regularise atypical employment in the public administration (PREVPAP) converted fixed-term contracts into permanent ones only when the post was judged a 'permanent need' and the employee submitted an individual application via an online platform; even successful applicants subsequently had to pass an open recruitment competition. The initiative originated in a parliamentary bargain between the minority Socialist government and the radical left and was the only labour market reform endorsed by all left parties by a vote in Parliament (PS, PCP, BE, and the Greens). Social dialogue was limited to consultation. The unions exhibited divergent stances: while the UGT-P-affiliated Federation of Public Administration Unions (FESAP) endorsed the measure, the CGTP-aligned Common Front, despite participating in the process and supporting certain aspects, criticised specific elements, particularly the stringent eligibility criteria and the marginalisation of concertation. This incomplete left bloc, made up of centre-left government, radical left parties, and a moderate union, left the class-oriented CGTP's preferences largely unaddressed. Even so, the CGTP engaged at workplace level, serving on the committees that assessed individual cases and seeking to shape implementation despite opposing elements of the reform. Overall, the scheme is less inclusive than its Spanish counterpart: individualised applications, the stringent 'permanent need' test, and competitive examinations introduce features characteristic of competitive solidarity.

In Spain, Law 20/2021 on the stabilisation of public employment required that any position filled on a temporary basis for more than three years be regularised; identification of such posts was automatic rather than subject to application. Positions vacant for three to five years were opened to public competition with experience credits, whereas those vacant for more than five years were reserved for the incumbent through an "unopposed" tender. The law also introduced sanctions to curb future over-reliance on temporary staff and set a target of cutting the share of fixed-term contracts from 30 per cent to 8 per cent. Within a cohesive Left–Union bloc, the PSOE–*Unidas Podemos* cabinet negotiated a bilateral pact with the three main public-sector unions before legislating; only afterwards were additional concessions negotiated in Parliament to win regional-left votes, broadening the bill's scope. A European Court of Justice ruling on abusive temporary employment practices, together with Recovery and Resilience Plan milestones, provided legal and financial incentives for swift action. In this context, a cohesive left bloc comprising coalition partners plus strongly incorporated unions was willing to bypass opposition from right-wing parties, producing a decisively inclusive outcome.

Both reforms required support from a left-wing parliamentary majority and some form of union incorporation; nevertheless, the strength of radical left parties and the depth of trade-union engagement proved decisive. Portugal's minority PS relied on concertation only for advice and retained competitive procedures that limited coverage. Spain's coalition, facing a far higher incidence of temporality, embraced automaticity, union bilateralism, and parliamentary enlargement, delivering a broader and faster regularisation.

Viewed together, the two policy arenas reproduce the same fault-lines. In Portugal, a Left–Union bloc delivered reforms that were inclusive in aim yet diluted in execution: payroll-tax rebates moderated the minimum-wage hikes, while PREVPAP's individual applications, "permanent-need" filter, and competitive examinations pruned the pool of beneficiaries. Spain, by contrast, wielded a cohesive triangle of PSOE, *Unidas Podemos*, and the two union confederations; employers were consulted but could not veto change, and robust EU incentives strengthened the coalition's hand. The same constellation that front-loaded a 61 per cent wage rise also enacted Law 20/2021, using automatic identification and incumbent reservation to stabilise hundreds of thousands of posts. Whether the object was minimum wage pay or public employment security, the depth of inclusion turned not on the policy field itself but on the cohesion of the governing social bloc and the room it left for employer vetoes. Strong, unified left alliances reinforced by supportive European leverage pushed solidarity to its inclusive maximum; fragmented coalitions that kept one ear open to business produced a thinner, competitive-tinged version of the same ideal.

Comparative Synthesis

Table 7.1 presents the eight Iberian reforms in a single snapshot and, read horizontally, reveals a remarkably coherent pattern.[2] In Portugal, every measure shepherded by the Centrist-Employer bloc is marked by filled circles (●), signalling competitive solidarity: the 2019 Labour Code amendment shows double filled circles (●●), and the 2018 TVDE statute triple filled circles (●●●), each tightening rules for outsiders while preserving, or even amplifying, market pressure on insiders. Whenever legislation instead rested on a Left-Union parliamentary alignment, filled triangles (▲) appear and the orientation turns inclusive: the successive minimum wage upratings and PREVPAP both register double filled triangles (▲▲), broadening protection for the workforce as a whole, though without reaching the highest tier of generosity. Spain offers the mirror image. Throughout the period a cohesive PSOE–*Unidas Podemos* coalition, consistently backed by UGT-S and CCOO, produced no competitive filled circles (●); every reform carries filled triangles (▲), albeit with varying intensity. The 2021 employment-protection package records double filled triangles (▲▲), whereas every statute driven through Parliament achieves the maximum triple filled triangles (▲▲▲): the 2018 VTC decree, the 2020–2025 minimum-wage series, and the 2021 regularisation of precarious public-sector staff.

The decision-arena symbols clarify these gradations. Pacts concluded in social concertation (hollow diamond, ◇) prove the most modest: Portugal's

Table 7.1 Varieties of solidarity, decision arenas, governing social blocs, and EU leverage in Iberian labour market reforms

	Policy Arena	*Solidarity Orientation*	*Decision Arena*	*Governing Social Bloc*	*EU Leverage*
Portugal	Employment protection and collective bargaining	●●	◇	PS minority + PSD + CDS-PP + UGT-P and all employers' associations *Centrist–Employer bloc*	✓
	Passenger-transport platforms (TVDE)	●●●	■	PS + PSD + CDS-PP + Platform firms *Centrist–Employer bloc*	✓✓
	Statutory minimum wage	▲▲	◇/■	PS + UGT-P + Employers (some years) + BE *Left–Union bloc, incomplete*	✗✗
	Regularising fixed-term public-sector employment	▲▲	■	PS + FESAP + BE + PCP + PEV + Common Front (the latter four organisations opposed some dimensions) *Left–Union bloc*	
Spain	Employment protection, and collective bargaining	▲▲	◇	PSOE + *Unidas Podemos* + UGT-S + CCOO + CEOE *Left–Union bloc*	✓✓✓
	Passenger-transport platforms (VTC)	▲▲▲	■	PSOE + *Unidas Podemos* + regional left + taxi unions *Left–Union bloc*	✓✓
	Statutory minimum wage	▲▲▲	■	PSOE + *Unidas Podemos* + UGT-S + CCOO (CEOE supported once but opposed almost all years) *Left–Union bloc*	✓✓✓

(*Continued*)

Table 7.1 (Continued)

Policy Arena	Solidarity Orientation	Decision Arena	Governing Social Bloc	EU Leverage
Regularising fixed-term public-sector employment	▲▲▲	■	PSOE + *Unidas Podemos* + regional left + UGT-S + CCOO + CSIF *Left–Union bloc*	✓✓✓

Source: Own elaboration by the authors.

Key:

- A filled triangle (▲) marks a reform oriented to inclusive solidarity, whereas a filled circle (●) marks one oriented to competitive solidarity. The number of identical symbols (one, two, or three) indicates how far the measure moves in that direction: a single symbol shows a limited shift, a double symbol a substantial shift, and a triple symbol the maximum shift attainable in the political circumstances.
- Decision-making arenas are signalled by shapes: a filled square (■) denotes a statute or decree pushed through Parliament or the Council of Ministers, while a hollow diamond (◇) identifies a binding tripartite pact concluded in social concertation.
- In the "EU leverage" column, ticks (✓) indicate that European instruments facilitated the reform, whereas crosses (✗) show that they constrained it. Again, intensity is graded: one tick or cross reflects a mild, largely rhetorical influence; two signal a strong push or drag (for example, a draft directive or explicit CSRs); three denote a decisive "policy sword" whose funding conditionality or legal obligation shaped the final outcome. Intensity is assessed by combining the formal strength of the EU instrument with its political salience in domestic debate. A blank cell means that no EU pressure of consequence was detected.

annual minimum-wage deals plateau at double filled triangles (▲▲) because compensatory tax breaks were built in for employers, and Spain's concerted labour-market reform likewise stops at double filled triangles (▲▲) after CEOE insisted on retaining slimmer dismissal rules and limited firm-level opt-outs. Once bargaining shifts to the Parliament or the Council of Ministers, indicated by a filled square (■), ceilings lift: Portugal's TVDE law climbs to triple filled circles (●●●) on the competitive side, while Spain's parliamentary statutes achieve triple filled triangles (▲▲▲) on the inclusive side. PREVPAP reminds us that a parliamentary route alone does not guarantee top-tier inclusivity: the final compromise retained competitive examinations that constrained coverage, leaving the measure at double filled triangles (▲▲).

European leverage adds a further layer. In Portugal, reforms were steered mainly by mid-level facilitators – pre-pandemic Semester recommendations and the 2017 CJEU Uber ruling – providing only a gentle tailwind, marked in the table by single or double ticks (✓/✓✓). Three Spanish reforms, by contrast, operated under the weighty shadow of the Recovery and Resilience Plan and the Adequate Minimum Wage Directive, shown as triple ticks (✓✓✓); this post-pandemic conditionality strengthened the government's hand vis-à-vis a divided employers' front and helped deliver ambitious statutes at the triple-triangle level (▲▲▲). Where European pressure pulled in the opposite direction, as in Portugal's minimum-wage negotiations, flagged with double crosses (X X) for Semester advice on wage restraint, the outcome was trimmed from a potential triple-triangle result (▲▲▲) to a more modest double-triangle one (▲▲).

Finally, the Iberian cases remind us that the left is anything but monolithic. Spain's PSOE–*Unidas Podemos* coalition operated in tandem with two partnership-oriented confederations whose partisan ties have largely lapsed (Marques and Fonseca, 2022), forming a stable triangle effective in both concertation and parliamentary arenas. Portugal's left bloc is more brittle: the class-oriented CGTP rarely signs pacts, the smaller UGT-P has frequently sided with centrist forces, and the radical left remains organisationally fragmented. These fissures encourage the PS to construct centrist alliances on contentious dossiers such as employment protection (Branco et al., 2024).

Taken as a whole, Table 7.1 refines, and partially qualifies, the analytical framework set out in Chapters 1 and 2. An inclusive outcome indeed requires a Left–Union bloc, but triple filled triangles (▲▲▲) materialise only when that bloc is cohesive, employers lose (or cannot exercise) their veto, and strong EU incentives reinforce domestic ambitions. Remove any one of these pillars – weak European impetus in Portugal, an employers' veto within concertation, or divisions among left actors –competitive logics re-emerge through fiscal offsets, quota systems, or residual deregulatory clauses. In this sense, the Iberian evidence confirms the book's central proposition; governing social blocs are the primary drivers of reform orientation, while showing that their impact is decisively filtered by decision arenas and supranational leverage.

From Dualisation to Varieties of Solidarity: Theoretical Contributions

Set against three decades of liberalisation and dualisation, this book identifies a clear counter-movement – "counterpoints", to borrow Rodríguez and Lucio's (2023: 18, 51–72) Polanyian phrasing – visible in recent Iberian developments. Since 2015, Portugal and Spain have restored elements of solidarity to labour markets long marked by segmentation and deregulation. In doing so, both countries depart from the dominant trajectory observed between 1990 and 2015 in most co-ordinated or mixed-market economies (Ferragina and Filetti, 2022; Ferragina et al., 2023). Our findings challenge interpretations that treat dual labour markets as stable equilibria or liberalisation as an inexorable trend. They also extend the emerging "solidarity" literature by showing that counter-trends need not confine themselves to upgrading outsiders' positions alone. By theorising how de/dualisation intersects with de/commodification, we propose a spectrum of "varieties of solidarity" and, empirically, distinguish different solidaristic orientations across four labour-market arenas in two national cases.

This section places those insights within the wider literatures in comparative political economy, comparative industrial relations, and social-bloc theory. We first reassess liberalisation and dualisation theses in light of our evidence. We then specify the political and institutional conditions under which dualisation and liberalisation can be reversed. Finally, we draw out the implications for the social-bloc perspective developed in Chapter 2.

Rethinking Liberalisation and Dualisation

Debates in comparative political economy pivot on two powerful claims: first, that advanced capitalist economies are travelling inexorably along a common, liberalising path; second, that once reforms bifurcate labour markets, a dualised equilibrium settles in and proves remarkably resilient. The liberalisation thesis portrays a broadly homogeneous rise in the commodification of labour, acknowledging only country-specific variation in pace and scope, largely attributable to "obstacles to employer discretion" that differ across institutional settings (Baccaro and Howell, 2017: 172). The dualisation argument points to a different endpoint: successive two-tier reforms have pitted insiders' interests against those of outsiders, and this insider–outsider configuration is cast as a stable equilibrium rooted either in a producer coalition at the core of manufacturing (Palier and Thelen, 2010) or in the strategic collusion of unions and social-democratic parties (Rueda, 2005). Conceptually, the first lineage derives from the varieties-of-capitalism approach; the second from the economic insider–outsider framework (Marques and Salavisa, 2017: 137–139).

Mounting evidence now qualifies both claims. Regulation has proved more fluid than expected – even, strikingly, in Mediterranean labour markets long seen as archetypically dual (Eichhorst and Marx, 2021). Reforms have not only upgraded outsiders' rights; in some cases they have also re-regulated conditions for insiders and outsiders alike. The chapters in this volume join recent work documenting such reversals (Bulfone and Tassinari, 2021; Marques and Fonseca, 2022; Branco et al., 2024; Marques et al., 2025a; Bondy et al., 2025; Alvariño et al., 2025).

Our theoretical contribution is to specify why reversals take distinct solidaristic forms. Liberalisation and dualisation generate a structural tension: as atypical employment spreads, downward pressure reaches standard workers; and as protections for permanent contracts erode, employers' bargaining power rises, ultimately weakening insiders as well. This growing interdependence re-opens political space for inclusive solidarity (policies that re-regulate both tiers). Yet a second trajectory is possible: competitive solidarity, whereby policymakers tighten rules on atypical work while loosening protections for permanent jobs. Dualism narrows in both paths, but risk is shifted back on to some insiders in the latter, leaving the overall drift more liberalising.

A large literature has examined when dualisation can be reversed, with particular attention to the centre-left and the radical left. Some studies underline the decisive role of centre-left parties when they govern in coalition with radical left partners (Marques and Fonseca, 2022), especially under proportional electoral rules (Iversen and Soskice, 2015). Others emphasise realignment pressures on the centre-left as outsiders grow electorally salient and politically mobilised (Schwander, 2019; Bürgisser and Kurer, 2021). A third line highlights the incentives for ideologically cohesive minority governments or ideologically divided majority coalitions to seek union cooperation to broaden social support and engage additional parties in parliament to bolster political legitimacy (Rathgeb, 2018). Although this literature is highly relevant, it does not account for the existence of the different forms of solidarity mentioned previously.

To elucidate when reforms tend towards inclusive solidarity or competitive solidarity, it is essential to consider the interaction of three critical factors: the composition of the governing social bloc, the chosen decision-making arena (social concertation versus parliamentary dynamics), and the influence of EU governance mechanisms.

Additionally, our findings indicate that the critical factor was not solely the occurrence of collaboration between the centre-left, the radical left, and trade unions, but rather the particular configuration that this collaboration took, which also reflects the cohesion within the Left–Union bloc and elucidates the interplay between the Left-Union and Social Concertation dimensions. In Spain, the radical left emerged from the sovereign debt crisis strengthened, entering a formal coalition with the PSOE in 2019, thereby acquiring decisive influence over labour market reform. Moreover, there was a clear alignment between the major trade union confederations and left-wing parties. By contrast, Portugal's 2015 *Geringonça* represented a form of contract parliamentarism through separate bilateral accords between the PS and each radical left party, agreements that notably excluded several labour market topics. The four Portuguese left parties were never in the same negotiating room, reflecting deeper frictions than in Spain and indicating a more fragmented governing bloc. Additionally, the most representative trade union confederation, CGTP, did not sign any tripartite agreement. This lack of cohesion played a significant role.

In the field of comparative industrial relations, there is a substantial body of work dedicated to exploring solidarity within the labour market, with a particular emphasis on the circumstances that prompt trade unions to adopt pro-outsider orientations. Comparative industrial relations scholarship has shown that unions can represent outsiders alongside standard workers where: (i) power resources are institutionally embedded in encompassing bargaining systems and protective legislation limiting employer exit (Doellgast et al., 2018); (ii) class-oriented unions, typically more inclusive, resist concessions at outsiders' expense (Marques et al., 2025b); (iii) unions include significant numbers of atypical workers whose voices are integrated through democratic internal structures (Lindvall and Rueda, 2014; Thelen, 2014; Mosimann and Pontusson, 2017; Vlandas, 2018); and (iv) unions prioritise mobilisation strategies after losing institutional power, including attenuated ties to centre-left parties (Baccaro et al., 2003; Dorigatti, 2017).

Yet much of this literature treats politics as an exogenous backdrop. Ground-level studies, such as ethnographies of outsourcing struggles in German manufacturing (Dorigatti, 2017) or reviews of firm-level campaigns against precarity (Carver and Doellgast, 2020), foreground intra-organisational bargaining while relegating labour-law regimes or national bargaining structures to the status of fixed constraints. Even the inspiring approach of Doellgast et al. (2018), which links inclusive outcomes to union capacities and encompassing institutions, gives limited purchase on how peak-level confederations seek to reshape those very institutions. Our analysis bridges this gap by locating the decisive locus of change in governing social blocs, not merely workplace coalitions, where union strategies, employer preferences, and partisan alignments intersect to condition reform trajectories.

Implications for Social-Bloc Theory

Our findings have four implications for the scholarship on social blocs reviewed in Chapter 2. First, when analysing specific public policies rather than the formation of electoral majorities, the decisive arena for bloc formation lies at the level of governing social blocs. In both countries, inclusive solidaristic public policies emerged when partisan and union actors coalesced into a recognisable Left–Union bloc, whereas outcomes tended towards more competitive templates where the Centrist–Employer bloc prevailed.

Second, Iberian developments indicate that bloc cohesion, rather than bloc type *per se*, sets the attainable ceiling of inclusivity. Inclusive legislation was most far-reaching when Left–Union blocs displayed internal unity and when unions were strategically embedded in governmental decision-making. Spain's 2021 employment-relations reform exemplifies this: cabinet-level radical left participation, coupled with close union alignment, enabled a far-reaching restructuring of the rules governing collective bargaining. Where cohesion was looser (Portugal), outsider gains were counterbalanced by new flexibilities for insiders. In short, the typology in Chapter 2 generalises well, but cohesion also plays a role.

Third, bloc composition interacts systematically with decision arenas. Parliamentary routes, especially for minority centre-left governments reliant on radical left votes, insulate reform from an employer veto and enable cohesive Left–Union blocs to legislate closer to inclusive standards. By contrast, social concertation expands legitimacy but inserts an employer veto that predictably trims inclusive ambition or marries outsider's gains with compensations to employers elsewhere. The bloc perspective thus helps explain when executives choose parliament over social concertation, and how that choice maps onto the distributional profile of the law ultimately adopted.

Fourth, the Iberian comparison refines the bloc approach's treatment of the EU as a conditional selector. The same Left-Union constellation yielded more inclusive outcomes when EU leverage supplied normative cover and material incentives (Spain, post-pandemic), whereas in its absence (Portugal, earlier timing) even left-leaning settings produced more bounded inclusion.

Taken together, the evidence urges comparative political economy and comparative industrial relations scholarship to view labour market change as the outcome of a three-way articulation among governing social blocs, decision arenas, and supranational incentives. First, dualism is neither an iron cage nor an inevitable staging post on a one-way road to liberalisation: trajectories can bend towards markedly different "varieties of solidarity", from business-friendly competitive fixes to far-reaching inclusive settlements. Second, whether a country moves down one path or the other hinges less on abstract institutional "obstacles to employer discretion" than on the concrete balance of power within the bloc linking parties and producer groups. Third, the depth of any solidaristic turn is conditioned by where the decisive bargaining occurs – parliamentary arenas insulate reform from employer vetoes; corporatist arenas uphold it – and by the strength and direction of European leverage, which can act either as a permissive tailwind or a binding "policy sword". By positioning political and industrial arenas within a single explanatory frame, we show how peak-level union confederations and radical left parties can, under favourable electoral and macroeconomic constellations, transcend sectoral logics and reshape institutions that earlier research often treats as fixed. In short, governing social blocs provide the missing link between micro-level studies of union strategy and macro-level analyses of party competition, offering a unified lens on when and how solidaristic labour market reform becomes possible.

Strategic Lessons for the Left and the Unions

The evidence assembled in this book from the case studies in Chapters 3–6 to the comparative synthesis in Chapter 7 reveals how the strategic and organisational choices of left-wing parties and unions shape contemporary labour market reform in Portugal and Spain (see Table 7.2 for a synthesis). First, we analyse the lessons for the radical left, then proceed to the centre-left, and conclude with the trade unions.

Regarding the *radical left*, the cases demonstrate that these actors can be pivotal drivers of measures oriented towards solidarity, but only insofar as they are willing to abandon purely oppositional stances and enter the parliamentary and executive arenas where binding decisions are made. In Spain, the readiness of *Unidas Podemos* to share office with the centre-left PSOE supplied the government with the muscle required for an ambitious

Table 7.2 Strategic lessons for unions and left parties

Strategic Aspect	*Spain*	*Portugal*	*General Lesson*
Engagement and Compromise	Active party–union engagement delivered major inclusive reforms	Cautious engagement yielded narrower advances	Strategic compromise enables substantial reforms
Risks of Engagement (radical left and unions)	Close association with government can constrain organisational autonomy	Greater autonomy came with reduced influence on design	Engagement trades autonomy for impact
Left Alliances	Formal left coalition enabled ambitious reform	Conditional support produced more moderate outcomes	Cohesive alliances are crucial for ambitious reform
Radical Left Coordination	Joint electoral list; bloc bargaining; cabinet roles	Separate lists; bilateral pacts; diluted leverage	Unified radical left gains bargaining power; fragmentation erodes it
Left-strategy trade-offs	Office-seeking radical left; centre-left pursued inclusionary agenda under near-parity	Radical left stuck to outsider-support strategy; centre-left often used centrist alliances	Office-holding expands leverage but ties identity to outcomes; outsider strategies preserve autonomy but limit influence
Social Concertation	Selective use; greatest inclusivity achieved via parliament	Central channel; employer veto moderated outcomes	Parliament maximises scope; concertation broadens compliance and can aid lock-in
European Influence	RRF and minimum-wage directive used to legitimise and accelerate reform	Pre-2020 Semester signals constrained ambition; facilitative cues existed but were weaker	EU leverage varies; when enabling, it is a powerful multiplier
Politics and Industrial Relations	Integrated political–industrial strategies delivered cohesive reform packages	Fragmented linkages limited reform breadth	Navigating intersecting arenas is essential

Source: Own elaboration by the authors.

programme that lifted the minimum wage, strengthened employment protection and regulated platform work. That achievement, however, carried organisational costs: by aligning closely with the Sánchez's cabinets, *Unidas Podemos* blurred the boundary between their own identity and the government's agenda, leaving them exposed to blame for unpopular decisions and potentially eroding their longer-term autonomy. Portugal illustrates the trade-off from the opposite angle. Throughout the '*Geringonça*' period the PCP and BE stayed outside cabinet and offered only conditional legislative support. That posture may have preserved ideological purity yet narrowed the reform menu: minimum-wage upratings were tempered by offsets to employers and the regularisation of precarious public-sector workers was gated by restrictive criteria. More importantly, the strategy ultimately proved electorally costly. When the radical left joined the right to defeat the Budget Law for 2022, the ensuing snap election delivered an absolute majority for the PS and heavy losses for both the BE and the PCP, setbacks from which they have yet to recover.[3]

A further layer of divergence lies inside the radical left itself. Spain's electoral alliance, *Unidas Podemos*, enabled *Podemos*, *Izquierda Unida*, and smaller forces to negotiate as a single bloc despite winning *only* 17.6 per cent of the vote (in 2019). Portugal's PCP, BE, and Greens, by contrast, contested elections separately and then signed separate accords with the PS in 2015. This fragmentation weakened each party's leverage and amplified the PS's agenda-setting power. Paradoxically, the Portuguese radical left, although winning a larger combined vote share in 2015 (18.4 per cent), extracted fewer concessions than its Spanish counterpart, demonstrating that organisational unity can outweigh sheer electoral strength when votes are converted into policy influence.

As for the *implications for the centre-left*, three merit emphasis. First, the Spanish trajectory indicates that a centre-left prepared to pursue an ambitious regulatory programme that entails meaningful market-containment, even in domains long deprioritised under the Third Way, need not mortgage its electoral base; under a cohesive Left–Union bloc, PSOE-led governments enacted far-reaching reforms in collective bargaining, wage floors, platform regulation, and public-sector regularisation without an electoral collapse. Second, alliance management is pivotal: when the centre-left seeks parliamentary support from the radical left while drawing firm "red lines" against labour-market re-regulation, the outcome tends to be precarious. The Portuguese experience – most notably the exclusion of labour-law dossiers from the 2015 accords and the competitive-solidarity profile of the 2019 Labour Code amendment – illustrates the limits of such a strategy. The disagreement on labour-related issues precipitated the collapse of parliamentary agreements between the centre-left and the radical left. This illustrates that pursuing a path of moderation necessarily implies that such agreements are unlikely to endure in the long term. In Portugal, the situation remained stable until 2019; however, in the subsequent term, the BE initially voted against the budget in 2020, followed by the PCP in 2021. Combined with the votes from the right-wing parties, this was sufficient to overthrow the PS government. The 2019 labour reform was pivotal in this entire process. Third, inclusive reforms pushed through without assent from centre-right parties and employer associations carry distinctive hazards: they heighten the risk of abrupt reversals when parliamentary arithmetic shifts and can sour relations with organised business, thereby shrinking the scope for future bargains. The chapter's synthesis underscores both points: where alliances drew employers in (as with Spain's 2021 reform, endorsed in tripartite concertation), inclusivity proved compatible with relative stability; where measures bypassed or only weakly incorporated social concertation (notably several minimum-wage upratings and sectoral statutes), backlash risks loomed larger. The Portuguese experience since 2024, under a centre-right coalition, already signals how fragile some gains can become when the context changes. In short, centre-left parties maximise both policy reach and coalition durability when they privilege inclusive-solidarity packages negotiated within cohesive Left-Union configurations. However, this entails risks for the future, particularly concerning the relationship with centre-right parties and employers, which may later result in radical liberalising reversals.

Having explored the lessons for the left parties, the focus will now shift to an analysis of the *lessons to be drawn for trade unions*. In Iberia, class-oriented unionism is concentrated in Portugal, whereas Spain's confederations have long pursued a pragmatically moderate approach. In Portugal, the CGTP's principled refusal to endorse tripartite social-concertation agreements – despite refraining from escalating to general strikes or sustained protest cycles – preserved strategic autonomy but limited its capacity to shape the concrete design of labour market reforms. By remaining outside the venues where binding agreements were struck, it contributed (among other factors) to a narrower reform scope and more competitive-tinged outcomes. In contrast, Spain's moderate confederations (UGT-S, CCOO) leveraged close incorporation within a cohesive Left–Union bloc to secure substantial advances in wage floors, collective bargaining rules, and public-sector stabilisation. This was achieved albeit at the organisational cost of blurred boundaries with the government and a tightening constraint on longer-term strategic autonomy. In Portugal, the UGT-P's moderation yielded more modest returns than those realised by its Spanish counterparts, reflecting a divided union movement and the absence of radical left actors from the cabinet. Even so, this stance was consistent with the confederation's historical profile. Nevertheless, the costs of moderation within the union camp are higher in Portugal due to fewer advancements for labour.

Forging broad coalitions that span the radical left, the centre-left, and the union movement is, however, exceptionally difficult. Spain's success between 2019 and 2025 rested on a conjunction of circumstances that will seldom be replicated: a radical left willing to moderate on some topics; a united radical left electoral front that maximised bargaining clout; trade-union confederations ready to temper their stance on contentious issues such as labour-law reform; a supportive European agenda that supplied funding and legal cover; and a near-parity of parliamentary strength between the PSOE and *Unidas Podemos*. When even one of these elements is missing – as in Portugal, where the radical left is organisationally divided, the CGTP resists concertation and EU signals have often been restraining – the scope for inclusive reform narrows sharply.

These concluding lessons are offered as practical resources for renewing labour market solidarity under adverse conditions. In a period of substantial losses for the Left and the trade union movement, the Portuguese and Spanish trajectories examined here show that strategy and organisation – coalitional design, venue choice, and judicious use of European leverage – can still create room for solidaristic reforms. These lessons will be of clear and enduring use in thinking about the future of solidarity: not a blueprint but a repertoire for managing trade-offs between autonomy and influence, ambition, and durability. Learning from Iberia is therefore not retrospective homage; it equips progressive parties and unions to face the next conjuncture with sharper priorities and sturdier institutional tools. If solidaristic outcomes are never guaranteed, the Iberian record demonstrates that they remain attainable through disciplined coalitions and carefully sequenced institutional design.

Notes

1 EU pressure offers an alternative explanation: the CSRs initially discouraged substantial minimum-wage increases in Portugal while encouraging them in Spain. Yet this asymmetry began to fade after 2018. Strong labour market performance eased fears of job loss, and the EU's emerging "social turn" (Perista and Perista, 2019; D'Erman et al., 2022) gradually softened the tone of the CSRs in Portugal. By 2020 – under the stimulus of the EU's pandemic response and the forthcoming Directive on Adequate Minimum Wages – Brussels' stance had reversed fully, now supporting more ambitious upratings across the board. Even so, important cross-national institutional differences continued to shape how that common stimulus was translated into domestic policy.

2 Refer to the key in Table 7.1 for an explanation of the codes used throughout this section.

3 On 27 October 2021, the BE and PCP sided with the centre-right opposition to defeat the 2022 State Budget Law, precipitating the dissolution of parliament and a snap election on 30 January 2022. The PS secured an absolute majority (120 of 230 seats), while the BE fell from 19 to 5 members of parliament and the PCP-led CDU from 12 to 6.

References

Alvariño M., Arrigoni A., Soler-Buades L. and Ferragina E. (2025) *The End of the Age of Dualisation? A Comparative Analysis of Fifty Years of Labour Market*

Protection Reforms in Spain and Italy. Sciences Po LIEPP Working Paper n°175. Paris: Sciences Po LIEPP.

Baccaro L., Hamann K. and Turner L. (2003) The politics of labour movement revitalization: The need for a revitalized perspective. *European Journal of Industrial Relations* 9(1): 119–133.

Baccaro L. and Howell C. (2017) *Trajectories of Neoliberal Transformation: European Industrial Relations since the 1970s*. Cambridge: Cambridge University Press.

Bondy A. S., Maggor E. and Tassinari A. (2025) Putting wage growth back on the table: Labour incorporation, political exchange, and wage-boosting policies in advanced peripheral economies. *Competition & Change* 29(3–4): 437–464.

Branco R., Miró J. and Natili M. (2024) Back from the cold? Progressive politics and social policy paradigms in Southern Europe after the Great Recession. *Politics & Society* 52(4): 630–661.

Bulfone F. and Tassinari A. (2021) Under pressure. Economic constraints, electoral politics and labour market reforms in Southern Europe in the decade of the Great Recession. *European Journal of Political Research* 60(3): 509–538.

Bürgisser R. and Kurer T. (2021) Insider–outsider representation and social democratic labour market policy. *Socio-Economic Review* 19(3): 1065–1094.

Carver L. and Doellgast V. (2020) Dualism or solidarity? Condistions for union success in regulating precarious work. *European Journal of Industrial Relations* 27(4): 367–385.

D'Erman V. J., Schulz D. F., Verdun A. and Zagermann D. (2022) The European Semester in the North and in the South: Domestic politics and the salience of EU-induced wage reform in different growth models. *Journal of Common Market Studies* 60(1): 21–39.

Doellgast V., Lillie N. and Pulignano V. (eds) (2018) *Reconstructing Solidarity: Labour Unions, Precarious Work, and the Politics of Institutional Change in Europe*. Oxford: Oxford University Press.

Dorigatti L. (2017) Trade unions in segmented labor markets: Evidence from the German metal and chemical sectors. *ILR Review* 70(4): 919–941.

Eichhorst W. and Marx P. (2021) How stable is labour market dualism? Reforms of employment protection in nine European countries. *European Journal of Industrial Relations* 27(1): 93–110.

Ferragina E. and Filetti F. D. (2022) Labour market protection across space and time: A revised typology and a taxonomy of countries' trajectories of change. *Journal of European Social Policy* 32(2): 148–165.

Ferragina E., Filetti F. D. and Arrigoni A. (2023) Assessing labour market policy change. In: Clegg D. and Durazzi N. (eds) *Handbook of Labour Market Policy in Advanced Democracies*. 68–86. Cheltenham: Edward Elgar Publishing.

Iversen T. and Soskice D. (2015) Democratic limits to redistribution: Inclusionary versus exclusionary coalitions in the knowledge economy. *World Politics* 67(2): 185–225.

Lindvall J. and Rueda D. (2014) The insider–outsider dilemma. *British Journal of Political Science* 44(2): 460–475.

Marques P., Benassi C., Costa A. and Pinto A. (2025b) Under which conditions do unions succeed in pushing back dualization? A configurational study of collective agreements in Portugal. *British Journal of Industrial Relations* 63(1): 133–155.

Marques P., Branco R. and Guimarães R. (2025a) The politics of pro-outsider labour market reforms: A configurational study. *Comparative European Politics* 23(2): 159–184.

Marques P. and Fonseca D. (2022) Understanding the positions taken by moderate union confederations and centre-left parties during labour market reforms in Portugal and Spain: Why the configuration of left parties and trade union confederations matters? *European Journal of Industrial Relations* 28(1): 65–84.

Marques P. and Salavisa I. (2017) Young people and dualization in Europe: A fuzzy set analysis. *Socio-Economic Review* 15(1): 135–160.

Mosimann N. and Pontusson J. (2017) Solidaristic unionism and support for redistribution in contemporary Europe. *World Politics* 69(3): 448–492.

Palier B. and Thelen K. (2010) Institutionalizing dualism: Complementarities and change in France and Germany. *Politics & Society* 38(1): 119–148.

Perista P. and Perista H. (2019) 'Just being heard'? Engaging in the European Semester in the shadow of macroeconomic surveillance – Case study Portugal. OSE Paper Series, Research Paper No. 41. Brussels: Observatoire Social Européen.

Rathgeb P. (2018) *Strong Governments, Precarious Workers: Labor Market Policy in the Era of Liberalization*. Ithaca, NY: Cornell University Press.

Rodríguez C. J. F. and Martínez Lucio M. (eds) (2023) *Work and Employment Relations in Southern Europe: The Impact of De-regulation, Organizational Change and Social Fragmentation on Worker Representation and Action.* Cheltenham: Edward Elgar Publishing.

Rueda D. (2005) Insider-outsider politics in industrialized democracies: The challenge to social democratic parties. *American Political Science Review* 99(1): 61–74.

Schwander H. (2019) Are social democratic parties insider parties? Electoral strategies of social democratic parties in Western Europe in the age of dualization. *Comparative European Politics* 17(5): 714–737.

Streeck W. (2009) *Re-Forming Capitalism: Institutional Change in the German Political* Economy . Oxford: Oxford University Press.

Thelen K. (2014) *Varieties of Liberalization and the New Politics of Social Solidarity.* Cambridge: Cambridge University Press.

Vlandas T. (2018) Coordination, inclusiveness and wage inequality between median- and bottom-income workers. *Comparative European Politics* 16(3): 482–510.

Index